More Praise for *Building a Healthy Multi-Ethnic Church*

"The twenty-first century will be increasingly characterized by local churches that reflect the ethnic and economic diversity of the Body of Christ, just as they did in the first century. Mark's book makes a profound contribution toward the development of these churches, the kind of churches Christ most surely desires on earth as it is in heaven."

—Rev. Ali Velasquez, Hispanic Task Force, North American Mission Board

"This captivating book describes the fascinating story, including the biblical basis, behind Mark's passionate quest to develop a church that is truly multicultural and multi-ethnic. It fosters hope that the future can be different."

—Dr. Warren Bird, coauthor, *Culture Shift,* and research director, Leadership Network

"In *Building a Healthy Multi-Ethnic Church,* Mark paints a picture, with his own story and the story of God, that will inspire and equip people to join with God in fulfilling the vision of a faith of all colors."

—Doug Pagitt, senior pastor, Solomon's Porch, Minneapolis, Minnesota, and author, *An Emergent Manifesto of Hope*

"I am so excited to see the concept of cross-cultural local church ministry so thoroughly articulated by Mark DeYmaz. I encourage every pastor, parishioner, and even non-Christians, as well, to read this book in order to see where the local church is heading in the twenty-first century, and why."

—Dr. Ken Hutcherson, senior pastor, Antioch Bible Church, Kirkland, Washington, and author, *Here Comes the Bride*

"The North American Church is hemorrhaging through the ethnic and economic segregation of her people. Jesus Christ is using men like Mark DeYmaz to bring healing to His bride and to build authentic communities of faith that reflect the love of God for all people. This is an excellent book."

—Dr. Greg Kappas, director, Grace Global Network

"The fact that Sunday morning is the most segregated hour in the land is challenged biblically and experientially with this book. Mark DeYmaz offers hope for the local church to become a picture of heaven on earth, a place where all races can worship the same God in the same church at the same time."

—Rodney Woo, senior pastor, Wilcrest Baptist Church, Houston, Texas

BUILDING A HEALTHY
MULTI-ETHNIC CHURCH

JB JOSSEY-BASS

BUILDING A HEALTHY
MULTI-ETHNIC CHURCH

*Mandate, Commitments, and Practices
of a Diverse Congregation*

Mark DeYmaz

○

Foreword by

George Yancey

A LEADERSHIP ❖ NETWORK PUBLICATION

John Wiley & Sons, Inc.

Published by Jossey-Bass
A Wiley Imprint
989 Market Street, San Francisco, CA 94103-1741   www.josseybass.com

Wiley Bicentennial logo: Richard J. Pacifico.

Readers should be aware that Internet Web sites offered as citations and/or sources for further information may have changed or disappeared between the time this was written and when it is read.

Jossey-Bass books and products are available through most bookstores. To contact Jossey-Bass directly call our Customer Care Department within the U.S. at 800-956-7739, outside the U.S. at 317-572-3986, or fax 317-572-4002.

Jossey-Bass also publishes its books in a variety of electronic formats. Some content that appears in print may not be available in electronic books.

Library of Congress Cataloging-in-Publication Data
DeYmaz, Mark, 1961–
    Building a healthy multi-ethnic church: mandate, commitments, and practices of a diverse congregation/Mark DeYmaz; foreword by George Yancey.
        p.   cm.
    Includes bibliographical references (p.   ) and index.
    ISBN-13: 978-0-7879-9551-5 (cloth)
1.   Church and minorities.   2.   Church work with minorities.
3.   Ethnicity—Religious aspects—Christianity.   4.   Multiculturalism—Religious aspects—Christianity.   I. Title.
    BV639.M56D49 2007
    259.089—dc22

                                                                                2007028793

Printed in the United States of America
FIRST EDITION
HB Printing   10 9 8 7 6 5 4 3 2 1

LEADERSHIP NETWORK TITLES

The Blogging Church: Sharing the Story of Your Church Through Blogs, by Brian Bailey and Terry Storch

Leading from the Second Chair: Serving Your Church, Fulfilling Your Role, and Realizing Your Dreams, by Mike Bonem and Roger Patterson

The Way of Jesus: A Journey of Freedom for Pilgrims and Wanderers, by Jonathan S. Campbell with Jennifer Campbell

Leading the Team-Based Church: How Pastors and Church Staffs Can Grow Together into a Powerful Fellowship of Leaders, by George Cladis

Organic Church: Growing Faith Where Life Happens, by Neil Cole

Off-Road Disciplines: Spiritual Adventures of Missional Leaders, by Earl Creps

Building a Healthy Multi-ethnic Church: Mandate, Commitments, and Practices of a Diverse Congregation, by Mark DeYmaz

Leading Congregational Change Workbook, by James H. Furr, Mike Bonem, and Jim Herrington

Leading Congregational Change: A Practical Guide for the Transformational Journey, by Jim Herrington, Mike Bonem, and James H. Furr

The Leader's Journey: Accepting the Call to Personal and Congregational Transformation, by Jim Herrington, Robert Creech, and Trisha Taylor

Culture Shift: Transforming Your Church from the Inside Out, by Robert Lewis and Wayne Cordeiro, with Warren Bird

A New Kind of Christian: A Tale of Two Friends on a Spiritual Journey, by Brian D. McLaren

The Story We Find Ourselves In: Further Adventures of a New Kind of Christian, by Brian D. McLaren

Practicing Greatness: 7 Disciplines of Extraordinary Spiritual Leaders, by Reggie McNeal

119097

The Present Future: Six Tough Questions for the Church, by Reggie McNeal

A Work of Heart: Understanding How God Shapes Spiritual Leaders, by Reggie McNeal

The Millennium Matrix: Reclaiming the Past, Reframing the Future of the Church, by M. Rex Miller

Shaped by God's Heart: The Passion and Practices of Missional Churches, by Milfred Minatrea

The Missional Leader: Equipping Your Church to Reach a Changing World, by Alan J. Roxburgh and Fred Romanuk

The Ascent of a Leader: How Ordinary Relationships Develop Extraordinary Character and Influence, by Bill Thrall, Bruce McNicol, and Ken McElrath

Beyond Megachurch Myths: What We Can Learn from America's Largest Churches, by Scott Thumma and Dave Travis

The Elephant in the Boardroom: Speaking the Unspoken About Pastoral Transitions, by Carolyn Weese and J. Russell Crabtree

CONTENTS

PART ONE
The Biblical Mandate

PART TWO
The Seven Core Commitments of a Multi-Ethnic Church

PART THREE
On Planting, Revitalizing, and Transforming

ABOUT LEADERSHIP NETWORK

SINCE 1984, Leadership Network has fostered church innovation and growth by diligently pursuing its far-reaching mission statement: to identify, connect, and help high-capacity Christian leaders multiply their impact.

Although Leadership Network's techniques adapt and change as the church faces new opportunities and challenges, the organization's work follows a consistent and proven pattern: Leadership Network brings together entrepreneurial leaders who are focused on similar ministry initiatives. The ensuing collaboration—often across denominational lines—creates a strong base from which individual leaders can better analyze and refine their own strategies. Peer-to-peer interaction, dialogue, and sharing inevitably accelerate participants' innovation and ideas. Leadership Network further enhances this process through developing and distributing highly targeted ministry tools and resources, including audio and video programs, special reports, e-publications, and online downloads.

With Leadership Network's assistance, today's Christian leaders are energized, equipped, inspired, and better able to multiply their own dynamic Kingdom-building initiatives.

Launched in 1996 in conjunction with Jossey-Bass (a Wiley imprint), Leadership Network Publications present thoroughly researched and innovative concepts from leading thinkers, practitioners, and pioneering churches. The series collectively draws from a range of disciplines, with individual titles offering perspective on one or more of five primary areas:

1. Enabling effective leadership
2. Encouraging life-changing service
3. Building authentic community
4. Creating Kingdom-centered impact
5. Engaging cultural and demographic realities

For additional information on the mission or activities of Leadership Network, please contact:

Leadership Network

(800) 765-5323

client.care@leadnet.org

FOREWORD

RACIAL SEGREGATION, both formal and informal, has been the norm for the United States throughout much of its history. But in these days, our country is becoming a multiracial society. In light of this, old models of church that focus on reaching a single racial group are not going to be as effective as they have been in the past. So if the Body of Christ is to adjust to our new racial future, we will have to make bold, biblical steps toward the development of churches situated to meet the needs of people of different races and cultures. The ability of contemporary and future Christians to provide a relevant witness to a multiracial, multicultural society is at stake. If our God is not big enough to provide us the spiritual strength to overcome racial barriers in our society, then how can we ask a hurting world to trust such a feeble deity?

That is why this new work by Mark DeYmaz is so exciting. I have known Mark for many years. I know that he has a mighty big heart for reaching all people for Christ. This includes people who do not come from the same culture he does and those not of his race. Mark simply desires to see people come to Christ. In this book he recognizes that to fulfill the Great Commission we cannot sit on past accomplishments, but we have to create churches that address the concerns of a new generation of Americans who are not impressed with our megachurches—churches largely made up of people of the same race and culture. We are going to have to go outside our comfort zones and be with people from other races and cultures. We will have to make a biblical commitment to minister to and with them in ways that may seem foreign to us. Only then will we be able to fulfill the Great Commission in our multiracial society.

I have had the privilege of working with Mark and others who desire to reach people from different racial groups and cultures in an effort to create what I call "multiracial" churches. As a Christian academic, I can assess these churches and learn why they succeed and fail. This is very valuable in helping to discover the practical steps necessary for making our churches places where people of all races can feel welcome. I am so grateful for the role God has allowed me to play in the movement of Christian churches toward racial inclusiveness.

But a sterile academic approach to the issue of multiracial churches does not inspire us to undertake the task of creating them. If we are to ask our fellow Christians to join us in a reformative movement to bring the different races together on Sunday morning, we need to find scriptural support. What Mark brings that I am not equipped to provide is an understanding of the biblical mandate for having racially inclusive churches, as well as a scriptural perspective on why multiracial churches are important in contemporary United States. His contribution to the emerging movement to establish multiracial local churches throughout America and beyond is just as important, if not more so, than the role academics like myself can play, because he can go to the ultimate source of knowledge—our Bible—for the theological support this movement needs.

There are two powerful, compelling reasons we can look toward Mark's work to help us deal with the issue of multiracial ministry. First, Mark has the authority to speak on such a subject from his own personal experience leading the highly successful Mosaic Church of Little Rock. I have visited this wonderful church. Truly, it represents all of the rich diversity of the Little Rock area. This is a church that reflects its pastor's heart to reach out to those of all tribes, tongues, nations, and cultures. When Mark challenges other pastors to move out of their comfort zone, he does so with authority, because he has dared to move out into new cultural territory with his own church plant.

Second, Mark brings to this subject vital information from his theological training. Mark has written and spoken previously on the subject of multiracial ministry; and he set up much of his graduate training in the examination of this subject. Therefore, when he speaks, he does so with the confidence of one who has read the Scriptures and examined all sides of the argument. In the future when people ask me for a biblical justification for multiracial churches, this is the book I am going to recommend.

We do serve a God that is big enough to overcome the racial barriers in our society. The problem is often that we lack the faith to fully live out the power he offers to us. Mark's work reminds us of God's power, as well as our own shortcomings. Mark challenges us to move beyond the limited racial and cultural boxes we have become accustomed to and live more fully the Great Commission that has been given to us. If we are willing to take the risks necessary and to rely on the Power that is always sufficient, then the Body of Christ in the United States can be a witness of a better society and a source of racial healing that is so badly needed in our contemporary society.

August 2007   Dr. George Yancey
                    Associate Professor, Department of Sociology
                    University of North Texas, Denton, TX

PREFACE

AS FOLLOWERS OF JESUS, we are to be Christ-like. The New Testament is filled with teaching and examples urging us to live in a way that pleases God. Fundamental to this teaching is the call to be united as one in Christ (John 17:21–23) and, as such, instruments of peace (Matthew 5:9). Unfortunately, many Christians living in the United States today overlook this part of the mission. Yet the breaking down of ethnic, social, and cultural barriers is one of the strongest themes in Christ's ministry, and I believe Christ's Church should reflect both his character and his passion for all people.

I grew up in the South, more specifically, in Little Rock, Arkansas. During the 1970s, my father served as Arkansas' governor; for a time I attended Little Rock's Central High School—the same Central High that shook the world in 1957, when nine Black children attempted to integrate the all-White high school. Following *Brown* v. *Board of Education*, the integration of Little Rock's Central High endures as a major milestone of the civil rights movement, and it is fitting that this book, written by my friend Mark DeYmaz, is being released in the fall of 2007, the very season in which the nation will mark the fiftieth anniversary of that historic event.

From my days in Little Rock, as well as in representing the state of Arkansas in the U.S. Senate, I have seen the results and ongoing challenges of racism in our country. As a follower of Christ, however, I have often wondered what a difference believers could make if, somehow, we were able to put aside our racial preferences on Sunday mornings and attend worship services together. This I believe would lead to improved relationships among the races, in living and working side-by-side throughout the week, resulting in the strengthening of our communities and our nation as a whole. More than that, I am certain it would please the heart of God.

Although it is true that we have made a lot of progress in recent years, race is still a divisive force in our culture. In addition, social status, income levels, and educational achievement are all factors that influence our preference, more often than not, to attend a church with people most like ourselves. This aspect of our human nature, however, is rooted in sin and limits the ways in which we allow ourselves to pursue and to serve God.

I used to think things would never change and believed that cultural barriers were too strong a force to overcome in this regard. Now, however, I am convinced they are not. The Church can change and, in fact, is already changing!

There is a church in Little Rock that is breaking down these barriers and changing our city's culture. It is the Mosaic Church of Central Arkansas—a God-centered, Bible-based, evangelical community of believers that is multi-ethnic and economically diverse. God is using this body to change lives and to reach the lost. It is an amazing thing to see and even more amazing to experience. While many other churches are doing good things in Little Rock, Mosaic is influencing a systemic rethinking of things and setting an example that few churches to date have been willing to address.

With this in mind, I commend to you this work and pray that God will speak to you through it.

August 2007   Mark L. Pryor
                   United States Senator (AR)

ACKNOWLEDGMENTS

EACH OF MY CHILDREN HAS, in one way or another, helped bring Mosaic to life. Zack and Emily have been especially supportive, loyal, and involved. They have greatly lightened my load through their positive attitude and self-sacrifice. Will and Kate, too, have been wholeheartedly engaged and flexible. I will forever be grateful for children who have consistently asked, "Can I go (early) with you to church?" Daddy loves you! My mother, Dorothy, is also greatly loved and appreciated. She has always encouraged my dreams and sacrificed to help make them reality.

For more than twenty years, my friend Miles McPherson has helped me to consider the unique plight of African Americans. More recently, Greg Kappas inspired my vision for the multi-ethnic church, taught me the Word, and coached me in planting Mosaic. Ken Hutcherson further enlightened me and led Antioch Bible Church in Kirkland, Washington, to embrace our cause in the beginning. Linda Stanley at Leadership Network has also been a very consistent encourager and was the first to suggest that I write this book. My good friends, George Yancey and Jim Spoonts, are co-laborers in the Multi-Ethnic Church Movement and have partnered with me to establish the Mosaix Global Network, through which a growing number of like-minded pastors, educators, and ministry leaders are now connecting. Thanks especially to Rodney Woo and to Kim Greenwood for their work in writing Chapters Twelve and Thirteen, respectively, and to Jonathan Seda and my partner Harry Li for their contributions in other chapters as well.

I have greatly appreciated the encouragement and support of Greg Ligon, Mark Sweeney, and Stephanie Plagens at Leadership Network. And at Jossey-Bass, Sheryl Fullerton and Catherine Craddock have made this a very easy and enjoyable experience. Alison Clinton and Larry Tarpley of Mosaic were also very helpful in providing additional ministry and administrative support.

Finally, I want to thank my fellow elders, Bill Head, Eric Higgins, Lloyd Hodges, Tom Holmes, and Harry Li, as well as my staff and all the people at Mosaic who are today building a healthy multi-ethnic church. Together we intend it as a gift to God, to the city of Little Rock, and to the people of Central Arkansas: a symbol of how far we have come and a strategy to address how far we have yet to go.

To Linda, who has faithfully, sacrificially, and courageously accompanied me down roads less traveled for more than twenty years: thank you for your commitment to God, to prayer, and to his Word—a commitment that has stretched, challenged, and encouraged me to become the man I am, and the man I am still becoming, today. I love you dearly.

INTRODUCTION

A ship in a safe harbor is safe, but that is not what a ship is built for.

—William Shedd

IT WAS THE SPRING OF 1993, and I had two options. After ten years of full-time ministry as a youth pastor, two dynamic churches had each invited me to join their staff teams to oversee student ministries.

Antioch Bible Church was a growing and diverse congregation led by former NFL linebacker, Ken Hutcherson. I had heard of Ken's ministry for years and was honored by his enthusiastic invitation. Located in Seattle, Washington, the ministry was just two hours south of my wife, Linda's, hometown of Bellingham, and accepting the job would keep us in the western part of the United States. In addition, I had friends on staff and knew there would be great freedom to design a ministry "as the Spirit leads." Quite simply, there was nothing not to like.

Fellowship Bible Church, on the other hand, was located in Little Rock, Arkansas. *Arkansas?* I'm not kidding—Linda and I had to get out a map just to find the state! Robert Lewis, the pastor of this "equipping-oriented" church, was like Ken, an inspiring leader, and the people we met on our first visit epitomized Southern charm and hospitality. Yet visions of *Hee Haw* danced in my head:

> "Won't ya' whisper me something sweet, Jimmy Bob?"
> "Sho' will, Effie Mae. Nice tooth!"

I pictured the Hatfields and McCoys "feudin' in them th'ar hills" and ticks and chiggers just waiting to embed themselves in my body; I imagined eating grits in the morning and chitlins at the church potluck and cheering for a university whose mascot's a pig. *I don't know, man. I'm from Phoenix!*

Ironically, my mother, Dorothy, was born and raised in Arkansas but had somehow managed, as I once heard someone say, to "survive and make it out of there." Some fifty years later, was God now leading me back to "her people"?

Now at that time, I was nowhere near where I am today in terms of understanding the biblical mandate for the multi-ethnic church. Indeed, I was largely unaware of Christ's vision for unity and diversity within the local church, unity's intended purpose, the pattern of the New Testament Church, the prescriptions of Paul, or the commitments to oneness that can lead the local church back to a place of prominent influence in the community. The fact is, I had no earthly idea that a diverse church was anything more than flat-out "cool." I only knew that Antioch was integrated and Fellowship was not; somehow, that bothered me.

During the interview process, I asked Robert if he would ever hire an African American to serve alongside him. He told me that he would be open to doing so but not because of the color of the man's skin. Rather, he would hire such a man only if the potential candidate was qualified and if, of course, there was a need. In other words, he would do so only if the applicant was, in fact, "the best man for the job." I remember thinking, *Good answer*, though honestly, I couldn't say why.

One day as we neared our decision, Linda was in the next room and I was thinking out loud: "I don't know, Linda. I like the fact that Antioch is a diverse church in a large city out West. I mean, after all, Little Rock is so much smaller than Seattle, and it's in the South—a long way from our families. Think about it! It's a city infamously associated with racism. In 1957, Central High School was forcibly integrated,[1] and the schools are still controlled by the federal courts. Is this really where we want to raise our kids?"

In response, Linda leaned her head around the corner and said, "But who knows, Mark? Maybe God will use you to change things."

"Yeah, right," I flippantly replied. "I'm not even from the South—an outsider—and I'm going to change several hundred years of racial prejudice and segregation?"

Well that was it; we never discussed the issue again. Soon after, though, Linda and I did sense a strange but certain call to Arkansas, and in the summer of 1993, I accepted the job at Fellowship. So we moved our young family to Little Rock, home of the Hogs[2] and to (then) President Bill Clinton[3]—a place of terribly humid summers and an exciting new challenge of turning a youth group into a student ministry. It would be many years, however, before either one of us would begin to realize just how profound Linda's words that day really were.

Branching Out

By the spring of 1997, our family had been in Little Rock nearly four years. Fellowship Student Ministries was growing healthy and strong, and with the addition of staff, I had more time to be involved with other youth leaders throughout the city. Together, we had established a local network of youth pastors who, by this time, were meeting monthly and enjoying genuine relationships of friendship and trust.

There was just one nagging reality: virtually the entire group was White.

My initial inquiries concerning the lack of African American involvement in the network yielded somewhat resigned and stereotypical answers. I remember hearing that student ministry was "not as much a priority in the 'Black church' as it is in the 'White church,'" and that "the 'Black church' just doesn't view youth ministry the way *we* do." Economics, too, were cited as a contributing factor. Someone said, "Since 'Black churches' don't pay their youth pastors, volunteer leaders might not be able to meet with us during the day."

No matter the cause, I was becoming increasingly troubled with the status quo. So in April of that year, I decided to do something about it. I invited eight youth workers, with whom I had become acquainted through the years, to gather for a morning of prayer and discussion. Significantly, four of them were White and the other four were Black. My sole motive for meeting was to determine the cause for the lack of African American involvement in our network and, hopefully then, to resolve the situation.

Sponsored by Bank of the Ozarks' president, George Gleason, and hosted by Greg Murtha, one of the bank's employees, the meeting was both enjoyable and productive. In the quiet seclusion of a warmly decorated log cabin at the Oasis Retreat Center, the guys who came that day shared honestly and from the heart. For instance, I learned that the many African American youth leaders in the city at the time were, in fact, bivocational, and this did make it difficult for them to participate in network meetings held during the day. However, it was not at all true that Black churches didn't pay their youth pastors or that youth ministry was somehow less of a priority in the African American churches. "How wrong it is to assume such things," one of the African Americans said, "simply because we don't necessarily approach it the way that you do."

Toward the end of our time, we all agreed it was important to pursue greater understanding and cooperation. We then asked ourselves what might be done to get more African American youth workers involved in the local network.

First, someone suggested that we invite former pastor and the (then) current governor of Arkansas, Mike Huckabee, to a kick-off meeting in the fall and to address the importance of our network. We reasoned that such an event, attended by the governor, would surely draw a crowd.

Someone else brought up the fact that in just five months, the city (and, indeed, the nation) would honor the fortieth anniversary of the integration of Little Rock's Central High School. The president of the United States, the "Little Rock Nine," and many other dignitaries would likely be in town for events that week. We were brainstorming, when another person suggested that a rally of youth groups and leaders could be planned on the capitol steps that would not only bring us together but also would provide a platform to declare, *Racism is, ultimately, a spiritual problem.*

Next, we likened the passing of the forty years since the crisis at Central High to Israel's wanderings in the wilderness. Through such an event, we could stand together in declaring the dawn of a new day. Oh yeah, baby, we were on a roll!

Finally, Greg mentioned that he had a connection with the manager of DC Talk, a band that, at the time, was one of the most successful groups in Christian music. DC Talk was diverse[4] and quite naturally had a personal interest in such matters.[5] Perhaps, we wondered, the band could come to the city around this time and in some way be involved with us in making such a statement. Greg said that he would draft a letter and ask the governor to personally extend the invitation.

In leaving that day, we all shared the feeling that great progress had been made. Indeed, we looked forward to building a stronger, more diverse network in the future and to an event in September that might address even broader issues. Yet by the end of June, none of us had spoken again to anyone else about it.

Nevertheless, we met again on July 2nd at a local restaurant to see just what, if anything, was possible. As the smell of Petit Jean Mountain ham permeated the air of the breakfast hotspot, we gathered together, not expecting much. No news since April probably meant bad news in terms of any significant advance of the ball.

But God knew better.

Greg was the last one to arrive that day, bounding in with incredible news. He told us that he had just heard from his connection. DC Talk had not only received the governor's letter but, in fact, desired to come! "And not only that," Greg said, "but he told me that they want 'to bring some friends' with them."

"What friends?" someone asked.

"Oh, just people like Billy Graham, Evander Holyfield, and CeCe Wynans," Greg replied, doing his best to mask his excitement. "And one more thing," he said. "They want to come for free!"

To make a long story short, the Racial Reconciliation Rally was born that day, and on September 19, 1997, at the River Market Amphitheatre in downtown Little Rock, a wonderfully diverse crowd of nearly fifteen thousand came to be a part of the truly historic event which, in addition to those mentioned earlier,[6] included the involvement of two members of the "Little Rock Nine," Pastor E. V. Hill from Los Angeles, pastor and evangelist Miles McPherson from San Diego, and the band, Grits. The mayors of Little Rock and North Little Rock also came, as well as the governor of Arkansas, congressional leaders from three different states, and a large number of pastors representing churches throughout Central Arkansas. And we did, in fact, make a statement. The next day, the *Arkansas Democrat Gazette* quoted an African American pastor in a big, bold headline: "I Believe the Walls Have Come Down!"

Lasting Impact

The rally in 1997 was, indeed, a significant event for the city. And through my own involvement, I became much more aware of lingering prejudice and systemic racism still deeply embedded within our society and, yes, within the local church. But I still did not fully understand the complexities of the situation: for example, how the segregation of the local church contributes to the perpetuation of such problems, what the Bible might have to say about it, or what such understanding would ultimately mean for my family and me.

Over the next few years, I began to look at my own local church through a new grid, wondering why, it seemed, the only minorities there were janitors, or why "the best man for the job" always looked like us. Soon, I was no longer content to "build a bridge to the community." Increasingly, I wanted to be a part of a church that *was* the community.

So in the fall of 2000, my eighth year at Fellowship, I prepared my résumé, made a few calls, and wondered what might happen next.

That's when I met Precious.

Precious Williams was a hairstylist at Super Cuts in Little Rock, and I had recently begun having her cut my hair. She was close, the cut was cheap, and I particularly enjoyed talking with her about racial attitudes in the South. As an African American who grew up in Little Rock, she was a valued resource and person of genuine warmth. Indeed, I not only learned much from Precious, but that fall God used her to change my life.

I remember sitting back in her chair one day and initially enjoying lighthearted conversation. At some point, however, we began talking about racism and, in particular, the segregation of the local church. I asked Precious if churches in Little Rock had always been segregated and what it was like for her, growing up in such a place. *Had it affected her spiritually? Had it shaped her view of Christians, of the Church of God?*

Now I honestly do not recall all that she said in response, but I do remember what I asked her next (and, incidentally, in no way thinking of myself or my future). I said, "Precious, do you think there is a need in Little Rock for a diverse church, one where individuals of varying backgrounds might worship God together as one?"

Her answer was no surprise.

"Oh, yes, Mark," she said, in a quiet but hopeful tone.

She then went on to describe what she thought such a church might be like—what it would mean for the community—and to say that she, indeed, longed for the day.

Closing my eyes, I pondered her words, and with her hands skillfully shaping my hair, I soon relaxed nearly to the point of slumber. What she said next, however, shook me to my core.

"Mark, do you ever think it could happen here?"

Now in the precise moment that Precious spoke these words to me, I experienced two remarkable things. Physically, I felt a very powerful rush of heat pass through my body—the same terrifying sensation you feel when someone scares you in the dark! Spiritually, however, something even more remarkable occurred.

For though I had heard with my ears—"Mark, do you ever think it could happen here?"—I simultaneously heard with my heart—"Mark, would you consider doing it here?" And immediately, I was transported in my mind to Acts 16 and to a time when God used another individual to issue a similar invitation to a man at the crossroads of his life. It was my own Macedonian moment!

So right then and there, I clearly heard the call. I wondered, *How should I respond?*

Still shaking from the experience with Precious at Super Cuts and with a noble vision now birthed in my heart, I rushed home to share my excitement with Linda. "What if we stay in Little Rock and start an "Antioch-like" church right here?" I proposed enthusiastically.

Her response, however, was immediate and decisive.

"Are you crazy? We've spent two years in Germany and now eight years in Little Rock. And our children are growing up apart from our families. Don't you want them to be around our parents, their aunts, uncles, and cousins out West? Isn't it time to go home?"

Of course, Linda wasn't against the idea of such a church. In those days, she was just hoping that God would, finally, lead us home. The truth is, I also longed in my heart to return to the West. Consequently, I walked away from our initial conversation thinking there was no way that I could ever attempt such a thing without Linda's full support. Fortunately, we would keep talking and praying about it together.

In the coming weeks, I found my initial excitement quickly morphing into intentional pursuit. Increasingly, I found myself envisioning a multi-ethnic church and considering the significance of such a work in a city through which the very roots of the civil rights movement run deep. I began to ask myself, as I had of Precious, *Is there a need? Is this the time? Am I the guy?*

Soon I was posing these same questions to pastors and spiritual leaders throughout the community. In so doing, it was my intention to survey a wide diversity of leadership both in and outside the local church and to look for wisdom in the counsel of many. Toward that end, I spoke with individuals representing large and small churches, as well as with those working outside the local church in other Christian ministries. I spoke with leadership in the suburbs and in the inner city, and, of course, I spoke to those of different cultural background and economic means.

In those days, I prayerfully confided in the Lord that I would have little confidence in moving ahead with such an idea unless every person I asked answered *Yes!* to all three questions. Planting a church would be hard enough, but planting a multi-ethnic local church would be even harder. Beyond that, to think that it could happen in Little Rock seemed outright impossible!

As God would have it, however, not one of the individuals I talked with was anything less than positive. In fact to a person, they all agreed that the need was great, and it was "long past time" to establish such a church. And as one well-respected African American pastor told me privately, "If anyone can do it, Mark, I believe you can. And if you do decide to go for it, you'll have my full support." Talk about empowering. I was inspired!

By this time, Linda had become fully engaged in the vision, having opened herself in prayer to God's will, in spite of her initial reaction. Returning to Little Rock from Seattle after a visit with the leadership at Antioch, she wept as our plane flew over Mt. Rainier, knowing in her heart that God was speaking—calling us to walk by faith beyond our own understanding, experience, or abilities. Was it mere coincidence that when she opened the one magazine she had purchased just before boarding the plane, there was an article about the historic events of 1957 at Little Rock's Central High?

So on May 17, 2001, Linda and I responded in prayer to a very specific call of God on our lives. That day, we committed ourselves and our family to a journey of faith, courage, and sacrifice that would lead to the establishment of a multi-ethnic and economically diverse church in the heart of Central Arkansas—a church founded in response to the prayer of Jesus Christ for unity and patterned after the New Testament church at Antioch (Acts 11:19ff.)—a church for others, for all people, a church we called Mosaic.

Who We Are

Now to be clear, this is not a book about the church Linda and I planted. Yet at the outset, it will be helpful to understand what I believe this church, as well as the emerging Multi-Ethnic Church Movement is (and must be) all about. And to do that, I will be providing many examples from Mosaic throughout these pages.

Toward that end, consider for a moment the vision statement of our church:

> Mosaic is a multi-ethnic and economically diverse church founded by men and women seeking to know God and to make Him known through the pursuit of unity, in accordance with the prayer of Jesus Christ (John 17:20–23) and patterned after the New Testament church at Antioch (Acts 11:19–26; 13:1ff.).

Notice from this statement that our church was founded for two primary reasons: *to know God and to make him known.* For us, the pursuit of unity is merely the means for accomplishing these ends.

Who We Are Not

To avoid any confusion of purpose, we have not only written a statement concerning who we are but also a statement concerning who we are not. It reads:

> Mosaic is not a church focused on racial reconciliation. Rather, we are focused on reconciling men and women to God through faith in Jesus

Christ and on reconciling ourselves collectively with the principles
and practices of local churches as described in the New Testament.

Through this second statement, we make clear that our church is focused
on two primary works of reconciliation: first, on reconciling men and
women to God through faith in Jesus Christ (evangelism) and second, on
reconciling a local body of believers with the principles and practices of
the New Testament local church. Some may be surprised that "racial
reconciliation" is not our primary focus. Rather, it is for us a most wonderful and supernatural by-product of these two *a priori* works of reconciliation. And I believe the differentiation is important.

First of all, the term *racial reconciliation* does not adequately convey the
biblical underpinnings of a healthy multi-ethnic church. In addition
the term today means different things to different people, who use it at
different times and for different purposes. For instance, the National Organization of Women (NOW) has characterized Promise Keepers' commitment to "reaching beyond any racial and denominational barriers to
demonstrate the power of biblical unity,"[7] as a myth. In so doing, NOW
states,

> While the Promise Keepers claim to want to end racism, they are only
> giving lip service. They are not working to end the institutional racism
> in society today, but are working on programs of "racial reconcilia-
> tion" through personal relationships.[8]

In other words, so-called racial reconciliation, at least to NOW, is not
enough. Such is just one example of how the term today is somewhat
nebulous.

Of course, we should not at all deny the value of personal relationships
in helping us to move beyond lingering racism at an individual level, or
even the part relationships play in addressing systemic issues still plagu-
ing the United States today. But make no mistake—it is my sincere hope
and belief that the emerging movement to establish multi-ethnic churches
throughout the United States and beyond will have the effect of disman-
tling institutional racism within the local church through the application
of long-forsaken New Testament teaching concerning its very nature and
calling.

At Mosaic, therefore, we believe that when men and women of diverse
backgrounds are one with God individually, they can and should walk
together as one in and through the local church, all for the sake of the
Gospel! Indeed, this is the vision of Christ for the local church. It's about
evangelism and discipleship—simple as that.

What It's All About

Such understanding is foundational to the coming ethnic and economic integration of the local church and is essential, too, for those who will lead the way. For we who dare to chase the dream must be fundamentally informed by the Word of God and not by shifting cultural trends and attitudes, by globalization, or by politically correct thinking.

In other words, the desire to establish multi-ethnic churches like Mosaic must not be rooted in the fact that Tiger Woods is biracial and, therefore, representative of the changing face of America or, for that matter, in Rodney King's emotional appeal, "People . . . can we all get along?"[9] Nor should we pursue the multi-ethnic church simply because "the neighborhood is changing," because the increasing diversification of certain states has rendered them "Majority-Minority,"[10] or because projections indicate that the entire nation will be so classified by 2050.[11] Certainly, this is all well and good, making conditions favorable for our attempts. Yet in order to build a healthy multi-ethnic church, planters and reformers alike must be rooted in an understanding of God's Word and his revealed will for the local church. We must find our inspiration in none other than Christ himself, who calls us to be one so that the world would know God's love and believe (John 17:23). The very success of our efforts and, indeed, the emerging Multi-Ethnic Church Movement, depends upon passionate individuals getting this right.

In our case, such understanding led to the conversion of some forty-three individuals within the first eighteen months of Mosaic (July 2001 to January 2003). This included men and women from seven different nations in a city where internationals have come to dwell in increasingly significant numbers.

Amazingly, our first convert was a thirty-two-year-old Muslim man from Saudi Arabia just three months after the horrific 9/11 attacks. The public testimony of faith he shared at the church just three weeks following his conversion led that same evening to the salvation of a university student from Japan and, in the days following, to the conversion of a twenty-four-year-old Australian woman, as well as a man from Mexico in his mid-forties.

I report such things not in any way to boast but simply to demonstrate the power and potential of the multi-ethnic church to advance the Gospel in remarkable ways. This, then, is the primary focus of our church, as well it should be for all churches seeking to reflect the kingdom of God *on earth as it is in heaven.*

Purpose and Intent

This book covers the most fundamental truths concerning the multi-ethnic church that I have learned to date. And let me make one thing perfectly clear from the start: pursuit of the multi-ethnic local church is, in my view, not optional. It is biblically mandated for all who would aspire to lead local congregations of faith.

Beyond this, I want you to know that it is quite possible to establish such churches in the twenty-first century. Indeed, if pastoral leaders are willing to be informed more by the New Testament than by the latest, greatest wisdom of man, that is, if we are willing to work to build his kingdom on earth and not our own, then God will come through! Yes, "Faithful is He who has called you, that He will do it" (2 Thessalonians 5:24).

Therefore, in Part One (Chapters One, Two, and Three), I provide a theological foundation for the biblical mandate. In Part Two (Chapters Four through Ten), I discuss the seven core commitments of a healthy multi-ethnic church. Finally, in Part Three (Chapters Eleven through Thirteen), I provide three examples of local churches that model understanding of the mandate and commitments through church planting, revitalization, and transformation. In so doing, I share why I believe the homogeneous church will grow progressively irrelevant in the years to come, as the message of God's love for all people is otherwise undermined by its own segregation. Beyond this, I will demonstrate the critical importance of getting this message right, both in principle and practice, if the Gospel is to prevail in an increasingly diverse and cynical society.

To do so effectively, the book is peppered with real-life stories of passion, prayer, and peace—stories that are drawn from my own experience as a multi-ethnic church planter. In addition, Chapters One through Ten each include a testimony of conversion or otherwise significant story of life change that we have been privileged to witness at Mosaic—stories that demonstrate the power of unity for the sake of the Gospel. At the end of Chapters Eleven through Thirteen are fifteen principles, drawn from each chapter's discussion, for quick and easy reference.

And speaking of reference, biblical passages throughout are from the *New American Standard Bible* (NASB) unless otherwise indicated.

Finally, let me clarify the use and meaning of key terms from the title:

> *Building:* Use of this word throughout is meant to imply that our work at Mosaic is not at all finished but is one that is still in progress.

Healthy: Use of this word throughout is meant to imply that the good, well-balanced condition of a local church is not only an intentional goal to strive for but also something we must work hard to maintain.

Multi-Ethnic: Use of this term throughout is meant also to imply economic, educational, and generational diversity, as well.

Church: Use of this term throughout is meant to imply, in most instances, the local church, except where the word is capitalized and refers to the wider Church.

I have written this book believing that the growing fascination with multi-ethnic churches must not be focused on racial reconciliation. Rather, it must be focused on reconciling men and women to Jesus Christ and, consequently, on reconciling local communities of faith to the pattern of the New Testament local church—a church in which diverse people worshipped God together as one so that the world would know God's love and believe.

So turn the page, and let me show you why.

BUILDING A HEALTHY
MULTI-ETHNIC CHURCH

PART ONE

THE BIBLICAL
MANDATE

THE FOLLOWING THREE CHAPTERS present a clear and concise biblical argument upon which the multi-ethnic local church can be firmly established. Because much has been written to date concerning God's love for all people, as expressed throughout his Word, I will focus specifically on three key passages in the New Testament to show how such understanding played itself out in the formative days of the first-century Church. The passages we will examine are not only descriptive of early Church understanding and practice but also, in my view, prescriptive for the modern and future Church as well.[1]

With this in mind, we first consider a prayer of Christ in Chapter One, then the pattern of the New Testament Church in Chapter Two, and finally the Pauline mystery, as expressed in the Book of Ephesians, in Chapter Three.

THE PRAYER OF CHRIST

Man is born broken. He lives by mending. The grace of God is glue.

—Eugene O'Neil

THE MOSAIC CHURCH OF CENTRAL ARKANSAS gathers each week in 78,000 square feet of space that originally housed a Wal-Mart. The large glass front features two entrances and many windows. Just west of us is the nearest neighborhood; to the immediate east, a Kroger grocery store stands adjacent to the building. As people from the community pass by the church on their way to and from the store, it is not uncommon for them to put their hands to the glass, press their faces to the window, and look to see what's inside.

One Sunday morning, not long after we began meeting in this location, one African American woman did just that. She had been invited to come by two women from our church whom she had met at the Kroger. The women had encouraged her to come worship at Mosaic, learning that she had no other church to attend.

Before entering the building, then, she pressed her face to the glass and looked inside. And what she saw encouraged her to take another step forward.

Later, after this woman had become a member of Mosaic, she described her experience that day. When she saw the diversity of the people, specifically Blacks and Whites worshipping together as one, she understood intuitively that all people were welcome at Mosaic and loved by the God we were all singing and talking about.

Similarly, if we could strip away everything we know about God's love for all people and transport ourselves back to a time when the world thought *YHWH* (the LORD) was simply, "the God of the Jews," perhaps we would better understand how a Gentile peering into an all-Jewish congregation might never have gone inside. In fact, if we had lived in those days, we would have seen, like Paul, that Gentiles living in the first century "were at that time separate from Christ, excluded from the commonwealth of Israel, and strangers to the covenants of promise, having no hope and without God in the world" (Ephesians 2:12).

Fast-forward to the present day. Does a homogeneous church unnecessarily confuse the message of God's love for all people in a similar way? Will such a church, therefore, become increasingly cumbersome to the advance and proclamation of the Gospel in this century?

Why Is the Local Church Segregated?

According to research conducted by sociologists Curtiss Paul Deyoung, Michael O. Emerson, GeorgeYancey, and Karen Chai Kim,[1] 92.5 percent of Catholic and Protestant churches throughout the United States can be classified as "monoracial." This term describes a church in which 80 percent or more of the individuals who attend are of the same ethnicity or race. The remaining churches (7.5 percent) can be described as multiracial—churches in which there are a non-majority, collective population of at least 20 percent. By this definition, approximately 12 percent of Catholic churches, just less than 5 percent of Evangelical churches, and about 2.5 percent of mainline Protestant churches can be described as multiracial.

So, again, let me ask you a question: *If the kingdom of heaven is not segregated, why on earth is the Church?*

Surely, it must break the heart of God to see so many churches throughout this country segregated ethnically and economically from one another and that little has changed since it was first observed that eleven o'clock on Sunday morning is the most segregated hour in the land.[2] In an increasingly connected yet stubbornly sectarian world, it is time to recognize that there is no greater tool for evangelism than the witness of diverse believers walking, working, and worshipping God together as one in and through the local church. More than that, I believe the very progress of the Gospel throughout the twenty-first century will be largely dependent upon this pursuit.

What though, you may ask, is the basis for such passion and hope? And why am I (and increasing numbers like me) so sure that in reflecting the diversity of heaven, the local church will newly proclaim the Prince of Peace on earth in reformation and power, resulting in the salvation of significant numbers of seekers and skeptics alike to the glory of God? Is this a realistic goal or only the wishful thinking of mystics and mavericks among us? Indeed, I believe it is not only a realistic goal but it is the very prayer and intent of our Lord and Savior, Jesus Christ, for the local church. This, then, should inspire our faith, courage, and sacrificial abandonment to the cause.

What Can Be Learned from John 17?

For centuries, the prayer recorded in John 17 has been widely referred to as the "high priestly prayer" of Jesus Christ. In his book, *Reflections on the Gospel of John,* author Leon Morris notes, "In the early fifth century, Clement of Alexandria said that in this prayer, Jesus was a high priest acting on behalf of his people."[3] It is interesting that this is the longest of all the prayers attributed to Jesus and an appropriate conclusion to what's known as the upper room discourse (John 14–16). With this in mind, some also believe that Jesus intended his words to be overheard by the disciples in order to provide them further hope and comfort. Be that as it may, the prayer marks the passing of the baton to those, both then and now, who are tasked with the responsibility of carrying on the work begun by Christ, namely, of proclaiming eternal life to all men (John 17:2).

In addition, remember that Jesus had just shared a final meal with his disciples. He had just washed their feet, reinterpreted the Passover, and dismissed Judas, who would betray him. Therefore, it is an emotional and significant moment, the night before Jesus would die.

The entire prayer can be divided into three sections. First, Jesus prays to the Father on his own behalf (John 17:1–5). Next, he prays to the Father on behalf of his disciples, that is, the eleven men left in the room with him in that moment (John 17:6–19). And finally, he prays for "those also who believe in Me through their word" (John 17:20–23). It is here that we will pause in a moment not only to consider who Christ had in mind but, more important, what and why specifically he prayed for the ones who would believe.

Christ and His Father (John 17:1–5)

In the first section of the prayer, again we note that Christ prays for himself: "The hour has come. Glorify Your Son, that the Son may glorify You, even as you gave Him authority over all flesh, that to all whom You have given Him, He may give eternal life" (John 17:1–2).

Here then, Jesus defines his mission and its scope. He had been given "authority over all mankind" and to all those the Father has given him, he will, in turn, give eternal life (see also Ephesians 1:3–7). As John 17:3 makes clear, eternal life is to "know You [the Father], the only true God, and Jesus Christ whom You have sent." And knowing God, in this sense, is a matter of faith.

The term rendered "know" is a translation of the common Greek word, *ginosko,* meaning simply, "to know." *To know,* in the full sense of this term, however, means to learn or acquire knowledge through experience. In other words, Christ does not so much pray that these will come to know God intellectually (the term, *oida,* in the Greek) but rather that they will come to know God more fully in and through their own personal experience. In order to know God experientially, we must come to know his Son, by faith, that is, Jesus Christ who has been "sent" by the Father. The term *sent* is a translation of the Greek word *apostello,* which translated means, "one who has been sent as another's personal [and] authoritative representative."[4]

As he begins to pray, then, Jesus makes it clear that he has been sent to represent God on earth and to proclaim (in person, word, and deed) the message of eternal life to all mankind. Indeed, this was his mission, and it is the theme of this prayer. Yes, Christ desires that people everywhere will come to know the Father's love, embrace him by faith, and receive the gift of eternal life. This remains today the passion of his heart.

Christ and His Disciples (John 17:6–19)

In the second section of the prayer, Christ turns his attention to the eleven men who were there with him that night (Judas having left to betray him [John 13:21–30]). These disciples are, in context, the "men whom Thou gavest Me out of the world" (John 17:6). They had received the message of Christ as having come from the Father and had "believed that Thou has sent Me" (John 17:7–8). In other words, they had received eternal life and were, therefore, among the first fruits of Christ's mission and its success. Furthermore, they were the ones to whom he would now pass the baton.

So having first prayed for himself, what does Jesus next pray for his disciples? Knowing that he would no longer be with them "in the world" (John 17:11a), he prays that the Father would "keep them in Thy name . . . [so] that they may be one" (John 17:11b). As John 17:12 makes clear, Christ asks the Father to guard these men, that is, to keep them firm in faith so that not one of them would fall away. In addition, he prays that they would be one or, as Paul later expounds, "of the same mind, maintaining the same love, united in spirit, intent on one purpose" (Philippians 2:2). In other words, from now on it would be up to them to carry on the work and, as Christ's ambassadors, to proclaim eternal life throughout the world (Matthew 28:19, 20; Acts 1:8). According to his prayer, remaining firm in God by faith and walking together as one would be essential for accomplishing the mission.

Jesus also asks his Father to "keep them from the evil [one]," knowing that the world (those who reject the message) would hate them and the Word of God, which they would proclaim (John 17:14–15). Thus he describes the disciples as "not of this world" (John 17:16), that is, in faith and focus different from the rest. So to the Father he prays, "sanctify them in the truth" (John 17:17).

Finally, he commissions them to the task: "As Thou didst send Me into the world, I also have sent them into the world" (John 17:18).

So first (John 17:1–5), Jesus states that he was sent from God to proclaim the message of eternal life throughout the world and to offer salvation for all those who would believe. In next praying for his disciples (John 17:6–19), he commissions them to carry on this mission, and in so doing, he reveals his belief: the success of their efforts will depend on the Father "keeping them in Thy name," and on their "be[ing] one" (John 17:11). It should go without saying that these men did, in fact, live out their commission. They remained true to the Father in faith and advanced the cause as one. With this in mind, Christ reserves his final words for those whose lives these men would affect throughout history.

Christ and His Church (John 17:20–26)

In the final section of this prayer, Christ reveals that this same oneness of mind, love, spirit, and purpose will be equally vital for all those coming after the disciples—those who will, likewise, embrace the message and the mission: "I do not ask or pray on behalf of these alone, but for those also who believe in Me through their word" (John 17:20).

The question is, *Just who does he have in mind?* You know, no matter how many times I consider the answer, I am always amazed.

On the night before Jesus died, he prayed specifically for me, and he prayed specifically for you. Indeed, he prayed not only for his apostles, but for all those, like us, who have or will someday come to know him through their word. For from the oral and written testimonies of the first apostles, the Gospel message has gone forth. On and on it has been extended for two thousand years down to the present day, with the result that you and I now believe. Yes, from the Father to the Son, to the eleven men in the room with him that night, to and through the countless hands of untold saints throughout the centuries, the message and the mission of the Gospel has come down to you and me. Indeed, the race is now ours to run; the baton has been passed to us.

Such understanding, however, leads to a second and equally profound question: *Just what did Jesus Christ pray for us on the night before he died?*

Remarkably, he prayed just one thing and one thing only. Three times in three verses, he prayed that we would be one.

> [I pray] that they may all *be one,* even as You, Father, Are in Me, and I in You, that they also may be in Us, so that the world may know that You sent Me. The glory which You have given Me, I have given to them; that they may *be one,* just as we are one. I in them, and You in Me, that they may *be perfected in unity,* that the world may know that Thou didst send Me, and didst love them, even as Thou didst love Me. (John 17:21–23, emphasis mine)

Now as both scholars and students of the Word know, any time something is repeated in the text, it is done so for emphasis. Stressing the importance of his words, then, Christ prayed first that we would *"be one"* (John 17:21, emphasis mine in these quotes), then a second time that we would *"be one"* (John 17:22), and, finally, that we would be *"perfected in unity"* (John 17:23). Let's break this down for a moment.

First, Christ prays that "they may all be one." As mentioned earlier, he is speaking of all those who would come after the disciples who would believe in him through their word. Quite simply, this refers to any and all who would later embrace him by faith and receive eternal life, regardless of who they were, from where they had come, or in what century they lived. All those who believe, then, have been called to be one and, as we are fond of saying at Mosaic, *all means all!*

In addition, the word *perfected* is translated from the Greek word *teteleiomenoi* (the perfect-passive subjunctive of the word *teleo*), which, in this context, means "to become mature or, completely one." According to the *Linguistic Key to the Greek New Testament,* "use of the perfect [tense] indicates a permanent state as the goal and final result."[5] In other words, Christ intends for us (believers) to become mature in our faith, completely united as one and one with the Father (John 17:21).

But Why Be One?

Yet there is something even more profound to be revealed in the exegesis of this passage. Indeed we must ask, *Why does Christ pray so fervently for future followers to be completely united as one?*

Let's look at the passage again, but this time focused on a different aspect of the prayer:

[I pray] that they may all be one, even as You, Father, are in Me, and I in You, that they also may be in Us, so that the world may know that You sent Me. The glory which You have given Me, I have given to them; that they may be one, just as we are one. I in them, and You in Me, that they may be perfected in unity, [so] that the world may know that Thou didst send Me, and [so that the world may know that Thou] didst love them, even as Thou didst love Me. (John 17:21–23, addition mine)

In this second pass, it is significant to realize that Christ prayed we would be one for two very specific reasons or "so that" two things will occur.

The words *so that* in verses 21 and 23 are translated from the Greek word, *hina*. This word, a preposition, is used linguistically to introduce what Greek scholars refer to as an "*hina* clause." When used, the word points to the intended result or purpose of something and, in a broader sense, is used to introduce a "purpose clause." According to H. E. Dana and J. R. Mantey, writing in *A Manual Grammar of the Greek New Testament*, "The function of a 'purpose clause' is to express the aim of the action denoted by the main verb. This aim may be of a deliberate design . . . or merely of contemplated results."[6]

In other words, an *hina* clause introduces an "if–then" propositional truth. In essence, the proposition can be stated as follows: If X occurs (though there's no guarantee *that* X will occur), *if* X does occur, then Y is the guaranteed result.

With this in mind, we can paraphrase John 17:21–23 to read:

I also want to pray for those who, in time, will come to believe in Me through the witness of My disciples . . . I pray that those who come after them will be completely united as one. There is no guarantee that they will be one; but if they will, then two things will certainly result. First, men and women throughout the world will recognize that I am the promised Messiah. In addition, Father, men and women throughout the world will recognize that You love them. Consequently, they will respond to Your love and receive eternal life through faith in Me.

In other words, Christ prayed specifically that future generations of believers would be one *so that* the world would know God's love and believe. In this way and by this means, Christ stated that his mission would be accomplished through others and, ultimately, his Father glorified. What Jesus intends for us (the local church), then, is clear: we have been called to be one for the sake of the Gospel. It may not be easy, but it is biblical, and it is right. Therefore, we are to "walk in a manner worthy of the calling with which [we] have been called" (Ephesians 4:1). Indeed, when men and women of diverse backgrounds walk together as one in Christ, they uniquely reflect the Father's love *on earth as it is in heaven*. More than that, their oneness of mind, love, spirit, and purpose proclaim the Gospel in a most powerful and compelling way. For as his own union with the Father uniquely empowered Christ to proclaim God's love for the world, our union with fellow believers uniquely empowers us to do the same. Yes, in pursuing the *"perfection of unity,"* we will see the world saved.

Unity as Confirmation: Jesus Is the Christ

Literally hundreds of prophecies are recorded in the Old Testament concerning the coming of an "anointed one," or *Messiah*. Beginning with Genesis 3:15 and subsequent to the fall of man, they speak of a Messiah, a *Savior,* who would one day be sent from God to destroy the serpent, abolish evil, and redeem mankind. In so doing, the Savior will restore man to a place of prominence in the divine order and, more than that, to a personal relationship with his Creator.[7] In addition, the prophecies point to a coming Savior who would not only deliver the Jewish people from destruction but grant to people from every nation, tribe, and tongue the gift of eternal life as well.[8]

The question, however, has always been, *Who is the Savior and how will we know?*

According to Christ, the answer to these questions will be plainly manifest in and through the unity of believers: "If they [we] will be one," he prayed, then "the world [will] know that You sent Me." Yes, if we unite as one in mind, love, spirit, and purpose, the world will experientially understand that he is truly the Savior of the world. For only the Messiah, the *Prince of Peace,* can redeem mankind—men and women from every nation, tribe, people, and tongue—and unite them as one before the Father, thereby establishing peace on earth, goodwill toward men.

In this sense, his use of the word *sent,* a translation of the Greek word *apostollos,* is intentional. As we have already seen (John 17:4) and here again (John 17:23), Jesus is referring to himself as the personal, authoritative representative of God in language these men clearly would have understood.

In addition and through the oneness of future followers, Christ foresees that "the world will know that You love them." Although today we take this for granted, we should remember that at the time of this prayer, the fact of God's love for all the world was, in general, a radical concept to the Jewish mind. In that day, most Jews believed that *YHWH* was their God, that he loved their nation exclusively. From their perspective, then, "the Egyptians have their gods, the Hittites have their gods, the Phoenicians have their gods, and we, the Jews, have our God." In contrast, it was not God's love but God's wrath that they believed would one day befall the rest of mankind.

So when Christ prays for the world to "know" God's love, he is speaking directly to the fact that salvation is not just for the Jews. And he says that all mankind will experience his love when men and women of diverse backgrounds are willing to walk together as one in Christ. In so doing, believers manifest the reality that, "He Himself is our peace, who made both groups (Jews and Gentiles) into one and broke down the barrier of the dividing wall" (Ephesians 2:14).

On the night before he died then, Jesus Christ delivered to us the most effective means for reaching the world with the Gospel. He did not ask us to write books, bring evangelists to our cities, or put fish emblems on our cars. Nor did he instruct us to win the world through large churches built by and for a specific segment of society. For that matter, he did not pray that we would be "seeker-sensitive," "postmodern," "emergent," or "purpose-driven." Rather, he called us to be one; then, he said, the world would know God's love and believe.

Yes, in the twenty-first century it will be the unity of diverse believers walking as one in and through the local church that will proclaim the fact of God's love for all people more profoundly than any one sermon, book, or evangelistic crusade. And I believe the coming integration of the local church will lead to the fulfillment of the Great Commission, to people of every nation, tribe, people, and tongue coming to know him as we do.

This, then, is the core of our message. This is the prayer of Christ.

○

Amer Chami

Amer was the first person to respond to Mosaic's witness of Christ-like love for all people. Having arrived from Saudi Arabia just one month before the tragic events of September 11, 2001, his conversion to Christ is all the more miraculous. It is a vivid testimony to the power of unity in advancing the Gospel, even among the most entrenched of Muslim believers.

As a young man, I had two hopes in my mind. One was to visit a church for fifteen minutes and to see how Christians worship and discover what, if any, joy they might have in doing that. The other was to convert as many people to Islam as I could.

I was invited to a meeting with international students and introduced to a man willing to help me with my needs. In order to learn English, we began reading the Bible together and I was soon drawn to the truth of this book. God loves and accepts me for who I am, not for what I do. He is forgiving and calls me his child. The message of Christ is as simple as that.

I soon visited Mosaic and found people who were reflecting these truths. It was at this point, too, I wanted to believe as they did, but I was afraid for my life, my family, and my future. So I prayed, "Dear Jesus, I believe that you are real. If you want me to follow you, please show yourself to me."

I was still unsure of his existence, and furthermore I thought that even if Jesus was God, he would certainly not reveal himself to me. This would be my excuse not to follow him. I could go on with my life.

One evening during the church service and soon after I had prayed that prayer, a bright light appeared to me—a light, I realized, that only I could see. In my heart, I recognized the light to be Jesus, though I had never before this time heard him described as the light of the world. Jesus appeared to me in answer to my prayer. I can tell you in that moment, I was no longer afraid of following him by faith. I was afraid of not doing so! That night, during Mosaic's first communion service, I became a follower of Christ.

To say that Jesus is the light of the world is not only a metaphorical proposition; it is an experiential reality for me as well. I know this to be true and pray that Muslims will one day allow themselves to read the Bible so that they, too, will see and follow the light.

THE PATTERN AT ANTIOCH

---

*Community is not a common ideology, but a response to a
common call.*

—Henri Nouwen

HAVING RECEIVED CHRIST IN 1980, I was part of a generation of young
people influenced by the musician and songwriter Keith Green. A powerfully anointed, prophetic voice to an entire generation, he once wrote the
following lyric:

Jesus commands us to go.
It should be the exception if we stay.
It's no wonder we're moving so slow,
when His children refuse to obey,
feeling so called to stay.[1]

Although Keith's challenge, like so many appealing to the Great Commission
(Matthew 28:19–20), seems focused on foreign missions, it should cause us
to consider opportunities for cross-cultural evangelism in our own countries
as well. Particularly in the United States, it is true now that the nations have
come to us. To reach the world for Christ, then, no longer necessitates the
crossing of an ocean. Today we can do so simply by crossing the street![2]

Of Nations and Neighbors

Yet how sad it is that so many well-meaning believers attempting to build
relationships with others ethnically and economically different from
themselves are reluctant to invite acquaintances, coworkers, and

neighbors to the homogeneous churches they attend. And although an invited guest might come once in deference to the relationship, it will be obvious (in most situations) why he or she will not likely come again: "It," they will say, "just doesn't feel right."

The question is, *Just what, exactly, is "it"?*

I can say with some confidence that *it* is not so much the church itself or the claims of Christ espoused there. Indeed, *it* will not be the preaching style, the music, or any other programmatic feature of the church that will keep the invited guest from returning a second time. Rather, *it* will be the perception of racism. *It* will be the reality of segregation. *It* will be the feeling minorities know all too well: "You're really not welcome here."

With this in mind, I believe the homogeneous church will increasingly struggle in the twenty-first century with credibility, that is, in proclaiming a message of God's love for *all* people from an environment in which a love for *all* people cannot otherwise be observed. Fortunately, multi-ethnic church planters and reformers are now mobilizing to affect this otherwise predictable outcome. No one who makes the effort to walk with God or with his people should ever feel rejection from local expressions of the Body of Christ. Indeed, if the heart of God is for all people, so should be the collective heart of all those who call themselves one with him. Because he embraces men and women from every nation, tribe, people, and tongue, so should the local church.

Getting Beyond Ourselves

In Matthew 28:19, Jesus commands his disciples: "Go . . . and make disciples of all the nations." But have you ever wondered why we must read eight chapters into the book of Acts—nearly one-third of the way through the book—before finding anyone willing to leave Jerusalem for the sake of the Gospel? This is true in spite of the fact that on the night before he died, Jesus specifically commissioned the disciples to take the message of eternal life to the world: "As Thou didst send Me into the world, I also have sent them into the world" (John 17:18).

And later, at the time of his ascension, he instructed them "not [yet] to leave Jerusalem, but to wait for what the Father had promised . . . [for] you shall receive power when the Holy Spirit has come upon you; and you shall be My witnesses both in Jerusalem, and in all Judea and Samaria, and even to the remotest part of the earth" (Acts 1:4, 8).

The question is this: *If Jesus commanded his disciples to go, why did they stay for so long in Jerusalem among their own people?*

The fact is that it was difficult for the first disciples to understand that the kingdom of God, God's unconditional love, and the message of eternal life was to extend beyond Jewish borders. Likewise, they seem to have found it difficult to leave the environment in which they were most familiar.

Sound like others you know? Does this describe you? Yes, I'm speaking of "the comfort zone." It's not an easy place for most of us to leave or to even acknowledge that we are living in at all. Yet from Adam and Eve's flight from the garden to Abram's wanderings in a land far from his home; from Joseph to Ruth, to Esther to Isaiah, and from Christ himself to the apostle Paul, it is hard to find anyone of significant stature in the Bible who was not first called to leave someone, something, or someplace behind in order to become all that God intended them to be or to do all that God intended them to do. In order to build a healthy multi-ethnic church then, we must be willing to do the same. Indeed, we must be willing to leave the comfort and familiarity of homogeneity in order to, "go and make disciples of all the nations." And this we can do right here in our own backyard, that is, by embracing *all* people in and through the local church.

A Gospel Not Just for the Jews

Having been instructed to remain in Jerusalem, the disciples do wait for the Holy Spirit in obedience to Christ. And soon he comes upon them in power, resulting in the birth of the church at Pentecost (Acts 2:1–4). From there, we read of these men speaking miraculously in tongues, of Peter's first sermon, and of the conversion of three thousand souls. In subsequent chapters, we learn also of their devotion to God, their commitment to one another, and the initial triumphs and tribulations that, together, they experience (Acts 2–6).

Following the stoning of Stephen in Acts 7, however, "a great persecution began against the church in Jerusalem, and they were *all* scattered throughout the regions of Judea and Samaria, *except the apostles*" (Acts 8:1, emphasis mine). Again we might wonder, *Why do these men— commanded to go—still remain in Jerusalem?* Furthermore, *Why is it that God has to use persecution to get the church to obey?*

No matter our conclusions, among those who scattered was a man named Philip, one of the men who had been appointed to care for the Hellenistic widows (Acts 6:5) in Jerusalem. Beginning in Acts 8:5, we read that Philip traveled north to Samaria, becoming the first to proclaim Christ beyond Judea following the resurrection of Christ. Even more remarkable, however, is the fact that Philip preached Christ to the Samaritans at a time when they were a people largely estranged from the Jews; why they were estranged bears mentioning.

In 722 B.C., the Assyrians conquered the Northern Kingdom of Israel and its capital city, Samaria. According to Assyrian governance, the people they conquered (Jews, in this case) were often deported from their homeland in large numbers and dispersed throughout the Assyrian Empire. Other people were then "imported" to the newly acquired land and, through intermarriage, pure bloodlines corrupted. In such a way, the Assyrians sought to redistribute the population within their empire in order to reduce the possibility of national rebellion or retaliation.

This strategy of acquisition and redistribution, however, was quite different from the governing philosophy of the Babylonians, who later succeeded the Assyrians in world domination. Led by King Nebuchadnezzar, the Babylonians conquered the Southern Kingdom of Judea in 586 B.C. Yet unlike the Assyrians, the Babylonians only deported the young and promising from newly conquered lands in order to prepare them for future leadership within the empire.[3] Once trained, these young men would be sent back to their homelands to help govern their own people according to Babylonian law. Therefore, following the conquest of the Southern Kingdom by Babylon, the vast majority of Jews were allowed to remain in Judea, albeit as a subjugated people.

Consequently, because Jewish *blood* in the Northern Kingdom had been corrupted through intermarriage with Assyrians, the Samaritans were largely estranged from the tribe of Judah at the time of Christ. In addition, Jewish *faith* had also been compromised, for in repopulating the region, the Assyrians had brought pagan gods, beliefs, worship rights, and rituals into the land once ruled by David and Solomon. For these reasons, the way, the truth, and the life were no longer clear in Samaria, as Christ's interaction with a woman at the well makes clear (John 4:19–26).

It is against this backdrop, then, that Philip journeys north from Jerusalem to proclaim the message of God's love for all people; amazingly, his "cross-cultural" ministry is a great success. Attracted by his message, the casting out of unclean spirits, and miracles of healing, "[all] the people of Samaria . . . from [the] smallest to greatest, were giving attention to him, saying, 'This man is what is called the Great Power of God'" (Acts 8:10). Philip's preaching results in the salvation and baptism of many people in that city (Acts 8:12)—many people, that is, who were not of Jewish blood or background.

When word of this reached the disciples in Jerusalem, they dispatched Peter and John to investigate. And sure enough, they find that Samaritans are truly entrusting themselves by faith to Christ. As Peter and John prepare to return to Jerusalem, however, the Holy Spirit compels Philip to go south toward Gaza, and along the way he meets an Ethiopian eunuch. Soon this man, too, receives the Lord in response to Philip's witness.

Now at this point, it's appropriate to affirm my belief in the inerrant word of God: indeed, I believe that "every jot and tittle" in the original languages is "God-breathed" (2 Timothy 3:16) and that everything recorded in the Bible has divine intent and purpose. With this in mind we should ask, *Why is ethnicity being mentioned in the context of describing those who were being led to Christ by Philip, that is, in describing the Samaritans and an Ethiopian as well?* The answer, I believe, is clear: the Holy Spirit is demonstrating to disciples, both then and now, that the "good news," like the church itself, is not just for the Jews.

Peter Sees for Himself

In keeping with this theme, Luke (the author of Acts) next accounts for the conversion of a Roman centurion named Cornelius. According to Acts 10:2, Cornelius was a devout Gentile who was charitable to the Jews and one who prayed to God continually. In response to his prayers, an angel of the Lord appears to Cornelius in a vision and instructs him to send for a man named Simon (Peter). He was to invite Peter to his house in order to hear a message from him (Acts 10:22).

On the next day and while Cornelius' servants were en route, Peter enters into prayer and soon falls into a trance (Acts 10:9–10). In this state, he envisions the heavens opening up and a sheet coming down out of the sky filled with various animals deemed profane by the Jews. A voice then instructs him: "Get up, Peter, kill and eat" (Acts 10:13). But Peter balks: "By no means, Lord, for I have never eaten anything unholy and unclean" (Acts 10:14).

Twice more this scene is repeated, and, according to Acts 10:17, "Peter was greatly perplexed in mind as to what the vision [might mean]."

Providentially, the servants connect with Peter as he awakens from this experience. They then share with Peter their mission and on the next day accompany him to the house of Cornelius. Coming into the house, Peter sets the context for his arrival and, in so doing, adds something vitally important to our discussion. He says, "You [Gentiles] yourselves know how unlawful it is for a man who is a Jew to associate with a foreigner or to visit him; and yet, God has shown me that I should [no longer] call any man unholy or unclean" (Acts 10:28, additions mine).

According to Peter, it was at this time not only ill advised for Jews to associate with Gentiles, it was an unlawful breach of religious protocol. Here again, we get a glimpse of why it may have been hard for the first disciples to take the message of God's love to the nations beyond Judea. In this moment, however, the Holy Spirit is writing a new law upon Peter's heart. For through the vision and his encounter with Cornelius, Peter stands corrected: "I most certainly understand now that God is not one to show partiality, but in every nation the man who fears Him and does what is right, is welcome to Him" (Acts 10:35).

So as Peter shares the Gospel with these Gentiles, the Holy Spirit falls upon all who are listening, with the result that Cornelius, together with his relatives and close friends, responds in faith, receives the Holy Spirit, and is baptized (Acts 10:24–48). The significance of this moment does not go unnoticed by the Jews, for as Luke records, "All the circumcised believers who had come with Peter were amazed, because the gift of the Holy Spirit had been poured out upon the Gentiles also" (Acts 10:47).

When we consider these early stories of conversion featuring the Samaritans, an Ethiopian, and the Roman soldier, Cornelius,[4] they should cause us to ask, *If God himself does not show partiality in reaching out to others, why is partiality allowed to exist within the local church today?* Indeed, *If God welcomes men and women of every nation, tribe, people, and tongue into his kingdom, why is it that the vast majority of churches in the United States are not likewise welcoming diverse people into their local fellowships?*

Now to this question, I suppose some will say, "Our church would never turn away anyone. On the contrary, anyone is welcome to come and worship with us or even to become members of our church, regardless of race or economics."

Please know that I am in no way doubting the sincerity of those who respond in this way. However, the fact is that although most people (and the local churches they attend) might not intentionally turn others away, these same people, more often than not, do very little intentionally to invite or otherwise attract people unlike themselves to their church. Indeed, given the fact that more than 90 percent of churches in the United States today are segregated, we can safely conclude that homogeneous church leadership has proven reluctant, unwilling, or unable (at least to this point) to adapt their own majority culture in order to accommodate individuals of varying ethnic or economic backgrounds within the local church.

Thankfully, a new spirit is in the air! Yes, increasingly, church planters and reformers are questioning whether or not the homogeneous church biblically reflects the heart of God for all people; consequently, they are determining to build healthy multi-ethnic churches.

The Case for Inclusion

So Philip got it, and Peter got it, but what about the others? You would expect that the conversion of an entire Gentile household would have greatly excited the leaders of the one and only church existing at that time. However, this was not the case, for according to Luke, "when Peter came up to Jerusalem, those who were circumcised took issue with him, saying, 'You went to uncircumcised men and ate with them?!'" (Acts 11:2–3).

Having been called on the carpet, Peter responds by describing "in orderly sequence" all that had occurred (Acts 11:4). Yet this is no calm presentation. He passionately responds to their challenge! They have taken issue with him and called his actions into question. Indeed, a full-blown debate ensues over a pivotal theological point, and the discussion gets loud.

Toward the conclusion of his argument, Peter makes his point: "If God therefore gave to [the Gentiles] the same gift as He gave to us [Jews] also after believing in the Lord Jesus Christ, who was I that I could stand in God's way?!" (Acts 11:17, additions mine).

Notice that the next verse conveys the tone and tenor of the discussion. "And when they heard this, they quieted down" (Acts 11:18a). Of course, there would be no need to quiet down unless it had first become loud! More important, however, is what they affirm in response: "Well then, God has granted to the Gentiles also the repentance that leads to life" (Acts 11:18).

This is amazing! Luke's nearly half-way through the book of Acts before he can state with confidence that leaders of the emerging Church understand this most profound truth: the Gospel, like the Church, is not just for the Jews but is for everyone—Jews and Gentiles alike.

The next verse, though, makes it clear that the issue had not yet been settled for everyone. Indeed, it demonstrates the struggle. For those who were driven from Jerusalem following the stoning of Stephen "made their way to Phoenicia, Cyprus and Antioch, *speaking the word to no one except the Jews*" (Acts 11:19, emphasis mine). And this would be outright disheartening if not for what happened next: "But there were some of them, men of Cyprus and Cyrene, who came to Antioch and began speaking to the Greeks[5] also, preaching the Lord Jesus" (Acts 11:20).

In other words, there were some who said, "I'm not going home. I'm going to Antioch . . . , and I'm not just going to speak only to my own people. I'm going to speak to anyone who will listen!" This was a truly significant step and, in my opinion, the most pivotal moment in the entire New Testament concerning the growth and development of the Church for the following reasons.

First, the evangelists and church planters mentioned in Acts 11:20 were men of diverse cultural background: Cypus was [is] an island in the Mediterranean Sea, and Cyrene is a city on the North African coast, today located in modern-day Libya. It is this regional diversity that Luke refers to in describing these men. In addition, what makes this passage so remarkable is that it screams intentionality. Notice that these men chose not to return to their own land, that is, to environments in which they were most comfortable. Nor did they determine to speak only to the Jews, that is, to those most like themselves. Rather, they turned from a more *natural* course to embrace a *supernatural* one instead. And in so doing, they entered the third-largest city in the Roman Empire with a passion to see both Jews and Gentiles become one in Christ. It should come as no surprise, then, to learn that "the hand of the Lord was with them" (Acts 11:21).

Why Large Numbers Believed

So what were the results of their efforts? Three times in the next six verses (Acts 11:21–26), we read the phrase "large numbers"—twice concerning those who were being saved and once in connection with those who were then being discipled at Antioch. Yes, this was big. This was God!

This time, when news of Gentile conversions reached the church in Jerusalem, leadership dispatched Barnabus to investigate the claim. And in so doing, they would have been thinking, *Can it really be true? Are the Gentiles in large numbers now turning in faith to Christ?*

Barnabus himself was a convert to Christ, born in Cyprus and of Jewish (Levite) blood (Acts 4:36). His birth name was Joseph, but Luke tells us that the apostles called him, "Son of Encouragement," and at various points throughout the book of Acts, we learn why. For instance, it is Barnabus who first speaks to the apostles on behalf of a new convert and future apostle named Saul, later called Paul (Acts 9:26).

After arriving at Antioch, Barnabus is so overwhelmed by what he sees that he does not even return to Jerusalem. Rather, he heads north to Asia

Minor to look for a man well suited for ministry in the diverse environment at Antioch—an environment in which both Jews and Gentiles were not only coming to Christ by faith but, consequently, into an unprecedented situation—one in which people formerly alienated from one another would now be expected to walk, work, and worship God together in unity. Barnabus must have reasoned that these people and this emerging local church would need strong teaching, directional leadership, and an innovative problem solver. They would need Paul!

Barnabus' reaction is further explained in Acts 11:24, where Luke comments, "He was a good man, and full of the Holy Spirit and of faith." Such indeed must be the defining characteristics of all those who would build a healthy multi-ethnic church. In fact, apart from the Holy Spirit and the exercise of faith, it cannot otherwise be established, as we'll discuss further in Chapter Four.

After Barnabus locates Paul, the two of them return to Antioch, and "for an entire year they met with the church and taught considerable numbers there" (Acts 11:26a). At this point, it is significant to realize that in the sovereignty of God, Paul was not established in ministry at Jerusalem but in the church at Antioch. And from there, too, he would be sent to the world. This, in fact, is not coincidental. Indeed, the New Testament describes Paul as "a man from Tarsus" (Acts 9:11), a "Hebrew of Hebrews" (Philippians 3:2–6), and a Roman citizen (Acts 22:25–28). Consequently, this unique blend of Jewish blood and Roman citizenship afforded him understanding and experience, advantage and opportunity, mobility, education, and rights, which providentially equipped him for ministry among the diverse people of Antioch and to those beyond, down to the present day.

A New Term for a New People

Now someone asks, "Where were believers first called Christians?" And another responds, "At Antioch, Acts 11:26; 10 points, right? Next question . . . "

Whoa, not so fast!

Although many have read or heard this was the case, far fewer have asked the question, *What is so significant about this piece of "Bible trivia?"* Because we know that there is nothing at all trivial about the Bible, we should pause to consider the answer. Indeed, we should ask why it bears mentioning at this very place in the Word of God. By definition, the term *Christian* is derived from the Greek word, *Cristos*, which means "Messiah." After two thousand years of use (and misuse), however, the term *Christian* today means different things to different people throughout the world. Yet at the time of Paul in Antioch, it meant only one thing about those to whom it was applied. Christians were "followers of Christ"—those attempting to live according to his teachings and striving to be "Christ-like" in their actions and attitudes. Christians, then, were not only those who loved God but were those who sought to love one another unconditionally.

So Jews were loving Gentiles, Gentiles were loving Jews, and they were all worshipping God together as one in the local church at Antioch. Yes, it blew everyone away! This was unprecedented, remarkable, amazing, and miraculous, for only a *Prince of Peace* can bring peace to historically estranged people groups; only a *Messiah* can unite the world as one by sowing love into the hearts of those who for so long had been filled with hate. Indeed, only a god, that is, *the one true God,* Jesus Christ, can turn Jews and Gentiles—people of every nation, tribe, and tongue—into Christians. With this in mind, it is not coincidental that the disciples were first called Christians at Antioch. For there, Jesus Christ was clearly recognized in the midst of unity, just as he had said he would be (John 17:23).

When considered in this light, a piece of "Bible trivia" becomes profoundly meaningful. Indeed, it is the very link connecting Christ's prayer for his followers and the hina clauses of John 17:21–23 to the very results they anticipate. In the church at Antioch, we see the fulfillment of all that was anticipated by Christ in his prayer, as both Jews and Gentiles came to know the Father's love through the unity of his children. It is the church at Antioch, then, and not the church at Jerusalem, that should serve as our model in this regard. Indeed, it is the church at Antioch and not the church in Jerusalem that is the most influential church of the entire New Testament.

Yes, it was the congregation at Antioch that first took up a collection for those in need, namely, the "brethren living in Judea" (Acts 11:28–30). More significantly, it was the church at Antioch that first mobilized in response to the Great Commission to send missionaries to the world (Acts 13:2–3). In fact, not one but three missionary journeys (the only ones recorded in the book of Acts) were launched from Antioch; consequently, the Gospel spread throughout all of Asia Minor and into Europe as well. Let's imagine how this might have happened.

In the church at Antioch, there were people of varying ethnic and cultural backgrounds—converted Jews and Gentiles alike. Presumably, many of these would have been drawn to the bustling city from all over the known world. Having received Christ and then growing in faith

(Acts 11:26), it is likely that these new believers would have soon considered their mothers and fathers, sisters and brothers, extended family members and friends alike still living in the lands from which they came. In other words, they would have surely recognized a need for their loved ones to hear the message of God's love and to receive the gift of eternal life. With this in mind, we can imagine Paul first posing the following question to those in Antioch, as he would again later to those living in Rome:

> How then shall they call upon Him in whom they have not believed? And how shall they believe in Him whom they have not heard? And how shall they hear without a preacher? And how shall they preach unless [someone] is sent? (Romans 10:14–15)

It is not apart from experience, then, that Paul wrote these words to the Romans. For prompted by the Spirit, it was this church—the church at Antioch—that had sent Paul and Barnabus to the world.

So why did the church at Antioch care about the world? Because the church at Antioch reflected the world! They were a multi-ethnic people who considered it essential to send their money, their men, and the message of hope abroad to family, friends, and countrymen in obedience to Christ (Matthew 28:19–20; Acts 1:8). For them, missionary endeavor was not simply programmatic or merely a line item in the annual budget; rather, it was, more authentically, something that flowed from who they were. In fact, the awareness of global needs is one of the more refreshing characteristics of a healthy multi-ethnic church. Indeed, leadership in such a place will not have to work as hard as some to develop or maintain within the congregation a heart for others beyond its walls. Rather, such understanding is inherent in the DNA of a church populated by diverse individuals who have chosen to walk together as one in Christ for the sake of the Gospel.

Diverse Leadership for a Diverse People

But perhaps the most intriguing thing about the church at Antioch was the diversity of its pastoral leadership team. According to Acts 13:1, "there were at Antioch, in the church that was there, prophets and teachers; Barnabus, and Simeon who was called Niger, and Lucius of Cyrene and Manaen who had been brought up with Herod the tetrarch, and Saul."

It is interesting that Luke lists these men not only by name but also by ethnicity. *Why was Simeon called Niger?* Because he was from Niger, a country located, both then and now, in sub-Saharan West Africa. And Lucius was from Cyrene, a city near the northern coast of Africa in what is today the country of Libya. With this in mind, perhaps Lucius was one of the original evangelists and church planters at Antioch mentioned in Acts 11:20 and, therefore, among the first to arrive in Antioch speaking to both Jews and Gentiles. Next we read of Manaen, who had been brought up with Herod the tetrarch. This tells us that Manaen was from somewhere in Palestine, either Judea, Galilee, or perhaps even from Samaria, for the Herodian dynasty ruled over the entire region from approximately 65 B.C. to 90 A.D. Luke's comment also points the reader to Manaen's privileged upbringing, for Manaen could not have been raised with the son of a king unless he had the proper connections, pedigree, and access to funds.

Yet it is true, the passage does not comment directly on the background of Barnabus or Paul. However, there is no need again to do so. Luke has already informed his readers that Barnabus was from the island of Cyprus (Acts 4:32) and that Paul was from the Roman city of Tarsus, located in Asia Minor (Acts 9:11). Therefore, the point is made. Luke has listed the five leaders of the church at Antioch not only by gifting and role but (significantly) by ethnicity as well. Surely it is more than coincidental that two of these men were from Africa, one was from the Mediterranean, one was from the Middle East, and one was from Asia Minor! In light of all we have discussed, I do not believe that this passage should be dismissed merely as descriptive of the local church at Antioch. Such indirect prescription[6] is informative for the church today and, certainly, for the multi-ethnic church, as we'll discuss further in Chapter Six.

A Church for All People, Then and Now

Finally, we should consider the socioeconomic status of the first converts in Europe resulting from Paul's second missionary journey. Indeed, *What can Acts 16 teach us about the heart of God for those of varying economic class?*

According to Acts 16:14, the first convert in Europe was "a certain woman named Lydia . . . a seller of purple fabrics." It is widely believed that Lydia was a woman of some financial means and a successful business owner. For example, after listening to Paul, Acts 16:15 tells us that "she and her household" were baptized, indicating that Lydia was also the head of her home. In addition, it is believed that she owned her own house, one that must have been somewhat substantial in size, for following her baptism, she prevails upon Paul, Silas, and Luke to stay with her there. Luke tells us also that the emerging church in Philippi met in her home, and it was the place where Paul and Silas met with the brethren following their miraculous release from jail.

Following the conversion of Lydia, we next learn of the deliverance of "a certain slave-girl, having a spirit of divination who was bringing her masters much profit by fortune telling" (Acts 16:16). The possibility of her conversion rests in the fact that Paul cast an unclean spirit out of her and immediately, "her masters saw that the hope of their profit was gone" (Acts 16:19a). This story's placement between two other clear accounts of conversion lends further weight to the probability that this girl came to know the Lord as well.

The cleansing and conversion of this slave-girl, however, caused quite a disturbance in the city, resulting in Paul and Silas being beaten and thrown into jail (Acts 16:19–24). Yet that same night, an earthquake shook the foundations of the building, causing all the doors to open and the chains of the prisoners to come undone (Acts 16:26). The rest of the passage (Acts 16:27–40) tells of the jailer's conversion and, as in the case of Lydia, the conversion of his entire household. The point here is that the jailer represents the middle class, for who else pulls the night shift? From the very beginning, then, the New Testament local church was not only ethnically diverse but economically diverse as well.

Now some will argue that such passages are only *descriptive* and not *prescriptive* today for the local church. However, I do not believe this to be the case. Rather, such thinking provides far too many people with an excuse to maintain the status quo, namely, the segregation of the local church. Yet we should recognize that this segregation does not at all reflect the will of God *on earth as it is in heaven*. With this in mind, then, I believe such passages are both descriptive and indirectly prescriptive in nature. In fact, the New Testament provides much more insight into the mind of God on the matter, and in the next chapter, we not only consider a select passage but an entire letter that clearly (and directly) prescribes the multi-ethnic church. Indeed, the book of Ephesians is the very foundation of the exegetical argument.

o

Angelica Rumpler

Soon after Amer accepted Christ (see Chapter One), he shared his story at Mosaic for the first time publicly. That very night, two others embraced Christ by faith: a nineteen-year-old student from Japan and an older man of African descent. Two nights later, a young woman from Austria—Angelica Rumpler—also gave her life to Christ in response to Amer's witness. Here is just part of her story.

> Honestly, I had always considered myself a Christian, coming from a country with a vast majority of Catholics. I was baptized as a baby and went to church at least every Easter and Christmas. But it never came to my mind that you could actually have a personal relationship with God.
>
> My image of God was that he is a distant God, a punishing God, someone whose faith you had to earn. But then I came to Little Rock and things changed. I still remember the first time I came to Mosaic. Philip Lamar, who was the first person to join Mark's staff, asked me if I wanted to go. Since I did not have anything else to do on a Sunday afternoon, I went along and I loved it. People were so passionate and enthusiastic about God, something I had never experienced before. You could feel that there was a difference.
>
> Over the next few months, God kept bringing so many wonderful people into my life, people who truly and deeply loved the Lord. They showed me that it is possible to have a personal relationship with God. They were a wonderful example for me, showing me what it truly means to be a Christian.
>
> Of course, I tried to run away from all that, thinking that if *it works for you, fine, but it doesn't have to work for me.* But God didn't leave me alone.
>
> So finally on December 18, 2001, at two o'clock in the morning, I accepted Jesus Christ as my Savior. My life, definitely, has changed since then." [Not long after this] I had to go back to Austria for a few months, a time I considered to be a testing of my faith. It was not an easy time. But [soon] I [was] back in Little Rock with my family at Mosaic.

Over the next few years, Angelica continued to mature in her faith. She was a faithful volunteer in the children's ministry at Mosaic and actively involved with young adults in reaching out to other internationals in Central Arkansas. One of her joys was seeing Stefania Cane, an Italian Ph.D. student, come to know the Lord in the summer of 2006. Angelica had met Stefania a year before and had befriended her.

Now living in Austria, Angelica continues to pursue the Lord and his plans for her life.

3

THE PAULINE MYSTERY

*Do not follow where the path may lead. Go instead where there
is no path and leave a trail.*

—Muriel Strode

INCREASINGLY, local church planters and reformers are envisioning
congregations through which men and women of diverse backgrounds
can worship God together as one. Yet for dreams to become reality, it is
essential that the growing fascination with the multi-ethnic church be
informed by sound theological reflection. In other words, the emerging
movement must be based on biblical *prescription* rather than on current
cultural *description* if it is to succeed in bringing the first-century church
to the United States of the twenty-first century and beyond.

This chapter is based on my belief that the local church at Ephesus was
made up of both Jewish and Gentile converts and thus was multi-ethnic.
Indeed, biblical evidence does not support the notion of a homogeneous
church at Ephesus. With this in mind, a fresh and more comprehensive
look at the letter will challenge popular wisdom concerning church
growth and, specifically, the future effectiveness of the homogeneous-unit
principle in an increasingly diverse and cynical society.

Jews and Gentiles in Ephesus

Paul's experience in Ephesus begins with a brief stop there en route to
Syria. As was his custom, "he . . . entered the synagogue and reasoned
with the Jews" (Acts 18:19). Though invited to remain in the city, he
deferred, promising "to return . . . again if God wills" (Acts 18:21).

It was on his third missionary journey that Paul fulfilled this promise. Coming into the city, he encountered twelve men—disciples who had been baptized only into "John's baptism" (Acts 19:1–3, 7). Discovering, however, that they had not yet received or even heard of the Holy Spirit, he offered them a more complete explanation of the Gospel. "When they heard this, they were baptized in the name of the Lord Jesus" (Acts 19:5).

The timing of their introduction in Acts makes it probable that these men were disciples of Apollos, whose ministry in Ephesus is reported to have taken place between Paul's second and third missionary journeys. Apollos had been instructed in the way of the Lord (Acts 18:25), and though fervent in spirit, his understanding was limited; according to this passage, he was "acquainted only with the baptism of John." In addition, Luke tells us that in Achaia, Apollos "powerfully refuted the Jews in public" (Acts 18:28). We can assume he had done so in Ephesus as well.

Following this event, Paul again entered the synagogue, "reasoning and persuading [Jews] about the kingdom of God," for a period of three months (Acts 19:8). According to the next verse, there were some who believed and some who did not. Those who did believe were taken from the synagogue to be taught in the School of Tyrannus, to which Paul transferred his public teaching ministry for the next two years. And it was through Paul's teaching there that "all who lived in Asia heard the word of the Lord, *both Jews and Greeks*"[1] (Acts 19:10, emphasis mine).

Consequently, the multi-ethnic nature of the church at Ephesus began to take shape. In Acts 19:17 we learn that the name of the Lord Jesus was being magnified among *both Jews and Greeks who lived at Ephesus*. Even Paul himself speaks to the diversity of the church in his farewell address to the Ephesian elders (Acts 20:21).

From the beginning, then, the church at Ephesus included both Jewish and Gentile converts. Together with the tone and tenor of Paul's letter to the Ephesians, such passages argue strongly for a community of inclusion at Ephesus. In light of this, the mandate for the multi-ethnic church expressed through this book becomes all the more clear.

A Love for All the Saints

Although few question the fact that a major focus of Ephesians is the church, far fewer recognize the theme of unity that flows throughout the book as well. Similarly, the simplistic division of the book into two halves, with chapters 1 through 3 devoted to doctrine and chapters 4 through 6 devoted to practical Christian living, does little to validate the context or to enhance our understanding of Paul's expectation that the local church is to be inclusive without distinction.

In Ephesians 1, Paul describes the blessed state of believers made one with God through Jesus Christ and calls attention to the Holy Spirit, who is "given to us as a pledge of our inheritance" (Ephesians 1:3–14). In so doing, he establishes the fact that all who have believed are now part of God's family, predestined to adoption as sons and joint heirs of the kingdom.

But where is Paul going with such thoughts? "For this reason, I, too, having heard of your faith . . . and *your love for all the saints,* do not cease giving thanks for you" (Ephesians 1:15–16, emphasis mine).

Notice that Paul's thankful remembrance of the Ephesians is not only rooted in the fact of their faith but also in the fact of their love for *all the saints.* Use of the word *all* here is, in fact, a significant point of interest. *To whom is Paul referring, and why does he employ such inclusive language?* It is my belief that Paul has in mind the multi-ethnic nature of this church—a community of faith in which both Jewish and Gentile converts worship God together as one. This conclusion finds even more support when observed, in retrospect, from the book of Revelation, but I'll hold that thought for later.

The Two Now One in Christ

Beginning in Ephesians 2:11, Paul turns his attention to the Gentile community within the church. The very plain and passionate language of the text makes it clear that the Gentiles are no longer to think of themselves (or, for that matter, to be thought of by the Jews) as "excluded from . . . [or] strangers to the covenant of promise, having no hope and without God in the world" (Ephesians 2:12). Paul's point is that the Gentiles have now been reconciled to God through faith and therefore to the "commonwealth of Israel" through the blood of Christ. To Paul, this reconciliation is not merely theoretical or an otherwise unobservable truth. It is to be manifest in the local church through which the "[Gentiles] are no longer strangers and aliens, but you are fellow citizens with the saints [Jewish converts in this context] and are of God's household . . . Christ Jesus being the cornerstone, in whom the whole building, being fitted together is growing into a holy temple in the Lord . . . a dwelling of God in the Spirit" (Ephesians 2:19–22). This, then, is Paul's vision for the local church. It is to be an authentic, visible community of faith where people of diverse backgrounds worship God together as one, and love one another in Christ.

Now, again, some may view this passage only as *descriptive* of the universal (capital "C") Church and not necessarily *prescriptive* for the local church today. Yet if Paul's teaching here is to be understood in this light, *Why does he later provide such specific instruction to the local church in Ephesians 4:1–3 and 4:11–13?* In other words, it is not likely that he would intend in one moment to speak of the universal Church and in another to speak of the local church without clearly stating so, or that he would expect his readers to intuitively recognize which one he was discussing at any given moment. Therefore, if Paul's teaching concerning spiritual gifts is intended for practical application within the context of a local church, we must also agree, for consistency's sake, that his teaching concerning the unity and diversity of believers is to be practically applied there as well. In the end, then, I believe the answer to this question is not an either-or but a both-and proposition.

The Mystery of Christ Revealed

Following his comments concerning the nature of the church, Paul intends next to share his prayer for the Ephesians (Ephesians 3:1, 14–19). However, he momentarily interrupts himself to remind the congregation of his apostolic mission. In Ephesians 3:2–13, a parenthetical statement is inserted in which he defines his calling (a "stewardship of grace") and declares that, "By way of revelation, there was made known to me the mystery . . . of Christ" (Ephesians 3:2–4). Here too, he mentions a previous letter he had written to the church in which he had also addressed his "insight into the mystery of Christ." According to Paul, understanding of this mystery had not been granted to past generations but had only "now been revealed to the apostles and prophets by the Spirit" (Ephesians 3:5).

A common error is to assume that the mystery Paul is speaking of is, simply, the mystery of the Gospel—the good news message of Christ's life, death, and resurrection, his atonement for sin. Yet this is most certainly not the case! For in verse 6, Paul makes clear that the mystery of Christ is something altogether different: "To be specific, the Gentiles are fellow heirs and fellow members of the body, and fellow partakers of the promise in Christ Jesus through the gospel" (Ephesians 3:6).

The *New International Version* (NIV) translates the passage this way: "This mystery is that through the gospel the Gentiles are heirs together with Israel, members together of one body and sharers in the promise in Christ Jesus" (Ephesians 3:6).

I believe this verse represents the very apex of the book from which all else written derives its context and meaning. In fact, it represents the very substance of Paul's life and ministry. Indeed, Paul is not describing himself here as merely a minister of the Gospel but a minister of "the mystery of Christ." Notice, too, that he calls himself a minister of "this" gospel (Ephesians 3:7, NIV), that is, of the good news concerning the unity of Jews and Gentiles in the church. Such understanding is further supported by his words near the end of the letter, at which time he asks the Ephesians to, "Pray also for me . . . so that I will fearlessly make known *the mystery of the gospel,* for which I am an ambassador in chains" (Ephesians 6:19–20, NIV, emphasis mine).

As Paul writes this letter from prison, he declares that he is not simply in chains for proclaiming the Gospel but for proclaiming *the mystery of Christ* (or *the mystery of the gospel*), namely, "that the Gentiles are fellow heirs [together with the Jews] . . . and partakers of the promise in Christ Jesus through the Gospel" (Ephesians 3:6; Colossians 4:2–4, addition mine).

Paul Imprisoned for This Reason

Now at this point, it's appropriate to recall why Paul's imprisonment began in Jerusalem. Acts 21:15–22 informs us that a mob had been incited by the false accusation that Paul brought Gentiles into the temple. In addressing the crowd, Paul offers a defense by telling the story of his conversion. And near the end of his remarks, he says something most interesting: "Then the Lord said to me, 'Go! For I will send you far away to the Gentiles'" (Acts 21:21, NIV).

Notice the crowd's response: "The crowd listened to Paul *until he said this.* Then they raised their voices and shouted, 'Rid the earth of him! He's not fit to live!'"(Acts 22:22, NIV, emphasis mine).

Indeed, the crowd listened to Paul up until the time he spoke of his calling to the Gentiles. It was only then, as he declared *"the mystery of Christ,"* that Paul became its ambassador in chains (Ephesians 6:20)!

Such understanding of Paul's unique role in the proclamation of the mystery of Christ can be also observed in his letter to the Romans. Again, his final words make clear what was most prominent in his mind:

> Now to him who is able to establish you by *my* gospel and the proclamation of Jesus Christ, according to the revelation of the mystery hidden for long ages past, but now revealed and made known through the prophetic writings by the command of the eternal God, *so that all nations might believe and obey him*—to the only wise God be glory forever through Jesus Christ! Amen. (Romans 16:25–27, NIV, emphasis mine)

In Colossians 1:24–27 also, Paul develops the concept of his unique calling as the one chosen to both proclaim and explain the mystery of Christ. According to this passage, he is the servant of Christ and of his body, commissioned "to present the word of God to you in its fullness the mystery that has been kept hidden for ages and generations, but is now disclosed to the saints" (Colossians 1:25–26, NIV).

To present the word of God yet fail to teach the mystery of Christ is, in Paul's mind, to fail to teach the church God's word "in its fullness." To build a healthy multi-ethnic church, then, planters and reformers must recognize—and refuse to make—this mistake.

By now it should be clear that failure to understand the central theme of Paul's ministry results in an impoverished understanding of the nature of the local church. Paul's passion is for the mystery of Christ to be understood and lived out in the context of community. Consequently, it should be our passion as well. Any attempt to render Paul's teaching in a purely homogenous light is to stray no small distance from his self-described calling, ministry, and passion. Indeed, it is to stand in direct opposition to Paul's clear teaching regarding the local church.

The Administration of the Mystery

In Ephesians 3:7–10, Paul tells us that he was called not only to proclaim the mystery of Christ among the Gentiles but also "to bring to light what is the *administration of the mystery* . . . in order that the manifold wisdom of God might now be made known through the church" (emphasis mine). In other words, Paul had not only been granted insight into the mystery of Christ but also insight into how, in a practical way, the mystery is to be lived out through the local church.

Here, however, we should note that the full text of Ephesians 3:10 has not been left for us in its entirety. Therefore, it is legitimate to ask the question, *For what reason has the church been called to unity and for what reason has Paul been given the task of bringing it about?* And beyond this, *Where, why, how, and to whom is the manifold wisdom of God to be made known?* The passage states that through the church, the manifold (or multi-faceted) wisdom of God will be made known to rulers and authorities. The question is, *Just where do these rulers and authorities reside?*

Clearly, the wisdom to which Paul refers is God's wisdom in reconciling both Jews and Gentiles as one in Christ (Ephesians 2:11–16). Yet with no other words in the Greek text following the phrase, "in the heavenly," we are left only to speculate how Paul might have finished the sentence.

The *New American Standard Bible* (NASB) supplies the word *places*, so that the verse concludes, "in the heavenly *places*." Likewise, the NIV supplies the word *realms*. But *Would Paul in the totality and context of his thoughts intend to limit God's display of wisdom to those rulers and authorities dwelling only in heavenly places?* It seems reasonable to affirm that Paul has in mind the rulers and authorities of this world as well.[2] In this regard, Eugene Peterson is instructive. Writing in *The Message*, he renders the verse this way: "Through followers of Jesus like yourselves [Jews and Gentiles] gathered in churches, this extraordinary plan of God is becoming known and talked about even among the angels!" (Ephesians 3:10; *The Message*, addition mine).

Finally, Paul closes his parenthetical statement in Ephesians 3:13 by speaking to the inherent difficulty of his mission and by encouraging the Ephesians not to lose heart on his behalf.

What is Paul's prayerful hope for diverse people pursuing God together as one in and through the local church? In concluding the chapter, Paul prays to the "Father, from whom the whole family [of God] in heaven and on earth derives its name" (Ephesians 3:15). This prayer flows from the context of Ephesians 2:11–22 and is rightly understood only in connection with the transitional phrase, "For this reason" (Ephesians 3:1, 14). In addition, Paul's words in Ephesians 3:17–18 are contextually tied to the hope that both Jews and the Gentiles will walk together as one in and through the local church. So Paul prays that the Ephesians,

> . . . being rooted and grounded in love may be able to comprehend with *all* the saints (Jewish and Gentile saints alike) what is the breadth and length and height and depth, and to know the love of Christ which surpasses knowledge, that you [all] may be filled up to all the fullness of God. (Ephesians 3:17–18, emphasis and addition mine)

This love, he suggests, will be experienced in a community of inclusion and faith, through which diverse people find common ground at the cross. Yes, in and through the local church, everyone who believes, no matter who they are or from where they've come, are from now on to be Christians—one family, under one Father, to the glory of God. With such hope in mind, Paul concludes:

> Now to Him who is able to do exceedingly beyond all that we (might) otherwise ask or think, according to the power that works within us to Him be the glory *in the church* and in Jesus Christ forever and ever. Amen. (Ephesians 3:20–21, emphasis mine)

How to Walk as One

In Ephesians 4, Paul turns his attention to practical Christian living. But what often goes unnoticed is that he does so with the multi-ethnic nature of the church in mind. A question to ask is, *In Ephesians 4:1, what is the calling in which the Ephesians are called to walk worthy?* Contextually, it is the call for Jewish converts and Gentile believers to love one another and to walk as one in and through the local church. *But how practically can this be achieved?* Paul says it can happen (only) when believers walk together in "humility and gentleness, with patience, showing forbearance to one another in love, being diligent to preserve the unity of the Spirit in the bond of peace" (Ephesians 4:2–3). Here he outlines the values and attitudes required of all those who would build a healthy multi-ethnic church.[3]

Of course, experience tells us that it's much easier to walk humbly, to be gentle, to show forbearance, and to love others who are more like ourselves, that is, with whom we share the same ethnic, educational, or economic background. As the planter and pastor of a multi-ethnic local church, I can attest that apart from the willingness of everyone involved to embrace these attitudes, unity and diversity cannot otherwise be achieved. This is why, I believe, the vast majority of local churches remain segregated today. Men and women *naturally* gravitate to what is most comfortable. But, again, *Isn't the Christian life to be lived in the supernatural?* At least, that's what I signed on for—living beyond myself in the power and pleasure of God. And when I consider the life of Christ, of the apostles and heroes of our faith through the centuries, I don't see many living comfortably. In fact, I see them wholeheartedly abandoned to the will of God and sacrificing their own preferences for a greater good. I wonder, then, if those of us living in the twenty-first century are willing to do the same in order to establish churches where *the manifold wisdom of God might be displayed to the world.* For the sake of the Gospel, I believe we must.

What else should motivate us to pursue such a dream? Paul summarizes the whole of his argument by writing, "There is one body and one Spirit, just as you also were called in one hope of your calling; one Lord, one faith, one baptism, one God who is over all and through all and in all" (Ephesians 4:4–6).

Throughout the rest of the chapter, Paul instructs the church concerning spiritual gifts and their purpose in the body (Ephesians 4:7–16). And he speaks of their need to turn from the past in order to pursue a future that reflects holiness, righteousness, and love (Ephesians 4:17–5:20).

In Ephesians 5:21–33, he continues to speak of unity, instructing husbands and wives in the art of love. Children, too, are taught to be one with their parents (Ephesians 6:1–3). Indeed, fathers are to be one with their children (Ephesians 6:4), employees one with their employers (Ephesians 6:5–8), and employers one with their employees (Ephesians 6:9). And toward the end of his letter, Paul writes, "Finally, be strong in the Lord and in the power of His might" (Ephesians 6:10).

Such will be required of all who pursue unity with God and with one another in the church, at home, and on the job. For our struggle to be one with God and with one another is not so much a battle between races, between husbands and wives, parents and children, or even employers and employees. It is a battle against "world forces of . . . darkness, against spiritual forces of wickedness in the heavenly places" (Ephesians 6:12). Yes ultimately, it is the ancient enemy, Satan, who seeks to divide and conquer us in every form of relationship. Indeed, this has been his tactic from the beginning, namely, to separate us from the love of God and from a love for one another that will otherwise make us strong. Therefore, Paul commands the Ephesians: "Put on the full armor of God, so that you may be able to stand firm [as one with God and others] against the [divisive] schemes of the devil . . . and having done everything [I have instructed you to do], to stand firm" (Ephesians 6:11, 13; insertions mine).

In conclusion, the Ephesians are asked to pray for Paul "that utterance may be given to me . . . to make known with boldness the mystery of the gospel" (Ephesians 6:18–19), that is, the mystery of Christ as we have seen. It is a request for courage that those seeking to build a healthy multi-ethnic church will find themselves praying frequently.

What First Love Had They Left?

There is one final, significant insight to share with you concerning the church at Ephesus.

As we know, the apostle John wrote the book of Revelation, addressing it to the seven churches in Asia (Revelation 1:4). Beginning with the church at Ephesus, he records the words of the Lord, as Christ speaks to each church individually through its angel (Revelation 1:17–20; 2–3).

Throughout the centuries, most scholars have believed that Revelation was written in the second half of the first century and in the twilight of John's life, perhaps as late as the A.D. 90s. Because most believe, too, that Paul's letter to the Ephesians was written between A.D. 60 and 64, and given the fact that the birth of the church at Ephesus dates back to Paul's second missionary journey (sometime around the year A.D. 50), it is possible that Jesus is addressing in Revelation a church at Ephesus that is some thirty to forty years old. *So what did Jesus have to say to the Ephesians at the time of John's writing?*

According to Revelation 2:2–4, the church is first *commended* for its [good] deeds, toil, and perseverance: it "cannot endure evil men . . . and [puts] to the test those who call themselves apostles." In addition, the church is described as steadfast and as having endured the widespread persecution that believers are known to have faced during this time. Indeed, in the face of persecution, the church has not grown weary.

However, in the very next verse, Christ *condemns* the church, saying, "But I have this against you . . . you have left[4] your first love" (Revelation 2:5). The question is, *Just what is the "first love" to which he is referring?*

Throughout the years, most have been taught that this "first love" was a love for Christ or, more specifically, a passionate relationship with him. In this sense, the word *first* has to do with priority, nature, or quality. The commendations cited in Revelation 2:2–4, then, are seen as a grocery list of religious piety. First and foremost, Jesus wants our hearts.

Of course, to walk in a passionate relationship with Christ beyond mere religion is what Christ intends for all who would believe. The problem is, however, this is not at all what I believe the Lord is referring to here. Remember, he has just commended the church as an example of steadfast faithfulness in the midst of persecution and false teaching. Furthermore, he commends them again in Revelation 2:6. And because Jesus also equates obedience with love (John 14:21), surely he views the heart of this church as devoted to him! In fact, if what most believe is correct, why didn't Jesus simply say, "You no longer love Me like you did before?"

The phrase "first love," however, is more correctly translated, "the love that you had at first," as clarified in Revelation 2:5. In other words, the question of "first love" is not so much a question of *priority* but one of *prior* love. In order to see what *prior* love the Ephesians had—the love that they had at first—and therefore to rightly understand this passage, we must again turn to Paul's letter to the Ephesians. Indeed, it is there we will find the precise answer to the question of "first love": "For this reason, I, too, having heard of your faith in the Lord Jesus which exists among you, and your love for all the saints" (Ephesians 1:15, emphasis mine).

Yes, some thirty to forty years later, it is precisely *this* "first love" that the church at Ephesus had left behind, namely, a *love for all the saints!* In other words, it is a love for one another, for Jewish and

Gentile converts alike, that Christ rebukes the church for abandoning (see Matthew 22:39).

Notice how Revelation 2:2–5 parallels Ephesians 1:15. First, there is a commendation for faith (compare Revelation 2:2 and 3 with Ephesians 1:15a) and then, a mention of love (compare Revelation 2:4 with Ephesians 1:15b). The only difference is that at the time of Paul's writing, Jewish and Gentile converts in the church at Ephesus were expressing unconditional (*agape*) love for one another. A generation or so later, at the time of John's writing, however, they were not. Therefore, Christ sternly rebukes the church: "Remember, therefore, from where you have fallen, and repent, and do the deeds you did at first; or else I am coming to you and will remove your lampstand out of its place unless you repent" (Revelation 2:5).

Sadly, this otherwise zealous congregation sometime around A.D. 90 was no longer expressing a *love for all the saints,* and Christ declares this to be sin. Apart from repentance, then, Jesus says that his Spirit (his Anointing) will be removed from the church.

With all this in mind, we should recognize that Paul, like Christ, intended the local church to be multi-ethnic and, as such, to uniquely display God's wisdom and glory to rulers and authorities in this world, as well as in the heavenly places. To the degree that local church leaders are willing to embrace this vision and to pursue the establishment of congregations free of distinction, it will be possible to radically transform the local church in the twenty-first century. Toward that end, let us pray with Paul:

> Now to Him who is able to do exceedingly abundantly beyond all that we ask or think, according to the power that works within us, to Him be the glory in the church and in Christ Jesus to all generations forever and ever. Amen. (Ephesians 3:20–21)

○

Ofelia Lima

Lori Tarpley, a member of Mosaic, works for the Myeloma Institute for Research and Therapy (MIRT) at the University of Arkansas for Medical Sciences (UAMS) in Little Rock. MIRT is focused on treating patients from around the world with multiple myeloma, a type of cancer related to lymphoma and leukemia. In time, those diagnosed with the disease become crippled and, sometimes, even paralyzed. There is no known cure.

In the spring of 2005, Lori was introduced at MIRT to a seventy-two-year-old woman from Cuba named Ofelia Lima and her daughter, Lissette. According to Lori, "It was clear that these folks were pretty lost, empty emotionally, and at the end of the road. Ms. Lima had had myeloma for more than two years, and doctors in Miami had told her there was nothing more that could be done. 'This disease,' they said, 'will take your life.'" Lissette learned about MIRT and decided that before they gave up completely, she would bring her mother to Little Rock.

As an intake specialist, Lori does not usually invite patients to church. "But somehow," she said, "in that initial interview, it was clear to me that I should take a chance and invite Ms. Lima to connect with our Latino community at Mosaic. I knew that our folks would be supportive."

From here, Ms. Lima picks up the story:

> From the moment I first entered Mosaic, I could sense something telling me, "You are going to be healed. You do not have anything, you do not have cancer." I bowed my head and prayed . . . and the brothers and sisters at Mosaic prayed for me, too. I heard a voice telling me, "Everything is going to be fine." And I left that place crying.
>
> The very next day, Ms. Lima returned to MIRT in order to get the results of tests taken the week before. An MRI (magnetic resonance imaging) confirmed well over 100 holes and lesions where the myeloma had done its damage. As Lori read a second test to determine what disease was active, however, she was amazed: The test showed absolutely no active myeloma in Ms. Lima!
>
> "That's not normal," said Lori. "One hundred lesions don't just empty out over the course of a weekend. It was clearly the fingerprint of God."
>
> Ms. Lima and Lissette soon returned to Miami, healed in every way. And on her final Sunday at Mosaic, she stood for the first time in nine months, pushing aside the wheel chair to which she had been bound. "In Little Rock," she said, "I was filled with joy, inside and out. It was here I began to walk again . . . and God is who I walk for."

Having been told she would be in Little Rock to undergo intense treatment of her disease for six months, Ms. Lima returned with Lissette to Miami after only twelve days! As of January 2007, Ms. Lima continues to do well. There remains no evidence of the disease. *Gloria a Dios!*

PART TWO

THE SEVEN CORE COMMITMENTS OF A MULTI-ETHNIC CHURCH

EARLY RESEARCH BY GEORGE YANCEY, published in his book *One Body, One Spirit*,[1] identified general "principles of successful multi-racial churches." Subsequent interaction with practitioners through the Mosaix Global Network,[2] however, led to the further examination of these principles and their refinement. From this process emerged what can now be described as the *Seven Core Commitments of a Multi-Ethnic Church*.

In Part One, we explored the biblical mandate for the multi-ethnic church. In Part Two, we'll consider the seven core commitments required to bring it about. Indeed, they are fundamental to the design and development of a healthy multi-ethnic church and, together with the biblical mandate, can light the way for the emerging movement—the coming integration of the local church.

4

EMBRACE DEPENDENCE

Unless the Lord builds the house, they labor in vain who
[attempt] to build it.

—Psalm 127:1

ONE WEEKEND, a cold front moved through Central Arkansas, producing ice on the roads and forcing the leadership at Mosaic to decide whether or not we should cancel our service on Sunday morning. Unlike many cities in other parts of the country, Little Rock is not equipped to deal with such inclement weather; in fact, the entire city shuts down at the slightest hint of snow or ice. So on this day, we were faced with a decision. And I know what some of you might be thinking, because we thought it, too: *No service, no offering!*

You know, it's amazing how reluctant we were to make the decision or, more accurately, how a concern for church finances so competed with what we knew in our minds we should do. Still, we tried in vain to overcome our objections: *We've got spirit, yes we do; we've got spirit, how 'bout you!* But in the end (in all sincerity), it was our commitment to embrace dependence that led us once again, to trust in the Lord and obey. That Sunday, we cancelled the service.

Now in those days, our average Sunday offering was about $8,000 a week. And as is true to this day, individuals contributing financially on Sunday mornings do so by placing their gifts in an offering box stationed near the front of our facility. However, on occasion, someone will leave a gift after the offering has already been counted and after most have left the building. With this in mind, our bookkeeper, Caron Higgins, sometimes checks the box at the start of her week.

Sure enough, when Caron came to work on the Tuesday following Sunday's cancelled service, she found a single check in the box made out to Mosaic in the amount of $6,000. This unusually large gift had somehow been placed in the box between Sunday and Tuesday, over a period of time in which the city was, for the most part, shut down. We truly had no idea how it had gotten there.

But there's more.

Later that same morning, Caron opened the mail to discover additional checks had been sent to us over the weekend, totaling some $4,000. So in the week following the cancelled service, we actually received over $10,000 in financial gifts—some $2,000 more than we would have otherwise expected to receive through the offering on a Sunday morning. At that point my partner, Harry Li, and I wondered if we should strategically cancel the service more often in the future!

In sharing such things, I am aware that others, too, from time to time, encounter the supernatural provision of the Holy Spirit in their own lives, as well as in the churches or ministries they lead. However, the point I am making is that a healthy multi-ethnic church can be established only where functioning faith is the modus operandi. Given the profound uniqueness of such a church, the inherent challenges related to diversity and, quite often, limited economic resources, there is simply no other means by which it can be built. Therefore, like George Müeller, the nineteenth-century pastor in England,[1] who famously trusted God for the needs of orphans in his care, or the legendary Christ-centered musician Keith Green,[2] who was known to distribute his recordings for whatever people could afford, those who would pursue the multi-ethnic church must actively embrace dependence if they expect to see their dreams become reality. Indeed, Müeller said it well:

> God's plan is that there shall be none of self and all of Christ. The very people who are doing the most for God in saving souls, in mission work, in the care of orphans, are those who are working on short supplies of strength, of money, of talents, of advantages and are kept in a position of living by faith and taking from God, day by day, both physical and spiritual supplies. This is the way God succeeds and gains conquest over His own people, and over the unbelief of those who look on His providences.[3]

I Can't Wait to See This!

The first time I proactively embraced dependence was in the summer of 1981. Prior to my junior year in college, I was playing baseball for Athletes in Action (AIA), an organization committed to sharing God's love with people through the platform of athletics. One night during a game in Indio, a city of 75,000 nestled in southern California's Coachella Valley just east of Palm Springs, I was hit by a pitch and consequently unable to throw for a week. The time off allowed me to return home to Scottsdale, Arizona, for some much-needed rest and recovery.

One week later and with my hand healed, I flew back to LAX on a Saturday night. That night, I was expecting to be picked up by one of our coaches and driven to rejoin the team. But as I departed the airplane, a stewardess called my name over the intercom to inform me that my ride would not be coming. Rather, she said, my coach had called to leave word that I should catch a flight to Ontario, California. Once there, he would come and pick me up.

Somewhat confused, I asked, "Did he pay for the ticket?" The stewardess didn't know and so she instructed me to check with an agent inside the terminal. When I did, I found out that my coach had not.

Now remember, it was 1981 and as a nineteen-year-old college student, my options were limited. I considered taking the bus, renting a car, and even hitchhiking to Ontario; yet having only a few dollars in my pocket and without a credit card, I had no other means at the time for making such a purchase. I remember dropping my bags in the middle of the terminal at which my flight from Arizona had arrived, and standing still for a moment as a sea of people swarmed around me. With no way to get where I needed to go and not knowing what else to do, I then said to God, "I can't wait to see how you pull this off!"

Having shared my prayerful frustration though somehow optimistic, I then did the only thing I could think of to do. I walked outside and headed toward another terminal at LAX where flights were scheduled for departure to Ontario. Perhaps, I reasoned, my coach had purchased a ticket on one of the competing carriers. But about half-way to my destination, I unexplainably looked back over my right shoulder. Somehow my eye had caught a man sitting alone on a bench, reading a Bible that lay open on his lap. And I immediately turned toward him like one desperate for water!

"Excuse me, sir," I said. "Are you a Christian?"

"Yes, I am," he answered back; sensing my predicament, he asked, "What seems to be the problem?"

With nowhere seemingly to go, I sat down and told him my story and for the next two hours, we talked. I learned, among other things, that he was a "Jewish Christian"[4] and that he had arrived in Los Angeles from Miami two hours earlier than expected. But what was even more amazing to me was how quickly he responded to my need. "Listen, I don't have any cash," he said, "but I do have a credit card. And when my ride comes, I'll be glad to take you to the next terminal and buy your ticket to Ontario."

In many ways, I could not believe this was happening! For instance, in no way did I even hint he should do such a generous thing. At the same time, however, I had almost expected something like this to occur. Yes, as a young man less than a year old in my faith, I just assumed this was the way it works: God takes care of his own!

Indeed, that summer I was living the life of faith for the very first time. I had raised my own financial support to be a part of AIA and was actively sharing the love of God with others. Still, I could not help but ponder the odds of such an occurrence, namely, that a total stranger would so treat me like friend. In the end, this experience showed me what Christ intends for us all to understand:

> If God gives such attention to the appearance of wildflowers—most of which are never even seen, don't you think he'll attend to you, take pride in you, do his best for you? What I'm trying to do here is to get you to relax, to not be so preoccupied with getting, so you can respond to God's giving. People who don't know God and the way he works fuss over these things, but you know both God and how he works. Steep your life in God-reality, God-initiative, God-provisions. Don't worry about missing out. You'll find all your everyday human concerns will be met. (Matthew 6:30–33; *The Message*)

You know, I have never forgotten the lesson I learned that evening at LAX, a lesson of faith beyond reason that is, likewise, required of all those who would pursue the multi-ethnic church. For more than anything else I've ever done or attempted in twenty-three years of full-time ministry, the multi-ethnic church requires me to embrace dependence with a knowledge that apart from God's direct involvement, it cannot otherwise be established. Yes in these days, the same genuine, almost naïve expectation that says to God, "I can't wait to see how you pull this off," daily informs my prayers, demands my patience, and inspires my persistence.

There Is No Business Plan

Once, when Jesus was approached by a man asking that his son be delivered from a demon-based illness, the man said, "I brought [my son] to your disciples, [but] they could not cure him." In reply, Jesus bemoans "this unbelieving and perverted generation." Seeing Jesus rebuke the demon and cure the boy, Jesus' disciples later came to him privately and asked, "Why could we not drive it out?" Jesus then said to them,

"Because of the littleness of your faith . . . [for] this kind does not go out except by prayer and fasting" (Matthew 17:14–21).

Likewise, the multi-ethnic church is a different "kind" of church. Only men and women of great faith—individuals who fully abandon themselves to the will of God—can build it by trusting God from day to day. In other words, human effort is not enough. Indeed, any independent attempt of men to build a multi-ethnic church is bound to fail, no matter how much money, expertise, or influence they have. There are no simple solutions, then, no shortcuts or strategies for success that can otherwise accomplish what only God can do in this regard. The multi-ethnic church is a work of the Holy Spirit and of faith that cannot otherwise be attained through human means or methods.

Such thinking, however, flies in the face of all that we, as Americans, have been raised to believe. L. Robert Kohls, a man widely recognized as one of America's leading pioneers in the study of crossing cultures, has identified thirteen values deeply ingrained in the American psyche and descriptive of most (but not all) Americans.[5] Kohls's list includes the following seven values:

1. Personal control over the environment
2. Time and its control
3. Individualism and privacy
4. Self-help control
5. Competition and free enterprise
6. Action and work orientation
7. Practicality and efficiency

It should come as no surprise to see such things in print. In short, Americans are fiercely independent. We value (and even reward) self-sufficiency at every level and seek in most instances to control our own lives and destiny. Yet this is not how God would have us live. In fact, such a mind-set is contradictory to Christ-centered spiritual life. Rather, we are taught throughout the Bible to recognize, *There is a God and I am not him*. Indeed, we are admonished repeatedly in the pages of Scripture to trust God, to wait upon him, and to seek him in recognition that he alone is both sovereign and sufficient. According to God's Word, then, we are absolutely not in control of our lives or destiny, no matter how detached we are from this reality at any given moment.

With this in mind, the way of dependence cannot only be for us a *transcendent* reality; it must also be an *imminent* mind-set—a governing philosophy, a practical way of living and of doing church. Contrary to what we have been taught as Americans, Christ's followers must embrace dependence for ourselves personally and in the local churches we attempt to lead.

Along this line, I'll never forget meeting with one man as I considered the potential of planting Mosaic. He said, "Sounds interesting, Mark; I can't wait to see your business plan." In response however, all I could say was, "Bro', you don't get it . . . there is no business plan!" Sadly, I believe and for too long now, such plans have governed the business of "doing church," particularly in the United States. But when did we abandon a walk by faith for a walk of sight, or the mind-set that would compel the local church to invite all to come, no matter who they are, just as they are?

The truth is, a professional approach to church growth will not likely guarantee the establishment of a multi-ethnic church. For such a church cannot be realized simply by following packaged principles to achieve the goal. The multi-ethnic church is, again, a completely different kind of church and, as such, supernaturally produced.

The only way to build a healthy multi-ethnic church then is to embrace dependence. This means taking to heart the direction to "be anxious for nothing, but in everything by prayer and supplication . . . let [your] requests be made known to God" (Philippians 4:6). In this regard, it is the job of planters and reformers to prayerfully discern the will of heaven, faithfully pursue it on earth and, finally, to obey the call from day to day. At that point, it is up to the Holy Spirit to make the dream come true. And by abiding in the vine, we should expect to bear fruit one day that only God can produce. For as Jesus himself taught:

> Abide in Me and I in you. As the branch cannot bear fruit of itself unless it abides in the vine, so neither can you unless you abide in Me. I am the vine, you are the branches; he who abides in Me and I in him, he bears much fruit, for apart from Me you can do nothing. (John 15:4–5)

Practicing Dependence

What does this look like practically? And how does a church—any church—embrace dependence? Of course, there are as many answers to these questions as there are churches. Let me share some reflections and examples from my own experience at Mosaic.

First, there are some simple steps we have taken to visibly demonstrate our dependence on the Holy Spirit as a church. For instance, as I have already mentioned, we are among those churches that do not pass an offering plate during the worship service. Rather, members of Mosaic place their financial gifts in offering boxes stationed near the front of our facility sometime before, during, or after the service. However, we do pass baskets to collect prayer cards that those in attendance are encouraged to fill out. When dismissed, Mosaics reach into these baskets and take one or two cards home with them in order to pray for the requests over the next seven days. In such ways, we demonstrate our dependence on God as a congregation, first, by more prominently emphasizing our commitment to prayer and, second, by trusting in the Holy Spirit to move in the hearts of our members (and in others, as well) to faithfully and sacrificially support the church financially.

In another example, our elders recently launched (in prayer and affirmation) our friend and co-laborer, Harold Nash, who accepted a position as the first African American teaching pastor in an otherwise all-White church in North Little Rock.[6] Like at Antioch (Acts 13:1–3), where the Holy Spirit instructed the church to set apart 40 percent of its leadership team for "the work to which I have called them," we were similarly asked by God to do the same.[7]

I have to be honest, though. This was not easy to do. For from the beginning and through the first five years of the church, Harold had stood with me personally and by me in the pulpit as a "teaching pastor" at Mosaic. In addition, he was serving as a co-chairman of our elder board at the time of his departure. His early involvement in the church, then, coupled with his strong reputation as a spiritual leader in the community, had helped to establish the credibility of Mosaic throughout the city. In short, Harold was one of our best assets, and it would have been very human of us to strenuously object to another church—one that is just across the river from us in North Little Rock—inviting him to join their work. Instead, I met with the elders there, and both churches are now praying that God will use Harold to help transition this healthy but otherwise homogeneous congregation into a multi-ethnic church over time. This is significant and, again, speaks to the issue of dependence, for humanly speaking, we might also worry that the loss of an African American teaching pastor (if not replaced soon) could lead to the exodus of African Americans from our congregation. Giving in to such a fleshly perspective, however, could cause us to run ahead of God in the matter.

Make no mistake: having an African American share the pulpit with us is our firm intention and desire. In fact, it is intrinsic to Mosaic's DNA. Yet to discover God's man rather than our own, we have chosen primarily to pray and to wait. In so doing, we are demonstrating to others that we are not concerned with quotas. Nor will we be informed by arbitrarily determined timetables or allow natural instincts to overrule the supernatural will of heaven. This is not to suggest that we will not be intentional in our prayers and in our pursuit of someone to pick up where Harold left off, only that we will not be driven by otherwise earthly concerns in this regard.

In other decisions also, building a healthy multi-ethnic church requires courageous faith on the part of its leaders. For all too often, church leaders will make decisions pragmatically and based solely on what, from a human perspective, can or cannot be done. Once again, this runs contrary to Christ's intent for our lives and for the local church.

You'll recall, for instance, Christ's encounter with the young ruler (Matthew 19:16–26; Mark 10:17–27; Luke 18:18–27). What prevented the man from selling all that he owned and giving it to the poor? Indeed, what kept him from believing in Jesus, who promised that in so doing, "you shall have treasure in heaven; [so], come, follow Me?" Was it not the man's unwillingness to trust and obey beyond what he could see, that is, beyond what otherwise made earthly sense, that caused him to walk away grieving? Indeed, let's imagine for a moment the thoughts that must have run through the young ruler's mind to inform and justify his decision. Or how his friends might have affirmed him later and his decision to walk away. They might have said something like this:

> He asked you to do what? That's nuts! Only a fool would do such a thing! Yes, think of all the good you can otherwise do for the people you rule in discharging the money yourself and if you are careful to invest it wisely. Of course, you should keep the lion's share for yourself. After all, you should never touch your capital; just give generously from your profits and only enough to keep others grateful and believing in your benevolence.

The truth is that leaders who do not necessarily make decisions based on what they have (or haven't) the means to do are needed to build healthy multi-ethnic churches.[8] Yes, such churches need leaders who will make decisions based on prayerful pursuit of the will of heaven and confident, then, that the Holy Spirit has led them to their conclusions. In short, multi-ethnic church planters and reformers need to embrace dependence. For if we do only that which we have the means to do, how will we know for sure that faith has been exercised and that God is, in fact, pleased?[9] Indeed, how will we be able to answer the question, *Was it God or was it us?*

With this in mind, Proverbs 3:5–6 is a wonderful source of guidance and encouragement for those seeking to build a healthy multi-ethnic church. It reads, "Trust in the Lord with all your heart and do not lean on your own understanding. In all your ways acknowledge Him and He will direct your paths."

When we seek then to practically apply these words in the context of life and leadership, men and women of faith can expect to see God work in amazing ways, as illustrated by the following story:

Alan Pollack spent twenty-two years in the business world, serving as a regional manager for the Red Lobster Corporation and overseeing restaurants in a three-state territory. His wife, Kathy, first visited Mosaic in the summer of 2003, checking it out as a possible church home for her family, especially with her husband in mind. Although Alan (a Jewish Christian) had in fact received Christ in the early years of their marriage, he had not grown much in the faith beyond that point. Blessed by her experience at Mosaic that day, Kathy brought Alan the following week and in his own words, "I was overwhelmed by the Spirit of God I felt in this place."

During his first year at the church, Alan spent significant time with Harry Li, who became his friend and mentor. Even so, Harry was just as amazed as I was when, in the summer of 2004, Alan shared a desire to leave his job and to work for the church in the coming year without pay! "I just want to serve the Lord," he said. "I believe he would have me to do so."

So in September of that year, Alan left his job and six-figure salary behind; for the next eight months, he served the church as a de facto part of our staff. On most days, he helped us make sense of growing demands on our facility and finances. However, at other times he would straighten chairs, empty trash, or hang dry-wall, according to the needs of the day. No matter what the project, Alan was so excited just to be a part of things and to invest himself in service of the King. All the while, he supported his family with money he had set aside through the years, effectively paying us for the privilege of serving on our staff. Oh, and did I forget to mention that Alan and Kathy have six children?!

Six or seven months into this partnership, there was moment in time when, as elders, we recognized that Alan was a gift from God. Subsequently, we began to ask ourselves whether or not he would have us extend Alan an invitation to become a paid member of our staff. The fact that we had absolutely no money budgeted for such a hire at the time did not keep us from exploring the possibility or taking the matter to God.

After much prayer and discussion, the elders gathered one Thursday morning to finalize a decision. At that time, we agreed that God would have us extend Alan an invitation to join our staff at the end of his voluntary year of service. Furthermore, we agreed to do so in writing in order to explain that while we could offer him some income over the next five months, we could not guarantee our ability to fund a full-time position in the coming fiscal year. If he was willing to walk with us by faith, we would be willing to walk with him.

Following our meeting, Harry composed a letter that read, in part, "As you well know, our current situation prohibits us from making any firm commitments on salary. However, as the Lord provides, we will [strive to] pay you. Thank you for your willingness to walk in faith with us on this incredible journey."

Later that morning, we gave Alan the letter and, like proud parents, Harry and I stood silently by allowing him to absorb the message and meaning of our words. As he did, he broke out in tears of humility and joy.

I'll never forget the moment: here was this forty-five-year-old man—a husband and father of six children, who had left a prominent position in a successful company simply to immerse himself in an environment of faith, hope, and love. In so doing, the Spirit of God had changed his life, his focus, and his priorities so much so that he now considered it a privilege and an honor to be offered a job without the promise of pay! Of course, it made no earthly sense at all, but Alan was blown away by what he described as the goodness and mercy of God.

After that, we all went on with the day. But when I returned from a lunch appointment, my staff began to buzz around me like bees near the hive. "Sit down," one of them said, pointing to a chair in the center of the room.

"All right" I asked, "what's going on?" But they said nothing. They just kept smiling, giddy-like! I quickly calculated the year and date: no, it was not the month of my birth or of my anniversary, and their merry mood told me nothing was the matter. So what in the heck, I wondered, were they up to?

Just then, Caron appeared from around the corner of her office and handed me a small box with something inside, and Harry said, "Take a look." But I hesitated, as visions of spring-loaded rubber snakes leaping forth from the box flooded my mind! Finally, I braced myself and reached inside the box only to feel an envelope. When I pulled it out, I realized it had already been opened and they all knew what I was about to find out.

Inside the envelope there was a check made out to the church, and on the check was the figure of $100,000! I was stunned. "Who sent this?" I asked. "Is this a joke?" The upper-left corner of the check, however, provided no clue. In fact, there was no personal indication anywhere on the check from whom it might have come, only the printed words, "The Anonymous Fund." I looked up at Caron, but she had already anticipated my question. "No, this is not a joke and yes, the check is good. I've already checked with the bank on which it was drawn," she said definitively. It was the largest single gift our church had ever received to that point and, more significantly, was a wonderful confirmation that we had indeed heard from God about hiring Alan Pollack. Since the envelope was postmarked a day or two before, the timing of its arrival was unmistakably an act of God, for if that check had arrived the day before, we might have invited Alan to join our staff team because "we could" and not, as we did, purely by faith. Yes, it was a miraculous moment in the life of our church. We had embraced dependence, and God came through—in his way and in his time—to the praise and glory of his name!

In this chapter, we have mined the first core commitment necessary for building a healthy multi-ethnic church, that is, *embrace dependence.* Indeed, it is a mind-set we must not only will ourselves to choose but also one we must be committed to maintaining in an individualistic culture all too enamored with the trappings of success. To do so requires that we pay much more than lip service to the virtues of prayer, patience, and persistence if we are to enfold diverse cultures into one local body for the sake of the Gospel. As the old hymn instructs, we must "trust and obey, for there's no other way," and this applies to every aspect of our lives. For above all, those of us in pursuit of the dream must recognize that the multi-ethnic church cannot be established in own's own strength, wisdom, or power. Rather, it can be realized only through the power of the Holy Spirit working in and through men and women of faith to accomplish something that, apart from him, cannot be done. For as Henri Nouwen once observed, "Community is not made but given."[10]

○

Danny Kiranja

Each and every story of conversion is, of course, remarkable. But Harry Li recently reminded me of one involving the brother of one of our members from Kenya—the result of very specific, answered prayer. Here's the story in Harry's words:

> One morning in 2003, our staff gathered for prayer at the start of the day. As an item of praise, Mark shared with us a list of those who had recently come to know the Lord at Mosaic and, more specifically, their countries of origin. Amazingly, there

were seven countries represented in a recent wave of over twenty-five converts through our ministry!

With this in mind, we thanked our Heavenly Father for his wonderful work and asked him to help us bear even more fruit in the days ahead. Little did we know how soon God would answer our prayer.

That very afternoon, a man from Kenya named Danny Kiranja walked into the church. Our bookkeeper, Caron Higgins, happened to be up front at the time, and seeing her, Danny announced, "I have come here to receive Jesus Christ as my Savior, and I must receive him right now!"

Since Danny did not know anyone in particular, Caron led him to Mark, and the two sat down to talk. Among other things, Mark learned that Danny had visited our church once or twice before through the encouragement of his sister, Miriam, a fellow member of Mosaic. At this time, Danny repeated his desire to ask Christ into his life. So, Mark began to share with him the plan of salvation but was quickly interrupted: "I already know all of that," Danny said, "I cannot wait any longer! I must pray right now!" So without further delay, they bowed their heads to pray, and Danny Kiranja asked Jesus into his heart.

Following their prayer, Mark introduced him to the rest of our staff as a new brother in Christ. But only after Danny left did we remember our prayer for more fruit earlier that morning. Wanting, then, to ask Danny what had prompted him to come see us that day, I chased him down at the local gas station. He told me that he had recently come under great spiritual conviction and that he needed to settle some matters once and for all. In fact, he said, that very morning, the first thought that had come into his mind was, "I must go to Mosaic and receive Jesus Christ. In that moment, I just knew what time he had awakened that morning but had to ask for confirmation. I was not at all surprised, then, to learn that Danny woke up at 9:00 that morning—the exact time we had been praying to the Lord to give us even more."

5

TAKE INTENTIONAL STEPS

If you would hit the mark, you must aim a little above it; every arrow that flies feels the attraction of earth.

—Henry Wadsworth Longfellow

AMONG THE FIRST LATINOS TO ATTEND MOSAIC were two women who had come to us from a trailer park in Alexander, a small town just outside Little Rock. They did not speak any English and had heard of the church through a local Spanish-language publication. There to welcome them was another Latino family, the head of which was willing to preach in Spanish. In what was to be our first attempt to integrate Latinos into our service, it was decided that we would all sing together and then the Latinos would be dismissed to hear a message in their own language. *Brilliant, you think?*

So we sang—well actually, the English speakers sang and the Spanish speakers clapped their hands—and with the best of intentions that day, we dismissed the four of them just before the message. Together they rose from their seats, walked up the aisle and back out of the church, while the seventy-five or so of the rest of us in attendance looked on and smiled. Believe me, it was pitiful to watch and still painful to remember. Later that week, we all agreed there must be a better way.

After some research, we recognized that the only way to fully integrate Latinos in the worship service was to provide for simultaneous translation. However, this would require a considerable investment of limited resources, especially of limited dollars. Headsets and headphones would have to be purchased, along with a transmitter, battery packs, and a charger. And someone would need to be tasked not only to provide simultaneous translation of the message but also for every other spoken word within the service. In addition, we would have to translate the bulletin and all other forms of written communication, as well as our PowerPoint slides. It was quite a hefty load for a very small, emerging church.

Nevertheless, we concluded that this intentional step was the only way to accommodate Spanish speakers and, therefore, one that had to be taken in order to realize our dream of becoming a multi-ethnic church. To this day we continue such practices, and at one point recently, 16 percent of our congregation could be described as Hispanic or of Latin descent. Entire messages are now delivered in Spanish, with the English translation provided from the front. And as a regular part of our Sunday morning experience, we sing often in both languages. Even the way we staff our church is a direct result of such early and intentional steps.

Out of Many, One

According to the Web-based encyclopedia, Wikipedia, *E Pluribis Unum*— the phrase found on the Great Seal of the United States—is originally from "Moretum," a poem often attributed to Virgil, though the actual author is unknown.

> Moretum is a type of salad; the poem contains a description of the ingredients being ground in a pestle which includes the [Latin] phrase, *color est e pluribus unus,* which means, "the color is, from many, one." This refers to the combining of the different colored ingredients . . . into [one] harmonious mixture.[1]

To create a harmonious mixture from different-colored ingredients requires intentionality; likewise, a multi-ethnic church does not just happen. Planters and reformers alike must first identify and then take intentional steps to turn their vision into reality.

With this in mind, we should view dependence (as discussed in Chapter Four) and intentionality as two sides of the same coin, for while it is true that the Vine (Christ) alone *produces* the fruit, it is the task of the branches (us) to *bear* it (John 15:4–8), and this we will do when we abide in him. Specifically, this means that we must keep his commandments (John 15:10). In other words, God expects us to do more than just *pray,* "Thy Kingdom come, Thy will be done." Indeed, he expects to *partner* with him toward that end. Therefore, he commands us to "go" (Matthew 28:19), to "be My witnesses" (Acts 1:8), to "serve the living God" (Hebrews 9:14), to "shepherd the flock" (1 Peter 5:1–3) and in,

"Whatever you do, do your work heartily, as for the Lord rather than for men" (Colossians 3:23).

There is no contradiction in commitments when we understand for whom we work and why. To be clear then, embracing dependence and taking intentional steps are not mutually exclusive concerns. Again, Müeller's words are instructive in this regard:

> Seek to depend entirely on God for everything. . . . Put yourself and your work into His hands. When thinking of any new undertaking, ask, *Is this agreeable to the mind of God?* Is it for His glory? If it is not for His glory, it is not for your good, and you must have nothing to do with it. Mind that! Having settled that a certain course is for the glory of God, begin it in His name and continue in it to the end. Undertake it in prayer and never give up![2]

Build It God's Way and in His Time

In the early days of our church, there were some who would occasionally count heads in the weekly service, not so much to chart the number of those in attendance but to note the diversity of the crowd from week to week. And I have to confess that I was often one of them. In part, I was driven by the fact that many I had known in the large, predominantly White congregation I had left in order to plant Mosaic were curious concerning the church and our diversity, and often they would ask about it when they saw me. Not wanting to lead others away from my old church, however, I was careful not to initiate conversations with members there and to talk only with those who first approached me. Nevertheless, some did leave to join the work, while most others, in one way or another, began to spread the word of a new church for all people in the heart of Central Arkansas.

Initially then, some of us at Mosaic were concerned with percentages and worried that the involvement of too many White people in the beginning might somehow undermine our desire to establish a truly diverse congregation. And although we did believe it was up to the Holy Spirit to make the dream come true, we did not believe this was an excuse to abandon further concern or to abdicate personal responsibility in pursuit of a healthy multi-ethnic church. On the contrary; although prayer is foundational, partnership with Christ is fundamental to the effort and must lead us to make purposeful decisions along the way. I can assure you, wishful thinking will not get the job done! There are, indeed, some things we can and must do to make the dream come true.

Now I have no doubt that people in many, if not most, homogeneous churches would sincerely state that they would not intentionally turn anyone away. If asked, they might say something like, "We welcome anyone to become a part of our church," or point to the fact that "a few families" of diverse ethnicity do attend their otherwise homogeneous fellowship. In fact, some pastors have specifically stated, "We would love to have more diversity in our church and have been praying recently that others would get involved." In other words, these well-meaning people are not doing anything intentionally to turn diverse others away. However, they are not doing anything intentionally to draw them in either.

What we should realize, however, is that while such statements are sincere, they do not accurately reflect the real sentiment below the surface. Again to be clear, I am not questioning hearts—just the fact that such statements have not been fully thought through. For when we dig deeper, what we find is that these folks really mean that diverse people are welcome to join "their" churches as long as they embrace the majority culture and do not try to bring another culture (namely, their own) with them, that is, as long as they do not try to change "who we are or the way we do things." In other words most local church leaders (and members too for that matter) are glad for diverse individuals to get involved "as long as they like our music, our preaching style, and our environment. But they should not expect us to change for them." Therefore, the message being sent, whether directly or indirectly, is that "you might feel more comfortable in another church down the street."

The fact is, we are all too set in our ways! So perhaps we should ask a few questions to determine our true desire and intent in the matter. For instance, how should leaders respond in a predominantly White church when an African American member suggests that a Gospel Choir might attract more of "our people" to the congregation? And when the children of a first-generation Latino or Korean congregation become bilingual young adults, will the church remain the same? Or what might we say to the pastor of a growing African American congregation that plans to hire a White pastor, when one hundred White people begin attending his church?

In pursuit of the multi-ethnic church, we must keep this truth in mind: "My thoughts are not your thoughts, nor are your ways My ways, declares the Lord" (Isaiah 55:8).

In other words, such a church is not ours to build in the way we see fit. Rather, we are to build it according to *God's* blueprint. It is not about us—what we like and prefer or what we are comfortable with. It's all about God! Consequently, multi-ethnic church planters and reformers must not only "look out for [their] own interests, but also the interests of others"—and not only for the interests of those in the ethnic majority but for those in the minority as well. Yes, we will have to align ourselves with God's agenda and abandon our own if we are to see every nation, tribe, people, and tongue worship God together as one in and through the local church, *on earth as it is in heaven*. And this will require us to take intentional steps toward that goal, ever mindful of our dependence on God.

In fact, we did have an African American woman approach us in the third year of our church to encourage the formation of a Gospel Choir for the reason just stated. And look, if it were up to me, we would have a band play what some describe as Contemporary Christian Music (a "Passion"-type sound) every week in our worship service. But it's not. So we invited her to *bring it on!* She then took up the challenge and spent the next year developing the new ministry. Over time, the Gospel Choir has become a staple of our worship mix, and many more African Americans have indeed become one with us at Mosaic.

I do not attribute such demographic growth solely to the Gospel Choir. However, I do recognize that it helped. What is more important is whether the heart of leadership is willing to get beyond itself so as to attract people outside the majority demographic to the church. In other words, rather than rejecting good suggestions that we may not experientially understand or those that stretch us beyond our comfort zone, leaders with multi-ethnic vision must learn to adapt and make them their own. In order to build a healthy multi-ethnic church then, we must own up to our fears, insecurities, and concerns. For instance, the question, "What will people think?" should not be allowed to inform the direction God would have us take as leaders. In addition, we cannot allow our past experiences, personal preferences, or personalities, or those things with which we are most comfortable or that we can more easily control, to dictate what we do and how we do it. For if we acquiesce, we will surely build a church filled with others just like us. Rather, we should take intentional steps to draw others in, and not only to accept or assimilate them into our local fellowships but to go one step further. We must learn to accommodate them.

Notice here the subtle difference in terminology. The word *assimilate* means "to integrate somebody into a larger group so that differences are minimized or eliminated."[3] Yet the word *accommodate* means "to adjust actions in response to somebody's needs." *Merriam-Webster* provides a further connotation of the word, namely, "to give consideration to: allow for [accommodate the special interests of various groups]: *to adapt onself*" (emphasis mine).

With this in mind, it is not so much our task to reach out and embrace other cultures as it is to look within our own hearts and churches in order to prepare to receive others who are somehow different from us. In so doing, we should not expect others to abandon their own cultural identity to become one with us any more than we should abandon our own to become one with them. Rather, we are all to recognize and celebrate who we are in Christ; as from the One, many—a "harmonious mixture of different colored ingredients." *E Pluribus Unum!*

Make Attitude Adjustments

Accommodation, then, is a very important value to embrace; likewise, intentionality is as much an attitude as it is an action. As such, it must permeate every corridor of the healthy multi-ethnic church. In fact, intentionality is not only essential for establishing a diverse congregation but for maintaining it as well. For instance, it was a commitment to intentionality that first led us to accommodate the language needs of Spanish speakers in our church; in other ways, intentional steps have been taken to promote the vision and establish the DNA of our church.

Along this line, we determined early on to locate the church in the central part of the city, in Little Rock's emerging University District. This was important to us for several reasons. First, we wanted the very location of the church to describe who we were and desired to be. In this regard, we chose not to plant the church in the suburbs or to place it in the inner city. We felt both extremes would create unnecessary obstacles for people to overcome in attempting to pursue God together as one. However, by positioning the church in more "neutral territory," as we did in Little Rock by planting the church in the University District, it helped to eliminate barriers of distance, economics, and perception, as well as to create a situation in which all people have to physically move toward one another in order to gather as one at Mosaic.

The University District is within ten minutes of virtually every demographic group living in Little Rock and is anchored, as the moniker suggests, near the University of Arkansas at Little Rock (UALR). The University of Arkansas for Medical Sciences is also nearby, which, like UALR, is responsible for bringing many internationals to the area. And while I in no way want to suggest that multi-ethnic churches cannot be established in the suburbs, I do think, as the research of George Yancey supports,[4] that location is an important consideration (especially for church planters) to address.

We are also very intentional about the language we employ in describing the church, and this is equally important to consider. Therefore, we describe ourselves as *multi-ethnic and economically diverse* in order to convey both sides of the coin. In addition, we do not describe ourselves as *multicultural;* we want to avoid any confusion with the tenets of *multiculturalism* on the college campus. Nor do we describe ourselves as *multiracial,* because we believe there is only one race (the human race) that comprises many different ethnicities (Greek *ethnos,* as used in Acts 17:26, for example, where we are told God "made from one man every nation [ethnos] of mankind").

Recently, I also have had to address the notion that we are a "poor church" with some in our body. The fact is, Mosaic is not a poor church or a rich church. Rather, *we are a church for all people.* And it's interesting to me that those who say such things tend to come from upper-middle- to professional-class churches. Consequently, I believe they are not used to being in a church with such a healthy percentage of demographic diversity. Therefore, they assume "our members just don't have the money to give," especially when things get tight for us financially.

Of course, we could always use more money, and like most churches, we have experienced times of abundance as well as times when we have wondered whether or not the bills could be paid. Yet in one recent three-week challenge, the church gave some $50,000 in cash over and above regular tithes and offerings—not $500,000 but not $5,000 either! So again, even in the way we speak about the church, I think it is important to speak truthfully and intentionally.

Challenge the Homogeneous-Unit Principle

I have chosen these examples not only to illustrate points of intentionality but because each, in one way or another, violates conventional wisdom concerning how best to plant or grow a church. This wisdom has been largely proliferated by the so-called Church Growth Movement since the middle of the twentieth century. Indeed, there has been much said and written in the past fifty years by those both for and against the principles espoused by this movement. For example, Amazon.com currently lists more than 8,000 titles under the heading "church growth." In addition, the phrase elicits more than 7,160,000 hits on Google and a whopping 18,300,000 on Yahoo! For my part then, I want only to address the homogeneous-unit principle as it relates to intentionality.

From its beginning, the Church Growth Movement has passionately promoted the homogeneous-unit principle as a means for planting or replicating churches and, more specifically, as a way to grow churches quickly. But in my opinion, this should not be the focus of our intentions or the measure of success. Indeed, the question should never have been, *How fast can I grow a church?* Rather, it should have been, as it should be now, *How can I grow a church biblically?* This is the fundamental question that pioneers of the Multi-Ethnic Church Movement are asking and in the future the question that twenty-first-century church planters and reformers should attempt to address.

Of course, what we now describe as the Church Growth Movement was birthed in the work of Donald McGavran, a third-generation missionary to India. While serving as field secretary for the United Christian Missionary Society in India in the 1930s, McGavran began to wrestle with the fact that some churches were growing and others were not. Applying scientific methodology to both interviews and observation, McGavran concluded, among other things, that churches grow fastest when they are homogeneous. In other words, McGavran observed through field research that people more easily come to Christ and, consequently, into the church when they do not have to cross racial, economic, or linguistic barriers to do so. Toward that end and because people have innate prejudices, the movement promulgated the notion that pastors and missionaries should work within specific cultural contexts to evangelize, disciple, and enfold. Rather than expecting nonbelievers to change their biases prior to accepting Christ, leaders in the Church Growth Movement felt that after people became believers in Christ and filled with the Holy Spirit, they would grow in their understanding that churches should be multi-ethnic wherever possible. This lofty hope, however, has gone largely unfulfilled.[5]

One of the major concerns I have with the broad acceptance of his conclusions, however, is that McGavran's original research was conducted in India—a country both then and now dominated by the caste system.[6] Indeed, we *might* expect the establishment of diverse churches in an environment with such deep-seated views of class to be a near-impossible task. But thankfully, the world today is much different than the one in which McGavran conducted his research. Indeed, the United States of the twenty-first century is not the United States of the 1930s, and in my view, the will of God should not be abandoned for the sake of expediency. It might very well be the case that churches grow fastest when they are homogeneous. But I am not convinced they do so biblically.

With this in mind, those bold enough to envision the multi-ethnic church should not allow what is otherwise expedient to discourage them in their quest. In fact, it is my opinion that the homogeneous-unit principle should no longer inform church planting and development, as

I believe it will become an increasing hindrance to both the advance of the Gospel and the growth of the Church in the twenty-first century— certainly in the United States, if not throughout the rest of the world as well. In the future, then, we should pay closer attention to the voice of God than we do to the voice of man concerning church growth and development. We should seek to build churches that are biblical and diverse, taking intentional steps to "become all things to all men, so that (we might) by all means win some," even if only 200 and not 20,000 people end up attending. Therefore, wherever it is possible, the multi-ethnic church should be pursued in spite of what the so-called "experts" say.

There are situations however, in which the multi-ethnic vision seems impossible to achieve. For instance, someone recently asked me the following question: "I come from a small town in which virtually everyone is White. What about situations like this, where it's not possible to have a multi-ethnic church?"

In response, I believe it is safe to assume the increasing diversification of the United States will (likely) soon lead to the integration of every town and city of this nation, in time diffusing this concern altogether. More specifically, however, we must keep in mind that in every town and city currently, there are those who own the shops and those who sweep them. In other words (as I have already mentioned) economic and educational diversity are *also* a part of the multi-ethnic vision I am championing. But again, such thinking is not usually in the minds of those interested in growing churches quickly or, more specifically, embracing the homogeneous-unit principle.

Having said this, however, I do not want to be misunderstood in the matter, nor do I mean to characterize churches that are currently healthy but otherwise homogeneous as somehow "bad," "wrong," or "unbiblical." Indeed, such churches of varying size and influence have not become so apart from a certain measure of unity. Yet it is my belief that these churches would do well to consider how they might take additional, intentional steps forward in this regard and press on to the "perfection of unity," as envisioned by Christ in John 17.[7]

Find a Balance

Although we might feel that it is not natural to walk, work, or worship together with others different from ourselves, we must not give in to systemic (or institutional) racism in this regard. Rather, planters and reformers must determine to tear down the earthly walls of segregation in order to build a local church that reflects heaven on earth. And this we can do in partnership with Christ and by taking intentional steps to change the attitudes and actions of others concerning the very nature of the church, that is, by helping them to understand for whom it exists and why. In so doing, we should remain confident in the supernatural power of God to accomplish in us that which he has already completed (Ephesians 2:14–16), that which he alone can do (Ephesians 3:20–21). At Mosaic, then, we continue to wrestle with the juxtaposition of dependence and intentionality, seeking every day to be led by God, to lead others according to his will, and to learn lessons ourselves in the process. Let me illustrate this tension through my own journey to find a permanent location for our church.

Prenatal growth at Mosaic began when approximately forty-five people assembled for worship on July 8, 2001, at Markham Street Baptist Church in Little Rock. That day in a small classroom adjacent to the fellowship hall, a very intimate time of prayer ensued. Over the next four months, a growing number of people drifted from week to week and from church to church meeting wherever we were welcomed. And as the group began to grow, so did the need to determine a consistent location for our gathering.

By November 2001, our emerging congregation landed at Faith United Church near UALR. Finally, there was a place to call home, and a measure of consistency began to take root. Most encouraging at this time was the conversion of a Muslim, the first person to respond to our witness of Christ-like love for all people (see Chapter One).

After nearly sixteen months at Faith, however, we had completely maximized the space and were in desperate need of a place to call our own. Numerous efforts to relocate to other facilities near UALR—an area to which we felt sure we had been led—had consistently failed. There was nothing else for us to do but pray and wait.

Specifically, we were asking God for the miraculous provision of a facility as testimony to the fact that he was, indeed, with us and so that he alone would be glorified. In obedience to the Spirit's prompting, I placed a call in April 2003 to the Wal-Mart Corporation, and with the help of fellow Mosaic Gary Perritt, an agreement was reached by the end of May. We would sublease nearly 80,000 square feet of abandoned facility for the amazingly low price of only 10 cents a square foot—a mere $650 a month, down from the original $18,000 a month we were originally told would be required!

So with a great sense of awe and wonder, Mosaic first entered the facility in June 2003 and conducted a prayer walk, giving glory to God and dedicating the abandoned space to his purposes. And by July of that year, we held our first service in the old Wal-Mart. From a place that once sold goods to all people, we would now share the love of God with all people.

For more than three years, then, we had been established in that place. But in January 2006, the facility reverted back to its owner, and at that time, he made it clear that we would someday need to relocate. Unfortunately, purchasing the facility was not an option, as the owner intended to convert the larger space into smaller shops. What this meant was that, contractually, we occupied the facility on a month-to-month basis. The owner could have called at any time and given us ninety days notice to vacate, and we would have had nowhere to go.

So in the spring of 2006, I spent some time driving around the area, searching desperately for a future home for the church or some property to acquire. While I was out looking one day, my wife, Linda, called me on my cell phone. "What are you doing?" she asked. And I replied, "Honey, the church is growing and, I mean, I've got to find something fast! What happens if the owner calls and needs us to leave? We have nowhere to go!"

With a gentle but firm voice of wisdom, she then responded, "Can I ask, *Why are you out driving around? Why are you wasting your time?* Instead, you should be on your knees praying. That's what you should be doing! For don't you know—don't you believe? God is going to take care of us. He's going to take care of the church!"

God Will Provide

Not long after Linda had rekindled my faith with her words, I learned that a 100,000-square-foot facility just a few blocks east of us had been sold. Situated on a 10-acre piece of property, the building rests on one of the busiest corners in the state of Arkansas. More important, it's located directly across the street from UALR and is in the heart of the University District, the most diverse area of the city. In addition, it borders an area with the highest instance of violent crime in Little Rock and, according to the 2000 census, 21.5 percent of people living in the area live at or below the poverty line. In other words, it is right where we want to be!

So when I received a call alerting me to its sale, I was sick! For more than a year, two men had tried to acquire this property, in part, to provide long-term space for the church. Unfortunately, they had not been successful, and this facility (which once housed a Kmart) was sold to a local businessman, the owner of Office Furniture Supply (OFS), Inc.

With discouragement swirling within me, I called Linda to share the news. And when I did, she said, "This doesn't make sense! You know that for more than three years I've told you, every time I drive by that building I see the flags of Mosaic flying over it. I just know God's going to give it to us, Mark; I'm sure of it! The story's already been written and God has the perfect place for us. It's already done! We just need to pray right now that he'll show us where it is and soon, whether that's the old Kmart building or somewhere else." So together, we then prayed and concluded our call. Linda had encouraged me, but still I was concerned.

Next I called Harry. After I had filled him in, he told me that he had once purchased a house on a desirable piece of property just outside Moscow, Idaho. On the very day that he did, however, another man approached him wanting to buy it. The man made an offer, and Harry accepted it, flipping the home he had just purchased for a profit. "Perhaps," Harry said, "the new owner of the facility would do the same for us."

"Say no more," I said, and springing into action, I quickly placed a call—cold turkey—to OFS, Inc. Fortunately, the owner, Mike Montgomery was in, and I introduced myself over the phone. Indeed, he had secured the property and was in the process of closing the deal. Trying not to sound desperate, I nevertheless found myself saying, "What if we were to give you $500,000 more than you are paying for the property? Would you be willing to sell?"

By that time, we had talked for about ten minutes, and Mike suggested we continue our discussion in person. Filled with optimism, I rushed over to see him. And within ten minutes of my arrival, Mike made it clear: "Someday, Mark, your church is going to own this property. And I can assure you, it has nothing to do with money!"

"You see," Mike said, "eleven years ago, I was a homeless drunk sleeping behind 'your' Wal-Mart. I was eating food out of the dumpster at McDonald's, and my only light came from the candles I would occasionally purchase for $1 right here in the Kmart. One day, though, someone came by and left a tract—I don't even know who it was—but after reading it, I began attending Alcoholics Anonymous (AA) meetings. In time, I sobered up and soon gave my life to Jesus Christ. And for four years now, I have watched your church grow and minister to 'my people' here in the community. It would thrill me, Mark, to see Mosaic permanently located here!"

Quite frankly, I was blown away! As we talked, tears began to flow from his eyes and mine. Somehow we both sensed that this was a holy moment, a divine appointment in which we had been led together into the presence and power of the Holy Spirit. And in that moment, Mike became our "Esther," a man positioned for such a time as this.

When I returned to the church, I again called Linda to share with her all that had happened in a very brief time, and we began to cry tears of joy. She told me that after we had talked earlier, she had spent more time in prayer and had been led in God's word to 2 Chronicles 7, where Solomon, together with the people of Israel, dedicate the Temple. Reading from the passage, she shared the very words that our hearts were bursting to express: "When all the people of Israel saw the fire coming down, and the glorious presence of the Lord filling the temple, they fell down on the ground and worshipped and praised the Lord, saying, '*He is so good! The faithful love of the Lord endures forever!*'" (2 Chronicles 7:3, emphasis mine).

With these words, Israel had finally received and dedicated the Temple and we now realized that Mosaic, too, would one day receive and dedicate a building of its own in which to worship God—the old Kmart, after all! It was a fitting end to the roller coaster of emotions we had ridden that day, April 20, 2006.

To make a long story short, we then had Mike and his wife, Monica, together with their children, come and share his testimony at Mosaic on November 19, 2006. And a few weeks later, he was back again, this time to sign a contract with us in front of the body. At that time, we agreed to buy the property within the next three years for $2,000,000—only $20 a square foot—for which we will receive the 10-acre site, the 100,000-square-foot facility, and 500 parking spaces to call our own. What a thrill it was to give him the $100,000 we had saved as a down payment! But wait, there's more.

The following week, we received another anonymous check in the mail—you guessed it, in the amount of $100,000—as well as a $250,000 matching gift pledge. Amazingly, the phone call informing me of these gifts came one year to the day that we had dismissed our Sunday service early to conduct a prayer walk on the old Kmart grounds. And as part of the contract, Mike agreed to deduct $300,000 off the purchase price at the time of closing. Therefore, we will need a total of only $1,700,000 to make the purchase; as I write, we are nearly half-way there! God is, indeed, answering our prayers, not only for a facility but also for the miraculous provision of it so that, in the end, we will all be able to say, Not by might, not by power, but by the Spirit it has been done. *Gloria a Dios!*

Admittedly, throughout more than twenty years of full-time ministry, I have not often viewed praying or waiting as intentional steps. Of course, I know I am "supposed" to pray, but I struggle with a temperament compelled to action. Through my experience at Mosaic, however, I am learning to embrace the tension and more fully abandon myself to this principle: *Sometimes intentionally, I must wait upon the Lord.*

To wait patiently on God to reveal his will, his way, and his time runs contrary to my very personality and to all that the world says will lead me to success. But in and through this ministry, and more so than in any other place I have been, I have seen God work in ways that cannot be otherwise attributed to the ingenuity of man. At such times, I feel his power and his pleasure. At such times, I know that he is really the One building a healthy multi-ethnic church!

o

Olga and Omar Cruz

In October 2003, two couches were donated to Mosaic. The couches were in such poor condition that when they arrived at the church, someone suggested throwing them away. However, one of our pastors, Cesar Ortega, stepped in to say that someone with nothing might be glad to own them.

A week later, Cesar received a phone call requesting that he visit a lady who had just arrived from Mexico—a woman with absolutely no connections, food, clothing, or material goods. Heading to one of the trailer parks in southwest Little Rock, he met Olga, who had run away from a life of physical, emotional, and mental abuse at the hands of her ex-husband. Upon entering the trailer where she was staying, Cesar noticed only one chair and a blanket. Before leaving, he shared the Lord with Olga, prayed for her, and told her he would be back tomorrow.

On the next day, Cesar loaded the worn-out couches, a dining-room set, and a bed onto an old pick-up truck and took them to her trailer. When Olga saw the items, she began to weep.

The next day, Elisabeth (Cesar's wife) came to visit Olga and to share with her the message of salvation. Olga wept like a child as she accepted Jesus Christ as her Savior. Two weeks later, Olga introduced Cesar and Elisabeth to her friend, Omar. Soon, he, too, received the Lord! Five months later, Olga and Omar were married during a Sunday morning service at Mosaic!

In 2005, the couple returned to Mexico for a short stay. While there, Olga shared her faith and all that she had experienced at Mosaic with her family. Seeing the change in her life, her father believed; Olga had led him to the Lord!

Three years have passed, and Olga and Omar are still a part of the Mosaic family. Olga's faith remains strong. She is not afraid to talk about the horrible life she once lived and how, in coming to the United States, she not only found a new life physically but, more important, a new life spiritually in the Lord. "Before I accepted the Lord, my life was horrible," she says. "I was a bad person with no hope and no future. Now, I have faith that the Lord is with me. He is changing me day by day, and I have learned to trust in him. He has restored that which was lost in me. I am so thankful for Mosaic!"

Of course, we also thank God for Olga and Omar and for our brother Cesar, who understood the value of worn-out couches to the One who makes all things good and new.

6

EMPOWER DIVERSE LEADERSHIP

The choices we make determine the shape and color of our lives.

—Luis Palau

IN THE SPRING OF 2006, I received a call from the local NBC affiliate in Little Rock. They wanted to feature our church in a weekly segment called *Faith Matters* that was designed to highlight people and institutions of faith making a difference in the lives of Arkansans. They were particularly interested in describing the diversity of our church—a story of interest, in part, due to the fact that we are located only three miles from Little Rock's Central High School. It was here, in 1957, that nine Black students (the Little Rock Nine) were denied entrance to the school, in spite of a ruling by the U.S. Supreme Court ordering the desegregation of public schools throughout the United States.[1] Once an epicenter of the civil rights movement in the United States, Central High was placed on the National Register of Historic Places in 1977. The school became a National Historic Landmark in 1988 and ten years later (1998) was designated a National Historic Site by an act of Congress.

When the producer of the segment came by to do the story, I was surprised to learn that she was a third-generation Baha'i—a faith based on the teachings of the nineteenth-century Persian Baha'u'llah and one, she said, "involving people from every race, religion, and nation."

"You know, Mark," she continued, "my faith community has been integrated from its inception. I'm so glad to see Christians and Christian churches finally reaching out to incorporate [diverse] people into their local congregations." Through our conversation I also learned that, as producer, she was the one who had initiated the idea and was ultimately responsible for the story. When I inquired further as to her interest in Mosaic, she summed it up by saying, "I want others to know that your church is not just diverse on the outside but diverse on the inside as well." In other words, what had caught her attention was the fact that our leadership—indeed, our pulpit itself—is fully integrated. What she had observed, then, was a partnership of people from top to bottom reflecting the very heart and message of the church. More than anything else, this established the credibility of the work in her eyes. Indeed, it was the diversity of leadership, through and through, that made Mosaic a unique story worth telling.

A Biblical Model for Today

Of course, Mosaic is not the first church to be led by people of varying ethnic background. As discussed in Chapter Two, the leadership at the church in Antioch (Acts 11:19–25; 13:1) serves as a model for enlisting diverse leadership within a local church setting. So here again, we should ask, *Why was Luke compelled, under the inspiration of the Holy Spirit, not only to mention the names of the men involved as prophets and teachers at Antioch but their country of origin as well?* Was it not to make clear that the church, like the Gospel itself, is for all people? Was it not to suggest that such a diverse team is best fit for leadership in a "house of prayer for all the nations" (Isaiah 56:7)?

In addition, we might also ask why Paul selects Timothy to join himself and Silas in delivering to the churches in Syria and Cilicia "the decisions reached by the apostles and elders in Jerusalem for the people to obey" (Acts 15:41; 16:4, 15). Surely, it was not only because "the brothers at Lystra and Iconium spoke well of him" (Acts 16:2). Was it not also because Timothy was "bi-cultural" (Acts 16:1) and, therefore, a living example of the fact that the Gospel, like the church, is available to all who would come?

Such examples should inform the development of leadership in a healthy multi-ethnic church. And when it comes to staffing, planters and reformers alike should staff for diversity, from the pulpit to the nursery and every-where in between. This is the "put your money where your mouth is" commitment! Practically speaking, however, how can this be done?

A Deliberate Choice

Intentionality, as I stated in Chapter Five, is as much an attitude as it is an action, and it should permeate every corridor of the healthy multi-ethnic church. Certainly, this is true when considering how best to enlist, equip, and establish leaders within the church, whether as part of a vocational or volunteer staff team. Intentionality can further be defined as the middle ground between quota and wishful thinking. Let me explain what I mean.

According to the *Encarta World English Dictionary*,[2] quotas are set to define "the maximum number or quantity that is permitted or needed" within a given setting. In other words, those in positions of authority or responsibility determine within their organizational context the limits as to who, what, and how much is needed. Of course, there is no place in the New Testament where quotas are prescribed for leadership within the local church. And attempts to otherwise set them can only be seen as human and therefore flawed, albeit noble, efforts to engineer what we might believe is the greater good. To be clear then, quotas are not recommended for those seeking to empower diverse leadership within a local church.

However, we should not expect to integrate our leadership teams through random prayer or wishful thinking. Diverse individuals of godly character, theological agreement, and shared vision do not just arrive on waves of whim. Rather, they must be intentionally sought. Like the best of college coaches, multi-ethnic church planters and reformers must continually be on the lookout for potential recruits. When we find them, we should establish a dialogue, mindful that there may be an opportunity for formal partnership together at some point in the future.

In doing this, one should always keep in mind the whole. In other words, while quotas should in no way dictate the diversity of your staff, potential hires must be considered in light of both the current and future composition of your team. In fact, each decision you make concerning additions or replacements to your staff will have an impact down the road. Practically speaking, this means that in saying *yes* to someone of a particular ethnicity or other valued descriptive (one who is Deaf or Blind, for example), you may have to say *no* to someone else like him or her later on, in order to maintain the general balance of the team. In so doing, you will safeguard the diversity of your staff and therefore the credibility of your church, mindful that no one people group should become so dominant in number as to undermine the vision.

An Ongoing Effort

As I discussed in Chapter Four, we currently have a vacancy to fill in our pulpit.[3] And given Harold's departure, we will most certainly look for an African American to replace him. This is a purposeful decision on our part, affected to some degree by the fact that we are a church located in the South. Because we desire at least three individuals to share the pulpit, we are also informed in this decision by the fact that my partner, Harry Li, is a Chinese American and I am White.

During these days as well, there is a White woman and another White family currently raising support to join our staff team as Residents. Once they do, our staff will consist of five Whites (one of whom is Deaf), three Blacks, two Latinos, one Chinese American, and one woman from Antigua—a pretty healthy mix. However, another White man has also recently shown interest in joining our team. Now all of these people are qualified in character, theologically in agreement, and on-board with the vision. But as our situation illustrates, the balance of diversity can quickly shift if leaders are not intentional. The point here is that planters and reformers must pay attention to changing scenarios and not become complacent in this regard.

So how are we adjusting? Because we are not about quotas, we are not too concerned at this time. However, we have begun not only to pray but also to speak with a number of African American leaders, letting them know of our need and desire. On the other hand, we do not wish to turn quality folks away simply because of their ethnicity (in this case, because they are White). Therefore, we have begun to consider who else might be available and how we might empower other individuals of diverse ethnicity in order to maintain balance in the future. Toward this end, I have recently approached two African American women, one man from Mexico, and another from Nicaragua about the possibility of one day joining our team.

I do not share such things to suggest that we absolutely have it all figured out with regard to empowering diverse leadership. Rather, it is only to provide further insight into how we are attempting to maintain the balance between quotas and wishful thinking and are pursuing others intentionally.

The "Best Man" Does Not Always Look Like You

Years ago and before beginning the church, I was cautioned to be careful in my zeal to develop a diverse leadership team. Specifically, I was advised by an African American pastor of a large congregation in Little Rock not to seek diverse individuals simply for the sake of diversity. Rather, we agreed, they should be men or women of sound integrity, theological unity, and shared vision. Furthermore, he told me that I should not ever presume to have achieved integration simply because diverse individuals were involved. "There are perceptions," he said, "that should also be considered and overcome for the sake of your vision." He then took me to school:

> Mark, if you hire or otherwise empower African Americans only to lead your church in worship, you may inadvertently suggest to people, "We accept them as entertainers." Or if you hire or otherwise empower African Americans only to work with your children, you may inadvertently suggest, "We accept them to nanny our kids." And if you hire or otherwise employ African Americans only as janitors, you are quite clearly stating, "We expect them to clean up after us." It is only when you allow us to share your pulpit, to serve with you on the elder board or alongside you in apportioning the money that we will be truly one with you in the church.

I have never forgotten his words.

Along this line I recently asked my friend, George Yancey, a sociologist at the University of North Texas and coauthor of the book *United By Faith*, whether statistics are available to describe not only the diversity of congregations throughout the United States but also the diversity of pastoral leadership teams. At the time of this writing, however, no such numbers are available. Responding to my inquiry, he wrote, "That is a good question and hopefully, in the future, we might be able to look at the effects of multi-racial leadership [on a local congregation]."

Yet we both agree, it is probably correct to assume that some proportion of the 7½ percent of churches that can be currently classified as multi-ethnic are led by homogeneous (mono-ethnic) staff teams. Although the diversity of these congregations is commendable, the challenge for such churches in growing forward is to recognize that more work needs to be done. Indeed, to achieve the perfection of unity that Christ intends for believers to experience in and through the local church, we all have a long way to go.

So where can we find people of diverse ethnic or cultural background who share our passion, beliefs, and vision concerning the multi-ethnic church? How can they become a part of our staff or leadership teams? Before I address these questions, let me first explain why such people are so rarely found or employed by a homogeneous church.

I know of a church in which well over one hundred individuals were hired over the course of eight years to fill significant positions of leadership. Some of these were hired to fill new positions in the growing congregation, while others replaced individuals who were, for one reason or another, leaving. In all that time, however, the church hired only two minorities to fill ministry positions, and only one minority in an administrative role. Yet this was in a town that was nearly 40 percent Black!

There were, however, a number of African Americans hired to work on the custodial crew. As you might imagine, this is not at all what it means to empower diverse leadership.

During those eight years, each time a new pastor was hired he would be introduced to the congregation with a similar story. The country had been searched, individuals were considered, and, as the leaders would say, "We are pleased to announce that we have found the best man for the job." As you might suspect, though, he was always White and in many other ways reflective of core leadership.

Connect with Others Beyond Yourself

But here's the question we should ask: *Why does the best man for the job always look like us?* The reason, of course, is simple. When a position becomes available in most churches, leaders tend to contact those they know and trust to inquire who they, in turn, might recommend for the job. The people we contact and those they recommend are, more often than not, people just like us in ethnic, economic, and educational background. This is because we have, quite naturally, formed common bonds with others most like us over time. Consequently, the people we know recommend people they know, and by the time resumes are submitted, personality profiles administered, interviews conducted, and decisions made, the new hire—"the best man for the job"—looks just like us as well. Indeed, we may have searched the country, but we searched only through a limited field of contacts. The new hire, then, is the best man for the job only in the sense that he is the best man we could find through a narrow network of friends and associates. *How can the cycle be broken?*

Those intent on building a healthy multi-ethnic church should develop relationships with people outside their own ethnic and economic background for just such a purpose. If starting from scratch, we can do this simply by picking up the phone and introducing ourselves to pastors and professors, ministry and business professionals alike, or in a variety of other ways to make ourselves and our desires known. Coupled with passion, persistence, and prayer, we can expect our intentional efforts to be rewarded.

Of course, once the church is established and diversity takes root, the process of finding candidates of varying ethnicity becomes much less contrived. Again, let me illustrate from our own experience at Mosaic.

Philip Lamar (White) was one of my former students. Responding to Christ as a senior in high school, he spent most of his collegiate years actively pursuing ministry. A gifted evangelist with a heart for internationals, Philip soon began traveling to Guatemala to work with orphans; there he picked up Spanish as a second language. When he came back to Little Rock, I invited him to join me in planting Mosaic and to apply his passion, gifting, and experience in reaching out to Latinos living here. It was the summer of 2001.

Several years before, Philip had met Inés Velasquez (Nicaraguan) while visiting friends in Texas. He introduced her to me, and by November of 2001, she had also joined our emerging staff team. Inés, in turn, recently introduced me to a young woman named Jamna Abdullah, one of her best friends from Nicaragua. Jamna was in town visiting just prior to beginning seminary training in Guatemala. During her stay, we began a dialogue that very well may lead to her involvement with us at some point in the future following her graduation. Toward that end, we will most certainly stay in touch.

Similarly, Miss Kitty Longstreth (White), a woman from the church I had left, introduced me in 2001 to her friend, Treopia Bryant (Black), after learning of my desire to establish Mosaic. By February 2002, Treopia had joined our staff (the first African American to do so) as the Director of Prayer. When Treopia's sister died at the end of 2002, our staff attended the funeral where we met her nephew, Amos Gray (Black). It took me three years to reel him in! Now he serves as the Student and Children's Ministry Pastor at Mosaic.

One day in January 2002, I was working from home. That morning, I had been reflecting on the fact that Whites, Blacks, and Latinos were now showing interest in Mosaic. Yet to date, not a single Asian had come. So I prayed a brief prayer expressing my desire to someday see Asians, too, become part of the church. Later that afternoon, my phone rang. Rob Smith, a Latino and the father of two of my former students, had a friend in town—a Ph.D. electrical engineer and tenured professor at the University of Idaho, who had some questions about vocational ministry. Rob explained that his friend would be leaving town in a couple of hours and, with apologies for short notice, asked if I might be able to meet with the man before he left. Hastily, we arranged to meet in thirty minutes at a local café. And when I arrived, Rob introduced me to Harry Li (Chinese American), who explained that he was considering a move to full-time ministry and told me why he was doing so. It was not long before Harry and I realized there was much more to discuss than our limited time would allow. Throughout the next nine months, we stayed in touch, and in October of 2002, Harry moved his family to Little Rock in order to join the work. I cannot imagine anyone better suited for partnership with me or for pastoral ministry in these days at Mosaic.

Connect with Others Beyond Our Borders

One final story demonstrates the fact that God connects leaders beyond borders and that such connections can also be a source for discovering and empowering diverse leadership in a healthy multi-ethnic church. Throughout the 1990s, I made several trips to Honduras involving students in short-term missions. In those years, Allen Danforth (White), the founder of World Gospel Outreach in Tegucigalpa, provided an excellent experience in connecting with the people of Honduras through medical missions for the purpose of evangelism. By the spring of 2002, he, too, had heard of my new endeavor and called to ask if I might need a Latino on staff. Allen told me that his adopted daughter, Elisabeth Ortega, together with her husband, Cesar (both Honduran), were considering a move from the business sector to vocational ministry. In addition to describing Cesar's heart for evangelism, Allen said that Cesar was also a worship leader in his church. With a sense of excitement, then, I left word for the Ortegas to contact me in order to further discuss the possibilities. I was disappointed, however, when I never heard from them.

One year later, in the winter of 2003, Allen called me again. He explained that at the time of our initial conversation, the Ortegas had not been ready to make the move to ministry but now he felt that they were. So I contacted them again, and the rest, as they say, is history. Cesar has served faithfully and effectively as a member of our staff since the summer of 2003.

Consider Volunteers

If you are planting a church, begin with a diverse team of people empowered to fulfill initial roles of leadership. In this way, there will be no confusion that people are being "propped up after the fact" to accomplish what some may then deride as your own agenda. Even if there is no money to hire additional staff, diverse volunteers can be positioned for maximum impact.

For example, the first call I placed in this regard was to Harold Nash (whom I mentioned in Chapter Four), the African American leader of an inner-city ministry in North Little Rock. At that time (the summer of 2001), I invited him to join me vocationally in planting Mosaic and to share the pulpit. However, concluding that it was not God's will for him to leave his ministry at that time, Harold accepted the invitation as a volunteer. In that capacity, he served alongside me for five years as a teaching pastor and for four years as an elder.

Two of our initial worship leaders also served in the beginning as volunteers; one was Black and the other was White. Rotating from week to week and, at times, singing together, their unity of mind, spirit, and purpose helped to model both an attitude and expectation that diverse leaders could and should serve side by side at Mosaic.

After appointing Harold an elder, he and I together appointed Harry in the spring of 2003. One year later, the three of us, in turn, appointed five others to join us in the role: Bill Head (White), Eric Higgins (Black), Lloyd Hodges (Black), Tom Holmes (White), and Bruce Patterson (Black). Like Harold, these men also served voluntarily, spending significant amounts of time serving the greater needs of the body. Some still do! So again, diversifying your leadership team can happen whether you have money or not. And I have not even mentioned all of the other areas of ministry in which diverse people serve together as one in our church.

However, let me also provide you with a word of caution. If you are revitalizing or transforming an existing church, it is important not to move too quickly in adding or making changes to your leadership team. In other words, you do not want to split a church in the name of unity! Yet this you will do, for instance, if without any preparation at all, the (homogeneous) body is told one Sunday morning that you have hired someone quite different from yourself and from them, who will, from now on, share the pulpit; it could happen if you too quickly enlist volunteer worship leaders to change the music in style and format, replace pictures of a White Jesus with those that depict him as Latino, or programmatically legislate the desegregation of midweek small groups or Sunday School classes. Once again, although intentionality must govern the approach to the revitalization or transformation of a church, as well as its leadership team, so must wisdom be displayed through prayer, patience, and persistence.

Go the Distance

Restrictive thinking related to roles and ethnicity is formulated by fear, ignorance, or outright racism. Sadly, many remain largely unaware of conditioning that has long shaped the American psyche and its effect on who we are or how we make decisions from day to day. Whether in the church, in government, or on the athletic field, people have often been evaluated through the lens of color. Take, for instance, the story of Don McPherson.

"Don McPherson was a . . . college All-American athlete at Syracuse University. As quarterback for the Orangemen from 1983–88, he compiled twenty-two school records, and in 1987, guided Syracuse to an undefeated season. That year, he was . . . a consensus All-American and winner of over eighteen national Player of the Year honors,"[4] finishing second in Heisman Trophy balloting behind Notre Dame great,

Tim Brown. In addition that year, McPherson was rated the nation's number-one quarterback in passing efficiency and widely respected as a running threat. In short, he could do it all!

Today, one would expect such a standout to be selected in the first round of the NFL draft. But again, it was 1987 and at that time, the NFL was largely resistant to drafting African Americans as quarterbacks. For example, prior to the draft that year one NFL team told McPherson that they would select him but only if he would change positions and become a defensive back. Conventional wisdom at the time suggested he was too thin, too athletic, and too short to play quarterback in the NFL. But refusing to change positions, McPherson was not selected until the sixth round of the draft by the Philadelphia Eagles, the 149th player taken overall. He went on to play seven years of professional football.[5] but like African American quarterback Warren Moon, Don had to spend time outside the NFL in order to play the position he loved.

Today, the NFL, like the NCAA, has come a long way in this regard. African American quarterbacks like Donovan McNabb and Vince Young are no longer exceptions but compete fairly with the likes of Tom Brady and Peyton Manning for recognition and respect as quarterbacks in college and at the professional level.

I believe the local church will soon likewise get beyond its own past in this regard. Indeed, the time has come to change our approach to staffing and commit ourselves to empowering ethnically diverse leaders. Yes, let us consider how to extend opportunities to various men and women of sound integrity, theological agreement, and shared vision and invite them to join us as partners in proclaiming the love of Christ in and through the local church. More than that, let us show the world through such interaction just what that love looks like.

○

Georgia Mjartan

Georgia Mjartan is the executive director of Our House, a shelter in Little Rock that provides the working homeless with safe housing, food, child care, education, and job training. Her story speaks to the compelling nature and power of unity:

> I visited Mosaic for the first time on January 14, 2007 and on that day, Christ came into my heart. Before then, my concept of "God" was very abstract and removed from day-to-day life.

When people referred to God as someone who was working in their lives, I thought they were being disingenuous.

In the summer of 2006, a man named Corey Ford came into the shelter. Corey is 6'2" and has tattoos up and down his arms and neck. A former drug addict, he spent four and a half years in prison. Yet here he was working in my shelter and truly concerned about the welfare of those around him. So when Corey told me how God was working in his life, I believed him. How else, but by the power of God, could someone be so truly transformed?

In January, Corey invited me to attend his church, Mosaic. On that Sunday, we arrived early and just in time for the weekly prayer meeting. Sitting with others in a small circle of prayer, I felt God's presence. Here were people of all different backgrounds, whose prayers sounded different—different intonation, different words—and all of these people were praying together to one God. Somehow I knew that God could hear these prayers. I did not have a question about that anymore.

As the room filled, I felt overwhelmed with joy. There were Black people and White people, Hispanic people, deaf people, Asians, and the blind. We were young and old, students and professionals, families with or without babies, wealthy and poor. I felt at home in this place and with these people. I felt God's presence in the music, in our connectedness, and in our prayers.

During the service, there was also a time of communion. Whenever I had witnessed communion as a visitor in other churches prior to this, I had always stayed in my seat. I knew what communion represented, and I knew that participation meant personally accepting Christ's sacrifice. However, when communion began at Mosaic, I knew I was now ready to take part. In that moment I chose Christ, accepting him and his sacrifice for me.

After communion, there was worship and praise. I closed my eyes. I told myself that it wouldn't matter what anyone else thought of me. This was between me and my God. As I began to worship, I felt Christ's glory all around me. My hands lifted up to him. Christ *had* come into my heart, and he is now a part of my day-to-day life!

DEVELOP CROSS-CULTURAL RELATIONSHIPS

There are two types of people . . . Those who come into a room
and say, "Well, here I am," and those who say,
"Ah, there you are."

—Frederick Collins

RECENTLY, I TOOK TWO OF MY CHILDREN, Will and Kate, together with some of their buddies, to see the Memphis Grizzlies play the Phoenix Suns at the FedEx Forum in Memphis, Tennessee. The game was played on Martin Luther King Day (2007), and a variety of special features throughout the evening called attention to Dr. King and his legacy. For instance, R&B legend Patty LaBelle sang the national anthem, and Sports Legacy Awards were presented to former NBA great, David Robinson, as well as to a current NBA star, Dikembe Mutumbo, by the National Civil Rights Museum. In addition, a video tribute to Dr. King was shown at half-time. And beyond these scripted elements, there was other more spontaneous entertainment that night.

For example, at one point during the second quarter, three individuals were led onto the court by the Grizzlies' team mascot and given thirty seconds to perform their best dance moves for the crowd. Of course, the winner, which was to be judged by the fans and measured by applause, was guaranteed to receive a prize.

The first man to dance was flat-out sensational. He was creative, uninhibited, and technically precise. The second contestant, a woman, did nothing outstanding to warrant any special attention and was, quite clearly, not in the same league as the man who had just performed. The final contestant, however, was unique. He was not as gifted as the first contestant either, but it did not matter to him or to the crowd. In fact, it was easy to tell that he was giving it all he had and enjoying the moment. He was clearly a good sport.

When the announcer said, "Let's hear it for Contestant Number One," the crowd cheered loudly and appropriately in appreciation of the first dancer's obvious talent. For Contestant Number Two, the applause was polite. But when invited to respond to Contestant Number Three, the crowd went wild! They stood to cheer, whoop, and whistle, and in many other ways make their feelings known. Contestant Number Three was the one to whom the crowd awarded its favor.

What caught my attention, though, was the fact that a large percentage of African Americans in attendance that night had chosen Contestant Number Three—a White man—as the winner. In so doing, they had passed on the other two contestants, who both were Black. And when the crowd erupted in applause for the young man, there was not a hint of bias in the place. People had simply acknowledged the one who had best entertained them without distinction. In that moment, it felt like we were all one happy family, enjoying the game and relationally connected through the entertainment. Indeed, it was a welcome respite from the racial tensions still all too prevalent in society and, indeed, lurking just outside the stadium doors.

Of course, sports have a way of connecting diverse people around a common interest or team. But we should ask, *Why has the local church been unwilling or unable to do the same, that is, to connect people of varying ethnic and economic backgrounds around the cross of Jesus Christ?*

Today in the United States, diverse people have to go to school together, for according to law, our public schools cannot be segregated. We must also work together with those different from ourselves, for the law mandates a workplace free of discrimination. In addition, homes in our neighborhoods must be sold to anyone with the desire and means to purchase, for, again, the law demands it. Yet have you ever stopped to consider that the local church is the only major institution in our society[1] in which segregation is allowable by law, in light of the judicial principle known as the "separation of church and state?" Indeed, the segregation of the church is not only *allowable* but seems quite *acceptable* to the vast majority of believers and church leaders throughout the United States who see nothing at all wrong with this picture. Is it not, however, the law of love (Matthew 22:36–40) that should inform us in the matter?

To experience sincere and mutual respect across ethnic and economic divides and in order for the church to walk worthy of its calling (Ephesians 4:2), we will have to develop cross-cultural relationships with others different from ourselves. And to do so, we should move intentionally, humbly, and lovingly toward diverse brothers and sisters in Christ. With this in mind, we would do well to remember the words of the apostle John, who wrote,

> If someone says, "I love God," and hates his brother, he is a liar; for the one who does not love his brother whom he has seen, cannot love God whom he has not seen. And this is the commandment we have from Him, that the one who loves God should love his brother also. (1 John 4:20–21)

Getting Beyond Ourselves

Of course, relationships are important to the overall development and well-being of any church. Yet the development of relationships, specifically, the development of relationships that transcend ethnic and economic barriers, are essential for building a healthy multi-ethnic church. To be sure, differences in personality and preference exist in a homogeneous church. Yet when entire cultures come together under one roof, the challenges are much greater. But so are the joys of overcoming them! Mutual understanding, respect, and appreciation, however, will develop only through a firm commitment to one another, over time. And these we should pursue, not simply for the sake of diversity but, indeed, for a greater good: the expansion of the Gospel through the expression of unity in and through the local church.

Much like a marriage, then, those of us in multi-ethnic congregations can expect the pursuit of such relationships to be awkward at times. Yet we should remain committed to working through misunderstandings and unintentional hurts and to overcoming petty issues that might otherwise keep us apart. The task, as Paul said, is "to walk in a manner worthy of the calling with which you have been called, with all humility and gentleness, with patience, showing forbearance to one another in love, being diligent to preserve the unity of the Spirit in the bond of peace" (Ephesians 4:2–3). Should we fail to develop such relationships, we will fail to realize the very church we have committed ourselves to building.

The Value of Cross-Cultural Relationships

Cross-cultural relationships form the very foundation and fabric of a multi-ethnic church because trust is not a commodity so easily assumed in an environment where people must interact with others different from themselves. Past conditioning from family or social setting, peer interaction, community mores, and the media have surely shaped our perceptions of those beyond our own ethnic, economic, and educational heritage. With this in mind, perhaps it is good to recognize that all of us from time to time have prejudicial thoughts and feelings. The question is, *What should we do with them when they arise?*

The word *prejudice* can be defined as "a pre-formed opinion concerning someone or something." More often than not, the term is used to describe the negative or inaccurate opinions we have "pre-formed" of others with whom we have had (in most cases) little to no relational contact. It is true, however, that some people have had negative encounters with others different from themselves and that these experiences have, quite naturally, shaped their thoughts and feelings. In attempting to encourage the development of cross-cultural relationships within the local church, then, we should be careful not to denigrate those who share honestly about themselves in this regard. Rather, to build a healthy multi-ethnic church, we should provide opportunities for open dialogue and commend those with the courage to discuss such things, as well as the determination to deal with them.

Recently, a church invited an African American to address the subject of "racial unity" within the Body of Christ. Following his remarks, he invited members of the church's leadership team to join him on the platform and to address related questions. In so doing, one White man, an elder in the church, began with a statement: "I hate to admit it, but I am prejudiced." He then went on to describe an experience in which, many years before, four men had broken into his home. At that time, a number of his possessions were stolen, and as a result he continued to struggle with his perception of African Americans. In fact, he said that when police had recently apprehended men responsible for a string of robberies in his community, he was surprised to learn they were White, having wrongly assumed they were Black.

For this man to admit such things in public required not only personal courage but also spiritual conviction. Indeed, the man not only acknowledged past struggle, he disclosed an ongoing effort to overcome it. To get beyond such thoughts and feelings, we must be intentional. And, like this man, we must ask God for help on the journey.

When he had finished speaking, the congregation learned even more about this man's resolve to move beyond his past. In fact, they were told that he had been mentoring a young African American student for the past ten years. In other words, the church heard from one who not only acknowledged a prejudicial attitude but one who had determined to do something about it. Indeed, this man desired to free his mind and heart of erroneous distinctions, and what had helped him greatly was the intentional pursuit of a cross-cultural relationship with a young man of color.

With this in mind, we must recognize that diverse people have been called not only to worship God but to walk and work together as one in and through the local church (1 Corinthians 12:12–27). For if we are willing only to worship together on Sunday mornings, we will fail to express authentic love for one another and thus fail to fulfill the "Greatest Commandment," as expressed by Christ in Matthew 22:36–40.

When Misunderstanding Happens

In pursuit of cross-cultural relationships then, let me stipulate right up front that there will be things said and sometimes done that will cause a measure of misunderstanding. It's just going to happen, so you might as well expect it! At such times, everyone involved will be challenged to apply Paul's command to be "patient and forbearing with one another" (Ephesians 4:2). This again is where relational trust is needed to overcome what, in most instances, will be an unintentional offense.

For instance, a White woman recently asked an African American woman, "Is that your hair?" Fortunately, the two had developed a friendship over time—one that enabled the Black woman to view the inquiry more as a *faux pas* than anything else. Nevertheless, she used the opportunity to gently admonish her White friend never to ask an African American woman—or any woman, for that matter—such a question!

On another occasion, ten men of diverse backgrounds had gathered for breakfast and discussion. When a White man in his mid-sixties began to speak of his childhood and of racism that had unfortunately prejudiced him at an early age, he stopped himself before continuing to ask, "So what, by the way, would you like for me to call you people?" In this case, it was a legitimate question and, as it turned out, everyone laughed. Because the man's honest inquiry was delivered with sincerity of heart, the African Americans sitting around the table simply responded, "You can call us anything you want, brother! In fact, there's nothing you can call us that we haven't been called before." Their point, of course, was not that any descriptive term would be acceptable. In fact, they later shared with those at the table that either "African American" or "Black" would be fine. Their comments and, more important, the spirit in which these men responded, demonstrated both an appreciation of the older man's willingness to acknowledge his past and to ask such a question openly. Through their response, they demonstrated an acceptance of the man based on who he was becoming and not on who he once had been.

Of course, these two examples speak of Whites offending Blacks. But it can work the other way, too. No matter who you are—your ethnic background, the customs of your culture, or the color of your skin—you can (and will) misunderstand or be misunderstood from time to time.

Having experienced this, I can tell you that there is no better place to learn or to grow in such matters than in the safe environment of a healthy multi-ethnic church. For those who join a diverse congregation have, in effect, both willed and declared themselves to be people intent on developing cross-cultural relationships so that "being rooted and grounded in love, [they] may be able to comprehend with *all the saints* what is the breadth and length and height and depth, and to know the love of Christ which surpasses knowledge, [in order to] be filled up to all the fullness of God" (Ephesians 3:17–19, additions and emphasis mine).

Walking the Walk

It is clear that the early Church was characterized not only by beliefs but also by behaviors (Acts 2:42–47; 4:32–37). Their authentic fellowship (Greek, *koinonia*) required *participation* together in faith, as well as *partnership* together in friendship. For any church to experience such community, members must strive to develop a corporate identity, as well as an individual affinity for one another. They must share a commitment to God and a commitment to each other, and organizational programming must take this into consideration. With this in mind, the first members of Mosaic made the decision early on to gather monthly in small groups known as Acts 2 Fellowships (A2f).

Acts 2:42 lists the four values of the first church in Jerusalem. In this verse, Luke writes that those who had accepted the message of Peter "were continually devoting themselves to the apostle's teaching, to [the] fellowship, to the breaking of bread, and to prayer." Through A2f then, the people of Mosaic initially gathered in small groups to experience two of these four values, namely, *fellowship* and *the breaking of bread*.

Twice a month throughout the first three years of the church, A2f met in homes throughout Central Arkansas. Each group reflected the diversity of Mosaic and included individuals of varying ethnicity, economic means, and generational status, both single and married people alike. Children were also welcomed as members of the group. Typically, the meetings began with spontaneous fellowship around a meal. Later, the entire group would gather for a brief time of interaction, as determined by the group's leader.

Through A2f then, Mosaics developed authentic friendships with diverse others attending the church, which led to expanded relationships of transparency and trust. The groups themselves were dynamic, and members were encouraged to bring others (whether Christian or not) to share in the experience. In addition, we modeled our faith and our unity before our children. In the end, A2f involvement increased our personal understanding of one another and encouraged a collective heart for social justice and spiritual transformation. In short, Mosaic became a family.

Although I have spoken of A2f in the past tense, the fact is that one or two of them are still active today. Yet as the congregation grew, the need for more consistent interaction became apparent. In response, we launched a more comprehensive program for connection and discipleship in the fall of 2006 known as LifeGroups. Nevertheless, A2f served an important function in the early days of our church, helping us to establish a strong foundation for future growth and ministry through the development of cross-cultural relationships.

One of the relationships that formed in the early days of our church involved two men and their families. Eric Higgins (Black), an assistant chief in the Little Rock Police Department, and Bill Head (White), who works for an insurance company, were drawn together not only through their shared vision of Mosaic but, as Bill tells it, by "a shared sense of humor!" More significantly, Bill and his wife, Donna, were foster parents to a young child whom Eric and his wife, Caron, eventually adopted. In fact, during the process Eric and Caron had no idea that Bill and Donna were caring for the baby girl they were pursuing, but the rest of us at Mosaic did! So on the day of the formal adoption, some of our members were there to witness the tears that flowed when Bill and Donna walked into the room and placed the child into Eric and Caron's arms. In time, the Higgins asked the Heads to be the child's godparents.

Recently, I asked Bill and Eric to comment further on their relationship. Here's what they had to say:

B.H.: There are many things that Eric has taught me through the years that have given me a greater understanding of his African American culture. At the same time, this information has challenged me because I have been blind to such things in the past. Having adopted two bicultural children into my own family gives me further incentive to cultivate our friendship. I am thankful that my kids have strong, Christ-centered role models like Eric and Caron.

E.H.: For my part, I do not think of Bill as my "White" friend; he is more simply, my friend. For instance, when we plan a cook-out or other family activity, Bill is the first person I think of to invite. In fact, his family always comes if we are grilling Bratwurst. I don't know if there is a connection there or not!

B.H.: It is true that our friendship has developed into one of knowing what the other's thinking or feeling in most situations. It's become a relationship of trust, where I don't have to be so careful about what I say for fear of being misunderstood. Eric knows my heart, and I believe he feels that I know his, too.

E.H.: I do, and since we are all unique with different life experiences, I think the first step in developing a cross-cultural relationship is to identify with each another for who you truly are, as children of God. The next thing I would say is to "just be you." Beyond that, Bill and I make it a point to stay in contact with one another from week to week and spend time together with our families, too.

B.H.: In fact, our families have taken trips together and often shared the holidays. On many of those occasions, we have been the only ones outside of family in the Higgins's home. More significantly, I was finally able, after three years of trying, to talk Eric and his family into going camping with us last fall. Our adventure, however, was short-lived, as we were forced to break camp in a driving rainstorm! Seriously, though, our friendship is extremely meaningful to me, and I'm confident it will stand the test of time.

E.H.: Personally, I look back on one particular event that caused our relationship to grow deeper. One day, Bill was helping me move some items to a storage unit. After placing my wife's curio inside the unit, we paused for a moment, pleased with ourselves and how everything was going. Just then, however, the curio, which had been securely wrapped in a couple of blankets, fell over. After hearing the distinct sound of breaking glass, Bill and I made eye contact with each other, and there was a pause. Bill then said to me, "Well, I'm sure glad I wasn't the one standing next to it!"

And we had a good laugh. I think Bill's willingness to help me secretly get the glass replaced was a bonding moment for both of us! In the end, "Uncle Bill" and "Aunt Donna" will always be a part of our family.

Keeping the Ring On

It is worth noting that Eric and Bill were among the first men appointed to serve as elders in our church. In that capacity, they have both witnessed and contributed to the greater struggle of developing transparency and trust among leaders in a multi-ethnic church like Mosaic. For as I alluded to earlier, things have been said or done in the past that have led to misunderstanding, frustration, and hurt at Mosaic, even among our staff and elders. And unfortunately, I have often been the one to blame!

For instance, in the months leading up to our decision to invite Cesar Ortega to become the first Latino hired as a pastor at Mosaic, one of our African American elders continued to voice resistance. It was not so much that he opposed Cesar personally, or even that he had concrete reasons for his concerns. As he said at the time, "I just don't feel right about it in my spirit." However, I countered that in the absence of tangible objections, we should, by all means, move ahead in pursuit of such a solid candidate.

The impasse, however, led me one day to wonder out loud in a meeting if his resistance was because of any racial tensions, whether real or perceived, between African Americans and Latinos in our city. In all honesty, my recollection of his reaction is still painful today. For what I thought was a legitimate question, he took as a personal affront to his character and motive in questioning the hire. Consequently, a fairly emotional exchange ensued, leaving the rest of our board members shocked and confused. All in all, it took about an hour to work through his reaction and another month or so of further dialogue, apologies, and prayer to get to the point where our relationship was not only restored but greatly strengthened through the conflict and its subsequent resolution. By God's grace (Romans 8:28), we had weathered the storm and I, for one, learned many things because of it.

In the end, this man did allow us to move forward with the hire, and soon Cesar became a part of our staff, for in spite of my words, he never doubted my heart. And though our relational account had been stretched to the limit, both of us were determined to *keep the ring on*. This is a phrase that we all embraced early on in anticipation of such times of misunderstanding. Indeed, we recognize that cross-cultural relationships are often as difficult to navigate as the relationship of a man and woman in marriage: two demonstrably different people, two different personalities, two perspectives, and two pasts. Like partners in a healthy marriage then, people in a multi-ethnic church must will themselves to stay engaged relationally with one another, especially in those times when every voice within them begs to leave or return to a more comfortable environment, that is, to a homogeneous church.

In Matthew 5:1–12, a passage commonly referred to as the Beatitudes, Jesus promises *something* for all of those he describes as "blessed": for the poor in spirit, theirs is the kingdom of heaven (v. 3); those who mourn will be comforted (v. 4); those who are meek will inherit the earth (v. 5); those in pursuit of righteousness will be satisfied (v. 6); those who are merciful will receive mercy (v. 7), and those who are pure in heart will see God (v. 9). Notice, however, that Jesus promises identification with Someone (himself) to the peacemakers: "Blessed are the peacemakers, for they shall be called *the sons of God*" (Matthew 5:9, emphasis mine).

Have you ever wondered why?

Like the "Prince of Peace" (Isaiah 9:6), peacemakers are those who love God and others, those who pursue peace without distinction. More specifically, peacemakers are intentional in their pursuit of others for the sake of the Gospel and for walking "worthy of the calling you have received" (Ephesians 4:1–3; see John 17:20–23), they are rightly called the "sons of God."[2] Indeed, peacemakers are those who are building a healthy multi-ethnic church.

Family Matters

After nine years in a private school, my son Zack made the move to a public school at the beginning of his tenth-grade year (2005). A random conversation late in the summer with the area director of the Fellowship of Christian Athletes led us to explore this possibility; largely, the draw was the football team—a chance to play in a higher classification and for a coach skilled in his position (quarterback). So with only forty-eight hours to make the decision, Zack practiced on Thursday with one team, on Friday with the other; on Monday the following week, he made the decision to enroll as a new student at Joe T. Robinson High School.

Now when I say "new student," I mean new in every way! Zack left a very solid stable of friends that had been developed over nine years in the same school. In addition, he was leaving the homogeneous environment of a private institution to attend an ethnically and economically diverse public school for the first time. Talk about a culture shock. In his first class and on the very first day of school, he was asked by the teacher to go get the school officer after a "cat fight" broke out between two girls and one pulled a knife!

Picking him up from his first practice with the team, I approached some players milling around a common area just outside the fieldhouse and recognized Zack sitting at a table with four to five of them. As it turned out, these guys were not only seniors, they were starters and also some of the most popular players on the team. I wondered, *What was my son doing among them?*

As Zack later told me, these players had reached out to him at various points throughout the first practice, welcoming him to the team and taking him in as if he had long been one of their own. I observed them joking with him, making him laugh and otherwise feel accepted. I'll never forget the emotions that I felt in that moment. In fact, I feel them even now. For like any parent, I wanted my son both to enjoy himself that day and to make a good first impression. In retrospect, the intentional effort of these players in moving toward Zack not only relieved his initial anxiety but also helped him to feel both significant and secure. It was a very positive and early sign of confirmation that we had done the right thing, though the road ahead would still be challenging.

The diversity of the students sitting around the table that day made the whole encounter even more significant in my mind. Giving in to earthly, prejudicial thoughts or stereotypes, I might not have expected these players (of different ethnicity and age) to reach out to my White, sophomore son. But like the people in Memphis who had voted for their favorite dancer without distinction, these boys made it clear in the moment that such things did not matter to them. Zack was now part of the team, and they were glad to add him to their number, even if that meant reaching out to one in many ways different from themselves.

So if young men like these—not all themselves Christians—understand the importance of developing cross-cultural relationships for the sake of the team, should we not expect believers to understand the importance of doing so for the sake of the local church?

Zack's friends today are a wonderful mix of ethnic and economic diversity. In addition, my ninth-grade daughter, Emily, has recently changed schools as well. Like her brother, she has learned to navigate cross-cultural environments and has an increasingly diverse array of friends. Yet at this point, it can become troubling for some. Indeed, many parents have concerns that cross-cultural relationships may lead to special interest among young people that goes beyond mere friendship. In other words, some parents will worry, *What if my daughter wants to date or marry someone ethnically different from her?*

Of course, a variety of arguments have been made through the years attempting to demonstrate (erroneously) that cross-cultural marriage is somehow unbiblical and, therefore, a violation of God's will. Yet in the end, we must recognize that any aversion to so-called "mixed marriages" among believers is purely social and in no way spiritual. With my own children in mind, it is not at all the color of skin I am concerned with; rather, it is the condition of hearts. In other words, I would much rather my kids marry men and women of color who love the Lord with all their heart, soul, mind, and strength than to marry lukewarm believers who share the same ethnicity but not the same passion for Christ.

As young believers, then, both Zack and Emily represent the future of the church. And as far as I can tell, the future looks bright indeed. But why should young people, that is, the next generation, have all the fun? No matter who you are or what stage of life you are in currently, you, too, can and should develop cross-cultural relationships. In so doing, you will "be able to comprehend with all the saints what is the breadth and length and height and depth, and to know the love of Christ which surpasses knowledge" (Ephesians 3:17–19). Indeed, you will then desire to build a healthy multi-ethnic church.

○

Ann Chami

The former Ann Owen has invested her life in children as a teacher for more than twenty years at the same school in Little Rock. As a single woman in her early forties, Ann followed the prompting of the Holy Spirit to join Mosaic in the early days of the church. In so doing, the Lord had even more in store for her than she realized! I'll let her tell you why:

> I was raised in Arkansas and, quite honestly, had never viewed *The South* as a particular culture. I simply assumed everyone approached life as I (we) did. At no time did I ever dream that I would one day come to understand (in such a personal way) that they did not. Yes, my loving, Heavenly Father had much to teach me when he brought a man from Syria into my life just five months after 9/11.
>
> In those days, the television was filled with images of the Arab world. I soon realized, however, that Amer (see Chapter

One) was nothing at all like I might have otherwise imagined. As our relationship progressed, differences did, though, begin to appear. For instance, we did not like the same foods, and he enjoyed reading the news in different languages. Beyond such things, I began to wonder what my friends would think. How would they respond to my growing love for an Arab and one who had only recently come to Christ, at that?

There came a point of crisis at which I found myself asking, "God, why? All my life I have dreamed of being married to someone who shares my interests and understands my world. There must be some mistake!" Over the next few days, though, God showed me that Amer was, truly, the man he had for me. Nevertheless, the choice would be mine.

These were definitely days of discomfort and uncertainty. I asked myself, "Am I willing to miss what could possibly be the greatest adventure of my life simply because of my own personal expectations, the reaction of others, or cultural differences?" Sadly, I never even considered that he, too, was dealing with these same questions. What pride there was in my life. My standards were higher than God's.

In December 2002, Amer and I did marry and we have been happily together for nearly five years. His eating habits have not changed, and he still reads the news in different languages, but none of that really matters. Often, though, we are challenged to understand one another, given our diverse backgrounds. At such times, we find that we have to communicate longer and possibly harder than some couples. But it is all worth it.

Often, I think back on all God has done in my life through this cross-cultural relationship. Prior to this, I had no idea how culturally arrogant I was or, for that matter, that I was cross-culturally ignorant. Today, however, I am thankful for a wonderful husband who God continues to use in conforming me to his image. My marriage to Amer has been the greatest adventure of my life, and I am, no doubt, the richer for it. I would not change it for the world!

8

PURSUE CROSS-CULTURAL COMPETENCE

The art of being wise is the art of knowing what to overlook.

—William James

NOT LONG AFTER MOSAIC MOVED INTO THE OLD WAL-MART BUILDING, we recognized that the time had come to buy chairs for the congregation. Having met for eighteen months in the sanctuary of an existing church, we had never needed chairs. Following the move, however, members of our church were asked to bring their own chairs to worship each week; this they did, carrying them in one way or another like parents to a soccer game or families to a picnic. Most often, these chairs were the kind that easily fold open and break down, the ones that are carried in a little bag or stuff sack. Some of them even had footrests and cup-holders. I'll never forget one woman who was pregnant at the time; she lay back in a chair, listening to the sermon with her feet propped up, sipping water from a large container through a straw!

Having determined to buy four hundred chairs, we ordered one chair as a sample to show the congregation. One Sunday morning, I put it up on the platform and explained that we would need to collect $25 from every person in order to cover the cost of the chairs. I added that our staff liked both the look and the feel of the chair and had even tested it out earlier in the week. "You know," I said, settling comfortably into the chair, "it feels pretty good to my buns!" When I did, the congregation laughed a bit, so I went on to milk the moment. "In fact, not only have I sat my buns in the chair, but most of the staff has sat their buns in the chair. And they, too, think it feels pretty good!" More laughter. "Now some on our staff have bigger buns than others," I said, "but even the biggest buns among us agree. So after the service, why don't you come and sit your buns, big or small, in the chair and tell us what you think!"

By this time, the congregation was fully animated, as I probably used the word *buns* six or seven times for comic effect. Yes, everyone in the room—the Hondurans, Guatemalans, and Cubans, those from the Middle East, Europe, and Africa—were all fully engaged and laughing—everyone, that is, except the Mexicans. No, they were not at all amused. Although my comments had been simultaneously interpreted into Spanish, apparently something had been lost in translation!

Now Inés Velasquez-McBryde, Mosaic's Director of Cross-Cultural Ministries, is a very skilled interpreter. Having grown up in Nicaragua, she began translating English to Spanish at the age of eleven, serving alongside her father in working with North American mission teams coming into the country. She is much more than a translator; she has an excellent command of common language, as well as theological concepts. On this day, however, even Inés was to learn something new!

Following the service, one of the Mexican women frantically approached Inés and, grabbing her by the arm, said, "Don't ever say that word again!" Her tone of voice told Inés that something was the matter. After some discussion, the woman finally calmed down but only when she realized the problem. You see, in translating the word *buns*, Inés had used the term *nalgas*, which in most countries throughout Central and South America carries, in tone and tenor, a force equivalent to the English term *buns*. Yet in Mexico, the term is more vulgar; it's equivalent to the English word *ass!*

Now I want you to imagine for a moment, your pastor getting up on a Sunday morning and saying,

> You know, this chair feels pretty good to my ass! In fact, not only have I sat my ass in the chair, but most of the staff has sat their ass in the chair, as well. . . . Now some on our staff have bigger asses than others, but even the biggest asses among us agree! So after the service, why don't you come and sit your ass, whether big or small, in the chair and tell us what you think.

This is exactly what the Mexicans heard me say that day! For within the Spanish language, there are variations in dialect, word meaning, and usage across regions, countries, and continents. Fortunately, the Mexicans forgave us, and through this experience, we learned a valuable lesson in pursuit of cross-cultural competence.

The understanding we need to be effective in a cross-cultural environment is gained through experience and interaction with diverse people, especially with those who are one in the Lord. To build a healthy multi-ethnic church, then, we must commit ourselves to the pursuit of cross-cultural competence, whether that means becoming proficient in the idiosyncrasies of language or the ins and outs of customs and traditions different from our own. Once acquired, cross-cultural competence allows us to interact in a more informed and effective way with others of varying ethnic or economic backgrounds. Though the challenge is formidable, the journey to acquire it, as we have seen, is not without its lighter moments! Indeed, in many ways cross-cultural competence is more caught than taught.

Lead and Learn

Of course, cross-cultural competence is gained not only through experience but through more purposeful pursuit as well. My partner, Harry Li, provides a good model in this regard. He often sits down with diverse others, both in and outside Mosaic, to discuss issues and needs related to culture. In fact, just a few hours ago he stopped by to see me at the San Francisco Bread Company, where I have spent much time preparing this manuscript. Coincidentally, Harry wanted to share some of what he has learned over time through conversations with African Americans in our church. In short, these interactions have focused on the ways in which Black and White Americans tend to interact with one another and, more specifically, how this interaction is often tainted by subtle messages of inequality still deeply embedded in our society.

For example, many African Americans in our church have experienced a number of personal or systemic acts of discrimination throughout their lifetime. And such repeated encounters have made it difficult for them to avoid viewing acts of unfairness, injustice, or insensitivity through a racial grid. On the other hand, many Whites remain largely unaware of their advantaged position in society. They tend to think that Blacks can achieve anything in the United States if they will just take personal responsibility for themselves and work hard in pursuit of their dreams. They cite successful African Americans to support this claim.

Yet, again, it is not that easy. African Americans must also work hard at overcoming four hundred years of negative images and stereotypes— a daily burden the rest of us do not feel or have to bear. In short, it is not so much that individuals are inherently racists; rather, many African Americans must deal daily with the systemic (institutional) racism[1] still prevalent in the United States today. By and large, this plays to the favor of Whites and to the disadvantage of Blacks, as well as many other ethnic minorities. Unfortunately, it is still "just the way it works."

On another occasion, Harry sat down with Jeremy and Whitney Simons. As pastoral Residents at Mosaic, serving the Deaf and Hard of Hearing (a multi-ethnic and unique culture all its own), Harry wanted to learn more about their efforts and to see what, if anything, could be done to better accommodate the people they were serving. At the time, we were doing the things you might otherwise expect of any church attempting to minister to this unique people group. For instance, we had a section at the front of the worship area specifically designated for the Deaf and Hard of Hearing and provided simultaneous translation in American Sign Language (ASL) throughout the service. We even sponsored a student ministry every other Sunday night for young people living at the local School for the Deaf. Yet through their conversation, the Simons provided Harry with insight into the Deaf community's needs, such as we had never considered before.

For example, the Simons helped us understand how screens in a sanctuary are often placed without thought or reference to the Deaf. In most churches, they pointed out, screens are positioned on the far sides of a stage to cover those not seated in the middle of the building. However, the Deaf are often seated just to the right or left of a pulpit, with an interpreter standing in front of them. From a Deaf person's perspective then, the pulpit might be to the left and a screen to the right, but they must look straight ahead in order to see the interpreter.

Therefore, consider what happens when PowerPoint slides are used on the screens. In this case, to be as fully engaged as those who can hear, the Deaf would have to perform the impossible task of looking in three directions simultaneously. According to the Simons, the solution would be to purchase a large screen for placement directly behind the interpreter, who would be aligned with the pulpit. A new and improved diagonal line of sight—first, the interpreter, then the screen, and, finally, the pulpit behind him—would offer a much better opportunity for the Deaf community to be fully a part of the service. Ultimately, we implemented this suggestion, and although it cost us money, it was well worth the price to more fully accommodate the Deaf and Hard of Hearing at Mosaic.

Another thing Harry learned from his conversation with the Simons was that believers who are Deaf have a very specific way in which they like to worship and, more specifically, to sing praise songs. Like many, for instance, I had always assumed that having an interpreter translate the words of a song in ASL and perhaps moving in rhythm to the sound of a full band fulfilled their needs and expectations. We learned however, that this is not necessarily true.

Rather, in Deaf worship, the kick drum alone is used to beat on the quarter notes in a 4/4 time signature. The singers then move to the beat of the drum while signing a song composed of repetitive words. For instance, the entire message of the chorus in a song like, "Shout to the Lord," might be otherwise communicated in just two signs—the signs for "praise" and "Jesus." Deaf worship is meant to be a very visual experience.

Once we learned of their preferred style of worship, we began incorporating it, on occasion, into our service. Admittedly, we need to do this more often. But when we do, the kick drum beats, the signs are taught, and the congregation sings (signs) as instructed. In such a moment, the entire church pursues cross-cultural competence and reflects the heart of God for all people on earth as it is in heaven. In so doing, we demonstrate that the church is not about us but is all about others. Indeed, such times provide for us an entirely new perspective on the psalmist's command: "Lift up your hands in the sanctuary and praise the Lord!" (Psalm 134:2).

There were other things Harry learned that day about the Deaf community, such as the fact that this people group learns best through storytelling and they view English as a second language. Again, it is only through the intentional pursuit of cross-cultural competence that such insights can be gained. To the degree that church planters and reformers are willing to act on what we learn in this regard, we can and should expect to build healthy multi-ethnic churches. For in so doing, we will communicate cross-cultural vision and value, pleasing the Father and winning the hearts and minds of those we seek to lead.

The good health of any church, then, is established by leaders who have an objective view of themselves—of who they are, who they are not, and who they desire to become. And although we can assume that those of us in positions of church leadership have gained a measure of understanding and competence through the years, we should rightfully acknowledge there is still much for us to learn. This is especially true for leaders seeking to bring diverse believers together in and through the local church—an environment in which "new wine" flows freely every day. To receive and dispense this new wine requires "wineskins" that are pliable. Therefore, local church leaders must become again the learners if, in fact, we are to succeed in establishing diverse congregations of faith.

Biblical Examples of Competence

Examples of those in pursuit of cross-cultural competence can be found in both the Old and New Testaments. For instance, the story of Ruth, a Moabitess, provides a very beautiful account of one intentionally investing herself in another's culture. Having married a Jew, Ruth is determined to remain, following his death, with her mother-in-law, Naomi, and to return with her to the land of Judah. Consider a few points of insight we can further glean from Ruth's story.

Despite Naomi's pleas for her daughters-in-law (Ruth and Orpah) to remain in the country of their birth after their husbands had died (Ruth 1:8–15), Ruth refuses to do so. Notice that Naomi's appeal is an argument to do what is the most logical thing. For instance, she suggests that their own mothers would better provide for them (1:8), that they are more likely to find husbands by staying in Moab (1:9–13a), and that, somehow, she is "cursed" and that the Lord is now against her (13b).

After initially dismissing her request, Orpah gives in and decides to remain in Moab. Ruth, however, determines to go with Naomi, responding with her now famous and poetic words, "Do not urge me to leave you or turn back from following you; for where you go, I will go, and where you lodge, I will lodge. Your people shall be my people, and your God, my God. Where you die, I will die, and there I will be buried" (Ruth 1:16–17).

In spite of potential difficulties or the unknown, Ruth makes an intentional choice to leave the familiarity of her own culture and to follow Naomi into another. It is also a decision informed by supernatural considerations, that is, by Ruth's desire to make Naomi's God her own God.

In Ruth 2, Ruth displays a measure of cross-cultural awareness by going into the fields to work (2:2–3ff.). Although conscious of the fact that she is a foreigner among the people (2:10, 13), she further demonstrates a desire to embrace the culture according to Naomi's instruction (2:20–23; 3:1–5). By the middle of Ruth 3, Ruth has become cross-culturally sensitive, even to the point of holding Boaz accountable to redeem the name and possessions of his kinsman, the son of Naomi who has died (3:9–10; 4:1–12). Through such redemption, of course, Ruth would become the wife of Boaz (4:13a), and the rest, as they say is history. Ruth, in fact, becomes cross-culturally competent—a matriarch in the culture and, in time, the great-grandmother of David (4:17). Through this account, Ruth models intentionality, purpose, and adaptability in her own pursuit of cross-cultural competence. We should also note how richly rewarded she was in moving toward others different from herself.

In the New Testament, the apostle Paul, by his own admission and testimony, is a man pursuing cross-cultural competence for the sake of the Gospel. For example, he writes to the Corinthians,

> [T]hough I am free from all men, I have made myself a slave to all, so that I may win more. To the Jews I became as a Jew, so that I might win Jews; to those who are under the Law, as under the Law . . . so that I might win those who are under the Law; to those who are without law, as without law, . . . so that I might win those who are without law. To the weak I became weak, that I might win the weak; I have become all things to all men, so that I may by all means save some. (1 Corinthians 9:19–22)

Beyond this statement of heart and intention, Paul's actions also support the claim. Indeed, he was able to share the message of Christ effectively "to the Jew first and also to the Greek" (Romans 1:16; see Acts 14:1). Perhaps nowhere is his cross-cultural competence better observed than through his encounter with the people of Athens (Acts 17:16–34).

While waiting for Silas and Timothy in Athens (17:15), the Bible tells us Paul "observed" that the city was full of idols. Later, he was able to use this observation to his advantage in proclaiming the Gospel among them:

> So Paul stood in the midst of the Areopagus and said, "Men of Athens, I observe that you are very religious in all respects. For while I was passing through and examining the objects of your worship, I also found an altar with this inscription, "TO AN UNKNOWN GOD." Therefore what you worship in ignorance, this I proclaim to you. (Acts 17:22–23)

Of course, Paul proceeds to share the Gospel in that city, resulting in increased curiosity among the Athenians and, specifically, among the Epicurean and Stoic philosophers (17:32) who had assembled to hear him. More significantly, his presentation resulted in the salvation of some in Athens, including both a man and a woman (17:34). In principle, Paul models intentionality in his pursuit of cross-cultural competence in obedience to Christ. His example challenges us first to observe before moving toward another's culture. Where evangelism is concerned, this means that we must recognize that it's not so much our task to take the Gospel *to* a culture but to share the Gospel *through* a culture different from our own. Before evangelizing then, we should read books, ask questions, take notes, and, in a variety of other ways, acquire understanding of diverse cultures on the front end in order to become increasingly competent in living with and loving people different from ourselves.

The Example of Christ

It is, however, Jesus himself who provides for us the greatest example of one in pursuit of cross-cultural competence. For,

> [A]lthough He existed in the form of God, [He] did not regard equality with God a thing to be grasped, but emptied Himself, taking the form of a bond-servant, and being made in the likeness of men . . . found in appearance as a man, He humbled Himself by becoming obedient to the point of death, even death on a cross. (Philippians 2:6–8)

Therefore, the author of Hebrews writes, "We do not have a high priest who cannot sympathize with our weaknesses, but One who has been tempted in all things as we are, yet without sin" (Hebrews 4:15).

Though he created man, Jesus had to become a man in order to save us from our sin. Similarly, pursuit of cross-cultural competence provides us opportunities for incarnational relationships, understanding, and ministry among brothers and sisters different from ourselves.

As *God* among men, Jesus provides us with a perfect model of one who pursues cross-cultural competence with great success. As a *Jew* among men, we should also note the absence of "ethnocentrism" in Jesus' life and ministry. *Ethnocentrism* is the belief that one's culture is superior to another's culture. Unfortunately, this is a problem that we, in our humanity, do not so easily avoid, as is illustrated by the following story.

In 2005, a denominational conference on evangelism and missions was held for Hispanic[2] leaders in South Carolina. On the first day of the conference, the convention center filled with excitement as nearly six hundred Hispanic pastors and lay leaders, together with their wives and children, gathered for a weekend of encouragement and equipping. At the registration table, however, a White administrator struggled to maintain her poise as she tried first to hear and then to find Hispanic names on the registration list. Fortunately, Inés was at her side to offer assistance and to help bridge the cultural gap.

Following the successful conference, the Hispanic church planter and organizer of the event—an employee of the denomination—was called to meet with his White superiors. Although he expected them to be excited, he was accused of allowing fornication to take place on the convention center campus!

"Where in the world did you get such a notion?" he asked.

"Well," they said, "we have it on good authority that the unmarried people who registered for the conference were, in fact, rooming together."

"Really?" he asked incredulously. "What makes you think that happened?"

"See for yourself," they said. "On many of the family registration forms, the last name of the woman is different than the last name of the man!"

This is a perfect example of how a lack of correct information can result in wrongful judgment of another's culture or character. In this case, the White denominational leaders had to be informed (after their unfortunate jump to conclusions) that women in Latin America traditionally add the last name of their husband to their own last name, connecting the two names with the Spanish preposition *de*, which means *of*. In addition and for simplicity's sake, a Latina will often use her birth name on forms instead of taking the time to write out her married name in full. This difference in the way marriage affects last names in another culture, of course, in no way implies infidelity. Nevertheless, these denominational leaders remained skeptical and determined for the future that people attending the conference would need to bring their marriage certificates in order to verify their marital status. This can be described as an ethnocentric conclusion.

As I have mentioned, ethnocentrism is the belief that one's culture is superior to another. Couple it with hate, and racism is born. The term *racism* itself can be defined as "discriminatory or abusive behavior towards members of another race; the prejudicial belief that members of one race are intrinsically superior to members of other races."[3] In either case, the problem with racism is that it is much more than a problem; in fact, it is sin. With this in mind, it is unrealistic to expect that racism can be eradicated through government intervention, educational prescriptions, or any number of other, well-meaning reconciliatory attempts of man. As a matter of the heart, it requires a spiritual solution. Before we can rightly pursue cross-cultural competence, then, we must recognize that both ethnocentrism and racism are concepts foreign to the kingdom of God and therefore to those who are truly God's children. And to get beyond such things in our own lives and in the church, we must invite the Spirit of God to tear down these strongholds and embrace this fact:

> He, Himself, is our peace, who made both groups [Jews and Gentiles] into one and broke down the barrier of the dividing wall, by abolishing in His flesh the enmity . . . so that in Himself, He might make the two into one new man, thus establishing peace, and might reconcile them both in one body to God through the cross, by it having put to death the enmity. . . . So then you are no longer strangers and aliens,

but you are fellow citizens with the saints, and are of God's household. (Ephesians 2:14–16, 19, addition mine)

Press on to Maturity

So how can those of us committed to Christ and to the local church pursue cross-cultural competence and avoid ethnocentrism? Although there are a variety of ways to go about it, we should first understand that it will be an ongoing developmental process. With this in mind, an observable continuum, such as the one developed by Cristina López of the National Council of La Raza,[4] is helpful. Presented here in a modified form, we have used it at Mosaic to both identify where we are and where we need to be in relating to one another at any given moment. We see a cultural continuum as moving from *destructiveness* to *blindness* to *awareness* to *sensitivity* to *competence*.

Destructiveness

Cultural destructiveness is the first component of the continuum. "Cultural destructiveness acknowledges only one way of being, and purposefully denies or outlaws any other cultural approaches."[5] According to López, "the emphasis is on using differences as barriers."[6] Unfortunately, examples of cultural destructiveness throughout history, both past and present, are all too easily observed. For instance, the attempt to exterminate Jews in Nazi Germany resulted in the deaths of more than six million people. The genocide in Rwanda, ignited by racism among the Hutus and the Tutsis, also resulted in an "ethnic-cleansing" of epic proportion. In Bosnia, Darfur, and the Sudan, an endless list of atrocities can be cited. Similarly, history tells us that Native Americans were massacred and forced to relocate to reservations here in the United States, effectively destroying the life they once knew. Their children, too, were once forced to assimilate into the emerging American culture by having their traditional long hair cut and being dressed in modern clothes. Anyone or anything that seeks to degrade one culture for the benefit of another can be described as culturally destructive.

Blindness

Cultural blindness "fosters an assumption that people are all basically alike, so what works with members of one culture should work within all other cultures."[7] However, this is not, nor should it be, the case.

For instance, I remember seeing a T-shirt in the mid-1980s with the words, "God sees no color." And like that shirt, I have heard many well-intentioned people voice similar sentiments through the years. In fact, I was one of them! Yet I have come to realize that God is the Creator of color (diversity), whether of flowers in a garden, fish in the sea, or cultures on this planet. Indeed, those with deeply rooted tradition, language, or tribal values different from our own perceive that in ignoring such distinctions, their own ethnic identity may, in time, be lost. Although there is only one race—the human race—we must not be blind to the fact that there are a wonderful variety of ethnicities within the race. Each one is worthy of recognition and appreciation.

Awareness

Cultural awareness is in the center of the continuum and often the starting point for those attracted to a multi-ethnic church. Cultural awareness "makes us sensitive to other ethnic groups [and] usually involves internal changes in terms of attitudes and values. Awareness . . . also refers to the qualities of openness and flexibility that people develop in relation to others."[8] For instance, culturally aware visitors entering our church will recognize that Mosaic accommodates those whose first language is either Spanish or ASL, as all verbal and written communication is translated in consideration of linguistic preference. Beyond this, we recently translated our Sunday morning service into Mandarin Chinese for the benefit of a local congregation worshipping with us that day. Unfortunately, the age and stage of our church, together with the size and demographics of Little Rock, has not yet afforded us the opportunity to provide for Mandarin translation every week. However, there are churches in larger cities, such as Village Baptist Church in Beaverton, Oregon, that are translating into many more languages than we are currently at Mosaic. Someday we hope that we can, too.

On the other hand, we have chosen not to translate the prayers of those speaking in Spanish, ASL, or other languages into English when they are intended for God and God alone. We have learned that there is something very special (spiritual) that occurs when we tangibly experience the fact that God is not just the God of English speakers in the United States.

In addition, the flags that fly in our worship area communicate not only our awareness but also our appreciation for the individuals and nations represented in our body at any given time. Such things, whether big or small, demonstrate our heart for all people. Still, we realize, there is further growth and development to pursue.

Sensitivity

Cultural sensitivity is increased over time through training, effort, and experience. It "involves actively seeking advice and consultation, as well as a commitment to incorporating new knowledge and experiences into a wider range of practice."[9] For example, a woman once asked Inés, "Is it offensive to give Latina girls a White Barbie doll for Christmas?" In so doing, she made her intentions perfectly clear, not only by demonstrating cultural awareness but in seeking the better way. In such instances, sensitivity is not only gained by the one asking the questions but is cultivated in the one to whom they are directed. For through the declaration of clear intentions and a sincere expression of heart, the past hurt and rejection in another can be replaced with new hope and that most valued of all commodities—trust. In addition, we should recognize that sensitivity is gained when leaders understand that Latin American husbands and wives may not share the same last name and refuse to draw conclusions from their own cultural lens!

Competence

Cultural competence—the last component of the continuum—is a lofty goal but, nonetheless, a most requisite pursuit for those who would build a healthy multi-ethnic church. Although competence does not assume expertise, it does describe a general proficiency in working with people of various cultures. More specifically, it defines individuals who "value diversity, conduct self-assessment, manage the dynamics of difference, acquire and institutionalize cultural knowledge and are able to adapt to diversity and the cultural contexts of the communities they serve."[10] Indeed, pastoral leaders can no longer afford to be cross-culturally incompetent in an increasingly interconnected world. In pursuit of cross-cultural competence, those seeking to establish a multi-ethnic church should surround themselves with cross-culturally competent people who can be trusted to provide insight and training across the board, from the nursery to the pulpit and at every station in between. In so doing, you will expedite the process and avoid many unnecessary mistakes along the way.

Pursuit of cross-cultural competence moves us beyond ourselves toward a deeper understanding of life from another's perspective. Such reflections should draw us nearer to others who are not like us and, together with them, nearer to Christ in and through the local church.

In pursuit of such unity, we will want to become more inclusive in all aspects of our lives, ministry, and outreach. And to the degree that we commit ourselves to becoming so, we can expect to build a healthy multi-ethnic church.

---
o

Martha Garcia and Gonzalo Morales

Gonzalo and Martha are originally from Mexico. They moved to the United States seeking opportunities for a better life. In so doing, God also gave them the opportunity to meet one another and to begin a relationship. By their own account, however, life has not been easy. They have had difficult financial times and have been unable to find good, stable jobs. Gonzalo had a serious drinking problem. In June of 2006, they ran out of money and out of hope. They did not even have food to eat.

At that time, a friend told them about Mosaic and said that the church helped people in need. So they decided to come to the church, where they were warmly greeted and given food and clothes.

From there, Martha picks up the story:

> Soon after this, we were talking about our need to find a church where we could find God—a place where we could trust people, be encouraged, and help others, too. We cried because we longed to find people who really cared and a God who was real. Gonzalo said we would wait and, in time, he would decide what church we would go to.
>
> One night, Gonzalo had a dream that we were walking. I was carrying a jar and was tired. Then we arrived at a fountain where Gonzalo sat on the edge to drink water. Suddenly, we were surrounded by a great multitude of people. When we saw them all surrounding us, our hearts were filled with peace. The next morning was Sunday and after Gonzalo shared with me his dream, we decided to attend Mosaic.
>
> When we arrived at the church, we saw a fountain and some jars located under a banner that read, "Prayer Court." As we sat down near the fountain to pray, some of the brothers and

sisters of the church surrounded us and began to pray, as well. When Gonzalo saw himself surrounded by these people, he started crying like a baby. He recognized that the dream he had the night before had become a reality!

It was right then that we received Jesus as our Lord and Savior. I never thought that we would find the love, hope, and peace we desperately desired. Since the day we met Jesus, Gonzalo has not gotten drunk. His life has completely changed and so has our relationship. Together, we have found a people who care; together, we have come to know that God is real.

9

PROMOTE A SPIRIT OF
INCLUSION

*We will so appeal to your heart and conscience that we
will win you in the process.*

—Martin Luther King Jr.

IN THE MOVIE *REMEMBER THE TITANS*,[1] former adversaries from diverse
ethnic backgrounds overcome the pervading spirit of the age, as well as
their own innate prejudices, at a unique time and place in history. Led by
two coaches who promote and model a spirit of inclusion, the 1971
Titans of T. C. Williams High School in Alexandria, Virginia, roll on to
an undefeated season. Coach Herman Boone's methods for bringing the
team together include the intentional integration of Black and White
players on bus rides and in dorm rooms at the team's summer camp, as
well as in one-on-one interactive conversations through which each young
man must ask of another specific questions in order to get to know him
better. Soon a common bond is forged among the players, and the team
goes on to experience the power and pleasure of unity, both on and off
the football field. They win Virginia's High School AAA State Champion-
ship and finish as runner-up for the national title—the second-best team
in the land. According to the team's official Web site, however, something
even greater occurred that year. "More importantly," it says, "the
willingness of these young men to talk to each other, along with their
determination to win, brought together a city torn apart by prejudice and
hatred. In December 1971, President Richard M. Nixon was quoted as
saying, 'The team saved the city of Alexandria.'"[2]

Similarly, the multi-ethnic church seeks to bring diverse people together in a countercultural way. In order to establish such a work, church planters and reformers must be willing to put aside their own personal biases and preferences in order to lead others together as one before the Lord. Like the coaches in the film, we, too, must promote a spirit of inclusion in order to experience the power and pleasure of unity within the local church. To the degree we are willing to do so, "the manifold wisdom of God will be made known through the church" and expressed before an unbelieving world (Ephesians 3:10). This will result in the salvation of souls and, progressively, the sanctification of the church.

Yes, in the end, the '71 Titans had a legendary run: the team was perfect that year—13-0. But then it was over. Seniors graduated, students moved on, and in a few years there were new coaches. A wonderful movie and a gym renamed after one of the players is about all that remains to help those who lived the dream, as well as others, remember the Titans.[3]

In contrast, those attempting to build a healthy multi-ethnic church contribute to a legacy that will last forever! The environment that dedicated leaders help to create foreshadows the coming kingdom of heaven—a place where diverse people will live together, forever, as one. Such a church is not only a worthy vision to pursue on earth but an intended, eternal outcome.

Inclusion Begins with Worship

As discussed in Chapter Five, well-meaning believers will often describe themselves as open to diversity and to having anyone who so desires become a part of "their" church. However, the unintended obstacle to this otherwise sincere belief is a lack of proactive consideration of diverse individuals who may walk through the doors. The statement, "We would welcome anyone here," is in most cases more accurately translated, "We would welcome anyone here as long as they like who we are, what we do, and how we do it." In other words, "We welcome anyone to join us as long as they are willing to conform to our ways but don't expect us to conform to theirs!" And nowhere is this attitude more pronounced than in a congregation's approach to worship.

To build a healthy multi-ethnic church, then, it is in worship that leaders must begin to promote a spirit of inclusion. For example, if the worship format in style and leadership is the same from week to week, it will appeal only to a certain segment of the population; thus a barrier (though perhaps unintended) is erected. Yet by diversifying its worship format—the songs that are sung, the way that they are done, and by whom—a church will demonstrate its (God's) heart for all people. Beyond this, leaders might also incorporate the prayers of first-generation internationals (prayers spoken in languages other than English) within the context of worship. In so doing, a church will expand its perspective and, in the process, experience a bit of heaven on earth, as diverse people learn to worship God together as one.

Of course, such enhancements within existing churches will require people to be prepared in advance. Reformers, especially, should expect opposition from those who "like our church just the way it is." Unfortunately, this comment reveals the misguided notion that the church is somehow "mine" or "ours," "all about me," or "all about us." However, people must be led to understand that the mature church, like the mature believer, "do[es] not merely look out for its own interests, but also for the interests of others" (Philippians 2:4). Indeed, *Should we not be thrilled just to have a seat at the table with brothers and sisters in Christ who are different from us?*

People must also be led to recognize that while the message is largely objective, the music is not. During the sermon, for example, we observe the biblical text, hear expositional preaching, and form conclusions (hopefully) based on the facts, free of bias or personal feelings. Because the music is subjective, however, church members tend to judge its quality or effectiveness through their own filters, namely, past experience, personality, and personal preference. For too long, such filters have been used to shape discourse on the matter, causing great harm and division in many churches.

Those seeking to build a healthy multi-ethnic church cannot allow such things to determine the course of music (or in a broader sense, the worship service) within the church. For if by these standards the music is judged, the very foundation of the church will be shaken. Instead, planters and reformers must lead people to understand that the "church is not about you or what you like." Rather, it is to be all about Christ and all about others. And I believe we should do all we can to attract as many as we can to come and join the feast (Matthew 22:9; Luke 14:23).

With this in mind, *a healthy multi-ethnic church is a place in which people are comfortable being uncomfortable.* In such a place, members recognize that they are part of something much bigger than themselves. Therefore, in obedience to Christ and for the sake of the Gospel, they actively embrace a spirit of inclusion in worship beyond the predictability of homogeneity.

It's Not So Much the Food, But the Family That Matters

To help further understand this, let's compare the multi-ethnic church to a multi-generational family. Assume for a moment that Grandma, who is alive and well, lives in the same house with you, your spouse, and several children of varying age. Now in your home, one tradition involves the family meal. Indeed, you expect the entire family to come to the table when dinner is served. However, one night you arrive home, only to be challenged in this regard.

On this occasion, Grandma has arrived early to help feed the baby while you help your spouse set the table. Soon your twelve-year-old twins enter the room arguing over television rights; nevertheless, they are seated and it is time to pray. At that moment, however, you realize someone is missing. Your teenage son is not at the table. Heading upstairs to see what's the matter, you find him playing a video game in his room; he is wearing headphones so as not to be disturbed.

"Why," you inquire, "are you not at the table? Didn't you hear mom say it's time to eat?"

"Oh yeah," he replies, with just a touch of attitude, "I heard her. But I'm not coming to dinner tonight. Mom's serving meatloaf, and I don't like it."

Now let me ask you a question: *If you were the parent, how would you respond?*

No matter how many times I have asked this question, the answer always comes back the same. It's likely that you, too, would tell your son get his *nalgas* to the table, right? And in so doing, of course, you would teach him a most profound lesson: *It's not about the food; it's about the family!*

"Look, son," you might say, "I don't care what we're eating tonight. You're coming to dinner because you're a part of this family. You see, it's not so much the *meal* but the *memories* we make that's important. And when you're not there, we miss out on all you contribute, and you miss out, too. Sure it's meatloaf tonight, but tomorrow we're having pizza!"

Of course, the next night you will not need to have the same talk with Grandma. In her maturity, she learned long ago to appreciate the blessing of life and love. And while her stomach will not allow her to eat the pizza, she will enjoy watching her grandchildren tear into it! Yes, in that moment, she will be thankful just to have a seat at the table, still to be alive and a part of the family.

Like the home in this illustration, the healthy multi-ethnic church is a warm and wonderful place, filled with people of varying personalities, personal preferences, and past experiences. Like the family in this illustration, we have been called to walk together as one. Like Grandma, the mature among us have learned to appreciate just what it is we have. Like the father, we must promote a spirit of inclusion for the good of the whole.

Consider Others More Important than Yourself

Paul's words in Philippians 2 should also inspire our approach and attitude toward worship in a multi-ethnic environment. Specifically, Paul commands the church: "Do nothing from selfishness or empty conceit, but with humility of mind regard one another as more important than yourselves; do not merely look out for your own personal interests, but also for the interests of others" (Philippians 2:3–4).

In a healthy multi-ethnic church, this passage should serve as the prime directive. Instead of looking inward, Paul expects individuals in a congregation to get beyond themselves for the benefit of others. Therefore, believers who embrace this imperative will find they are able to worship God joyfully, even at times when the music is not compatible with their own personal tastes, that is, on days, for example, when "meatloaf" and not "pizza" is served. In such moments, they should look across the room and, claiming Philippians 2, find someone else enjoying the worship. They should then thank God they even have a seat at the table and for the privilege of being part of such a wonderfully diverse family. In so doing, they should realize that the music next week will likely favor their own personal preference, and it will be someone else's turn to claim Philippians 2 in the interest of others.

With this in mind, those involved in worship planning should do their best to ensure that a wide array of styles and leaders are a consistent part of the mix. These can be interwoven throughout one service or, as we do at Mosaic, interchanged from week to week.[4] As in any church, worship planners should do all they can to guarantee that those involved in leadership are men and women of integrity, those who possess a measure of skill and, more important, a passion for Christ and for the local church. Musicians and singers, then, must be teachable in spirit and, as a whole, flexible and diverse in style. In addition, worship planners should ensure that all things are done decently and in order. And they, too, must keep from allowing their own preferences to dominate the format.

Of course, "what we do and how we do it" will, necessarily, change from time to time. It is the "who we are and why" that must be safeguarded from influences that would threaten the development of a healthy multi-ethnic church. Perhaps more than anyone else, then, worship planners are responsible for doing just that.

In respect to such things, Revelation 7:9–10 is often cited by those who desire to worship God in a multi-ethnic environment, that is, by those "longing for a better country—a heavenly one" (Hebrews 11:16). It reads:

> After this I looked and there before me was a great multitude that no one could count, from every nation, tribe, people and language, standing before the throne and in front of the Lamb. . . . And they cried out in a loud voice: "Salvation belongs to our God, who sits on the throne, and to the Lamb." (Revelation 7:9–10)

What has long intrigued me about this vision is not so much the diversity of those who worship but the fact that a plurality of nations, tribes, peoples, and tongues are somehow able to cry out in a singular voice. More than a dream, then, this is something we should pursue here and now. Indeed, the dream is reality in a healthy multi-ethnic church.

Do Little Things That Make a Difference

To promote a spirit of inclusion, planters and reformers must also pay attention to those little things that add up to create the look and feel of the whole. At Mosaic, for example, all of our signage is produced both in English and Spanish, as are the bulletins and PowerPoint slides. And we fly flags in our worship area to represent the diversity of nations within our body. In addition, we meet in a very large and open space in which you can see almost everything and everyone at once. Such considerations, though seemingly inconsequential, demonstrate to others a great deal about who we are and what we value. In fact just this week, a woman shared with us that seeing her national flag on her visit at Mosaic helped her to know she was welcome.

Pictures, banners, and other visual media must also be considered to ensure that these, too, promote a spirit of inclusion. Each week, for instance, we profile an individual or family in our bulletin telling how they came to Christ or to our church. Along with their story, we include a picture of them to communicate that all people are valued at Mosaic. On a different note, we ensure that dolls of all colors can be found in our nursery and early childhood classrooms. Even the logo we designed for our student ministry looks like the chrome emblem of an automobile, something that is attractive to teenagers across the board.

Beyond these things, it is important to consider the physical interior of a facility and to strike just the right balance between an environment that is too pretentious (as if only for the wealthy) or too neglected (as if not to care). In other respects, the goal is to eliminate barriers of every kind, and this includes providing clean, safe, and orderly surroundings in which those with means will feel just as comfortable as those without much.

In addition to the look and feel of the facility, church planters should think strategically in terms of a location for the church. Indeed, location will communicate in a very specific way the kind of church you desire to plant or to become. Of course, many factors must be weighed before making such a decision. In general however, churches that are located in areas of high need, diversity, and neutrality (that is, identified with neither the suburbs nor the inner city) are ripe for multi-ethnic ministry. When existing facilities within the community can be rented, purchased, or otherwise revitalized, a church will (in most instances) engender a positive response from citizens, neighborhood associations, and the community as a whole. Indeed, the community will be blessed by the heart of a church determined to bring life to dead or dying spaces, enhance the neighborhood, and in many other ways consider the needs of others outside their walls.

Having said this, however, location should in no way limit the possibilities for creating a healthy multi-ethnic church. Indeed, such churches can be found both in the suburbs and the inner cities across the United States. To somehow think or suggest that multi-ethnic churches are not possible in the suburbs is to create a condition, confuse the argument, or offer an excuse to justify not pursuing its course. Likewise, churches in the inner city should do all they can to erase barriers for those who desire to come, no matter who they are, where they live, or how much money they have.

In the end, it's the personal interaction of members from day to day that will best promote a spirit of inclusion within the church. In this regard, nothing is more attractive or speaks any louder than authentic relationships of transparency and trust enjoyed by individuals of varying backgrounds. When exemplified among leaders, the foundation for a healthy multi-ethnic church is set and secure.

To help foster the development of such relationships, a Community Meal is hosted once a month at Mosaic. Immediately following the service on the third Sunday of each month, the entire congregation (and anyone else who shows up) is served a meal free of charge. Prepared by our own Hubert Bryant and his illustrious team of volunteers, the meal is a social gathering where the diversity of relationships can be readily observed. At this meal you will see doctors, lawyers, and other professionals eating with the homeless, newly arrived immigrants, or other people looking for work. Blacks and Whites easily interact with one another, and internationals blend in with the crowd. In addition, a diverse team of volunteers serves the meal, and you can tell they are happy to do so. Therefore, it should come as no surprise that this is the best-attended Sunday service of the month!

Inclusion Is More than Mere Tolerance

A commitment to promote a spirit of inclusion, however, in no way implies a commitment to embrace doctrines or practices that, in one way or another, violate the Word of God. In other words, a commitment to inclusion is not a commitment to "tolerance," as it is often defined today.

According to Josh McDowell, "Not long ago, the word 'tolerance' meant 'bearing or putting up with someone or something not especially liked.' However, now the word has been redefined to 'all values, all beliefs, all lifestyles, all truth claims are equal.'"[5]

So for instance, a healthy multi-ethnic church will not accommodate the notion that Jesus is only one way (out of many) to the Father, or that the Bible is not inerrant, or that the traditional definition of marriage is open to interpretation. Promoting a spirit of inclusion does not mean that the church should adopt a doctrine of "Anything Goes." On the other hand, it will be patient with genuine seekers—those new to the faith and the disenfranchised who are reconnecting with Christ and with his church after a season of sin, hurt, or absence. Ultimately, the goal is to create an environment where all people feel welcome, where truth is proclaimed, where grace and mercy abound. Such an environment, once created, will likely lead to unique opportunities for you and your church to share the Gospel. In our case, it led to an agnostic from Japan living in our facility!

Daisuke Mitsutani came to the University of Arkansas at Little Rock (UALR) in the spring of 2002 to pursue a B.A. in professional and technical writing. His goal was to someday return to Japan as a teacher. As an international student and, more specifically, one who did not speak English, his entire first year was spent in UALR's Intensive English Language Program. From there, he enrolled in the B.A. program and at the time of this writing is scheduled to graduate in May 2007. A disciplined student with an inquisitive mind, Dai carries a 3.8 G.P.A. We first met Dai soon after he arrived in the city. He had come to Mosaic, having heard of the church from LaJuanna Magee, the local Director of International Friendship Outreach. In those days, we were meeting directly across the street from UALR at Faith United Church and, conveniently, within walking distance from his dorm room. Dai also liked the fact that our service began at 4:30 PM, allowing him first to study and then to attend. But unlike others at Mosaic, Dai was not at all interested in our message or our God. A self-described atheist (but more correctly, an agnostic), he simply thought that the church would be a great place to immerse himself for a couple of hours each week in the English language.

So from the back row of the small building in which we met, Dai began to listen and to learn, reading words on the screen, words in the bulletin, and words in the Bible. He would listen to us sing, listen to us preach, and, following the service, listen to us talk. At times, he would do his best to enter into the discussion. All the while, his bright smile, genuine enthusiasm, and helpful spirit were winning him many friends within the growing congregation. Soon Dai became more actively involved beyond Sunday afternoons. For example, at a local festival called World-Fest,[6] he came to help us by passing out fliers, inviting people to our table and, in fact, working the table himself. Even at our first anniversary celebration, Dai organized and sold T-shirts we had made in honor of the occasion. Quite simply, he was a joy to have around.

In time, Dai began asking more and more questions about God, about Christ, and about eternal life. And for two years, great progress was made in that regard as we prayerfully and patiently pursued a course of "Life-style Evangelism."[7] By the summer of 2003, however, college expenses were taking their toll, and Dai needed a place to live. Around that same time, we worked out a lease agreement to begin meeting in the old Wal-Mart; once again, Dai pitched in to help. Together with other members of the church, he helped clean, sweep, paint, and move furniture. In addition, he became an expert alongside our staff at setting up, tearing down, and reconfiguring movable partitions for offices and classrooms. All of this led us one day to design an apartment for him in the nearly 80,000-square-foot space. Converting a former employee break room for this purpose, we installed a shower, hot water heater, and new tile to create a simple room he was thrilled to call his own. By the fall of 2003, then, this Japanese agnostic was living in the church! Word of this spread, and the situation became a living example to the Christian community (and to others) of our commitment to inclusion for the sake of the Gospel.

Not long after these events, however, a well-meaning couple from another church invited Dai to attend a service with them. According to Dai, the preacher came across that day as somewhat dogmatic in his beliefs, and later at lunch he felt pressure from the couple to convert. This experience adversely affected him to the point that he became very hostile to Christ and to the church. Dai immediately stopped attending Mosaic and began writing papers in school to explain why he did not believe or, worse yet, why Christianity in general was flawed. Needless to say this was quite a blow for all of us who had been praying that the Holy Spirit would open his heart. At no time, however, did we ever ask him to move.

Through 2005, Dai's negative attitude remained steadfast and unchanged. In fact, it has only been in the last year or so that he has found his way back to a middle ground. Although Dai still does not attend church, he has begun to wonder what his life will be like following graduation and disconnected from a congregation that has been like family to him. He is somewhat puzzled, though very thankful, that we have allowed him to remain with us all this time. Beyond this, he has expressed some concern that in soon leaving, he would disappoint those of us who have been so kind and patient with him—disappointed, that is, if he does not become a Christian before returning to Japan.

I wish I could conclude this story by sharing that Dai has become one with us in Christ. However, as of yet he has not. What we have learned is that it's possible to promote a spirit of inclusion without compromising doctrine. Indeed, we are finding it possible to be doctrinally sound while not alienating nonbelievers or those who are still questioning. We do know that God loves Dai, and by faith we believe that Dai will one day become his child. In the meantime, we trust that God will not allow the years of our witness to return to him void.

Through more than mere words or good works, people today need to personally experience the love of Christ in order to believe. They need to feel the power of God transcending the barriers of this world and uniting diverse people together as one (John 12:32). By its very nature, then, a healthy multi-ethnic church can deliver the goods in this regard. Yes, in promoting a spirit of inclusion, local church planters and reformers can expect the lost and disenfranchised to head our way. Confident in our faith and sure of the truth, let us determine to do just that!

o

Raymond

Not long after Mosaic had moved into the old Wal-Mart, a homeless man named Raymond began attending faithfully from week to week. Typical of those on the street, he was disheveled and, in his case, often reeking of alcohol. Each Sunday, he would first head for the bathroom to clean himself up before coming back to get a cup of coffee and sit down for worship.

One morning during the service, I invited the congregation to break up into smaller groups for prayer. As I left the platform, a young high school Latina named Sandra motioned to me. She was concerned for Raymond, who was sitting close to her, and wanted me to pray with him. Sitting down with the man, I began to talk with him and, more important, to listen.

During our brief exchange, Raymond spoke sincerely from his heart. He confessed that drugs and alcohol had consumed his life and had left him isolated from family members living nearby. At Mosaic, he said, the people were friendly and treated him kindly. Coming to Mosaic each week gave him peace and hope. He said, "I feel so good here! I feel the Spirit of God here. I may live like hell Monday through Saturday, but I like to come here on Sunday because it makes me feel so damn good!"

Taking hold of his hands, I prayed for him and, touched by the interaction, concluded the prayer time by asking Raymond to come forward to share his story with the rest of the body. As he spoke, it was evident to all that Raymond truly desired to be cleansed from his addictions and restored to his family. Having shared from his brokenness and despair, Raymond asked the church to come and pray for him. In response, about a dozen Mosaics came forward and embraced him warmly. It was the first physical touch or affection he had received in a very long time. Laying their hands upon him, they led the entire church in praying for Raymond that day. It was a beautiful sight to see—the body of Christ extending the love of God to this man who had come, "just as I am." There wasn't a dry eye in the house.

Not long after this, two men from Mosaic helped Raymond to enroll in a twenty-eight-day detoxification program. He then entered rehabilitation and, after completing it, came by the church a completely different man. Soon Raymond, again, stood before the church, this time to ask forgiveness for the times he had taken advantage of generosity. More important, he shared that he had recently committed his life to Christ!

At the time of this writing, he continues in sobriety and holds a steady job at a local fast-food restaurant.

MOBILIZE FOR IMPACT

If you hear a voice within you saying, "You are not a painter,"
then by all means paint and that voice will be silenced.

—Vincent Van Gogh

RECENTLY, I CAME across new findings that confirm what many in multi-ethnic churches already realize from first-hand experience. In a report by the Hartford Institute for Religion Research, results of the Cooperative Congregational Studies Partnership's (CCSP) Faith Communities Today 2005 survey were released and determined that "while most congregations in America are composed of a single racial/ethnic group, those that are multi-racial are most likely to have experienced strong growth in worship attendance."[1] David A. Roozen, director of the CCSP and professor of religion and society at Hartford Seminary said,

> [The report] tests the continuing salience of long, "taken for granted" principles of [church] growth . . . as well as [those] more recently proposed. Most importantly, it suggests several newly emergent dynamics to consider [including] the potential for growth in downtown areas and *within multi-racial/ethnic congregations* (emphasis mine).[2]

In other words, the multi-ethnic church is favorably positioned for growth in the twenty-first century.

The Multi-Ethnic Church: Our Past and Future

These findings signal the coming deterioration of the homogeneous-unit principle as a precept for church growth in the years ahead. However, the growing movement toward multi-ethnic churches must not be fueled by a desire to grow a church numerically. Nor should we embrace the vision simply in light of changing times and neighborhoods or because it is somehow "cool" or politically correct. The movement and the healthy multi-ethnic church must be built instead on the firm foundation of the Word of God and a desire to lead individuals to Christ. With this in mind, we should recognize that the unity of diverse believers walking together as one in and through the local church provides for us the most effective means for reaching the world with the Gospel in the twenty-first century. As we have seen, such unity was envisioned by Christ, described for us (by Luke) at Antioch, and prescribed by Paul in his letter to the Ephesians. In other words, we must embrace the vision because it is "spiritually correct" and, while not necessarily easy, a right and noble pursuit. Yes, the multi-ethnic church is the church of our past and our future!

Likewise, the goal is not to become multi-ethnic simply for diversity's sake. Rather, the goal of a healthy multi-ethnic church, once established, is to turn the power and pleasure of God, as displayed uniquely in such settings, outward in order to (1) bless the city, (2) lead people to Christ, (3) encourage the greater body, and (4) fulfill the Great Commission. These are the four ways your own multi-ethnic church can mobilize for impact in the community and beyond. *Are you ready?*

Bless the City

Throughout the gospels, we read that Jesus amazed the crowds. He amazed them with his understanding, teaching, and authority. He amazed them with his power to cast out demons, to make the blind see, the mute talk, and the lame walk. And he amazed them by his command of nature and the elements. Even Pilate was amazed with him![3] These references, and many more, tell of a presence and a power that clearly indicated to others there was something very different about this man. Of course, not everyone he talked with responded favorably to his message, but we can assume he had everyone talking about it!

In the same way, the presence and power of Christ is amazingly displayed in and through a healthy multi-ethnic church. Consequently, a diverse congregation becomes a blessing to the city—one that raises the sights and hopes of all those who come into contact with it. Indeed, the world does not often see and, therefore, does not quite know how to respond to a group of diverse individuals so committed to one another apart from social mandate. For instance, I recall sitting several years ago with our staff team at a café in Indianapolis. You should have seen the looks we received from other customers in this section of the city! These were not stares of intimidation or racism, however. People simply did not know what to think. Likewise, multi-ethnic church pastors report that short-term teams sent out from their churches often receive similar stares when traveling internationally for the sake of global missions. The curiosity that people have about the diversity of these groups, even outside the United States, paves a remarkable path for the Gospel.

As mentioned in Chapter Seven, we (in the United States) are required by law to go to school with those different from us, to work with those different from us, to live in neighborhoods with those different from us—and the list goes on. The truth is, we are required by law to integrate in every way and in every place—every place, that is, except for the church. Now I am not at all suggesting that local churches be forcibly integrated. Yet on a Sunday morning, for instance, when any number of people coming from diverse ethnic and economic backgrounds gather to worship God together as one, it's an amazing witness, precisely for this reason: we have come together willingly. Indeed, no one has forced us to do so. We *want* to be in such a place, and that's what makes it amazing! With this in mind, local church planters and reformers should recognize the intrinsic witness of a healthy multi-ethnic church and make good use of it in blessing the city for the sake of the Gospel.

Although discretion prevents me from revealing names, there are a wide variety of individuals, Christian and non-Christian alike, living within our community—officials in city and state government, higher education, and leaders of organizations—who are very complimentary of our efforts and speak well of our vision. I share such things in no way to exaggerate the claim but to tell you, truthfully, that we have been pleasantly surprised in this regard. In our minds, this is further confirmation of the unique value and potential of a multi-ethnic church for kingdom-building work within a city.

Of course, the mere development of a favorable reputation is not all God has in mind for the multi-ethnic church. Indeed, the Lord would not only have us to *look good* in the eyes of men but to actually *do good* for them in his name. Coupled with the look, our actions will speak powerfully of Christ's love for all people.

With this in mind, we hosted a Thanksgiving meal in 2002 for the residents of a local trailer park; we wanted not only to serve but also to eat with our neighbors. In addition, winter clothes were made available to the residents that day. Given favorable reviews, we repeated the effort in 2003 and expanded to serve two trailer parks the following year. The growing celebration was moved to our own facility in 2005, and invitations were also distributed door-to-door throughout the community immediately surrounding the church. All totaled, some 350 people gathered for the food and festivities that year. By then, we had expanded the University District Thanksgiving Celebration (as it was now being called) to include games for the kids, as well as the involvement of local police and fire departments.

In 2006 we again moved the location and this time served some 600–700 people on one of the busiest corners in the city. And we continued to develop the event. That year, a radio station came to broadcast live, and the owner of a local restaurant, being closed for business on that day, gave us the keys to his place, allowing people to eat inside. We even added pony rides for the children! Beyond this, a growing list of community partners, including UALR and the First Tee of Arkansas, are also investing annually in the effort—one we believe is meeting a variety of individual needs on Thanksgiving Day in Little Rock.

On another note, I was recently approached by one of Little Rock's city commissioners,[4] who informed me that our church has significantly blessed the ward she serves. First, she said, we have helped to spur commercial revitalization in the area by turning around the very large and formerly abandoned space we currently occupy, namely, the old Wal-Mart. In this regard, she pointed to the fact that a national chain has just rented 10,000 square feet of this space to provide goods to people at an affordable cost. Because the long-term vision of our landlord is to carve the rest of the space up for such stores, it is as if we have fulfilled for her an important mission in being the first to come and breathe life back into the building. And because we have recently signed a contract to buy a 100,000-square-foot facility that was once a Kmart just a few blocks to the east, she believes that Mosaic will play a major role in the future revitalization of the University District. Beyond these community improvements, however, she took note of the heart and passion we display for all people, young and old, Black and White, rich and poor. She sees for her ward a better day and is grateful that we have come to help make it so.

Toward this end, we also open our facility to the community, making it available for a wide array of events and activities. Because large spaces that can be configured for a variety of purposes are not always easy to find or secure, this is another simple but significant way in which we demonstrate our heart for all people. In this sense, our building has become a community center of sorts, hosting such things as the annual Arkansas Asian Festival, a number of local health fairs, school banquets, an inner-city mentoring program, Head Start Teacher Training, monthly meetings of the University District Partnership, an annual Fall Festival (for the past two years sponsored by Little Rock's Police Department), and the office of the Evangelical Alliance for Immigration Services. In addition, we operate a food and clothing distribution center that is on track to serve two thousand people this year. By allowing groups to use the space free of charge, we further express our desire to bless the city. In turn, some of these groups are now blessing us by leaving a financial donation following their events, simply to say thanks.

Of course, many churches, whether multi-ethnic or not, will cite their own efforts in this regard, and all such work is truly commendable. But I have learned there is something uniquely expressed when a diverse congregation is involved. It is a silent witness—a nonverbal attraction that compels others to think well of its vision and of its presence in the city. Because a local church is dynamic by nature, however, I cannot say Mosaic will always be so. What I can tell you at this time is that many recognize and appreciate our attempt to share the love of God, not only through what we do but, more important, through who we are. Indeed, we do not seek simply to build a bridge to the community—*we are the community*. And this subtle reality is a defining characteristic of the multi-ethnic church. As such, it provides the congregation a unique platform and helps to establish moral and spiritual credibility throughout the city. To mobilize for impact, then, we must seek not so much to take the Gospel *to* the community but rather *through* the community by embracing an "incarnational" approach.

Lead People to Christ

From the beginning, however, Mosaic has not been defined by facilities, events, or good works but by the collective heart of those who call themselves one with us and a desire to reach people separated from Christ and disenfranchised from the church. In fact, the only building currently owned by the church was purchased in August 2002—an abandoned home in the B&B Trailer Park in Alexander.[5] The story of our efforts there demonstrates the fruit of multi-ethnic, incarnational ministry, namely, the physical, material, and spiritual transformation of an entire community.

After first improving the condition of the trailer, we sent teams of two into the park, going door-to-door in order to meet the neighbors and identify needs. Given the demographic make-up of this small community, our teams included both English and Spanish speakers of varying ethnic background. Many of the residents we met were aware that Mosaic had bought the trailer but had no idea who we were or why we had done so. Through these initial conversations, we shared simply that we had come to make a difference, driven by our understanding of God's love for all people. In response, we gathered information concerning needs for home improvement, material goods, medical and dental attention, winter clothes, and educational tutoring. We also asked if any would be interested in studying the Bible or being given rides to and from church on Sundays. Because we had first invested ourselves in the community through the purchase and renovation of the trailer, we encountered little resistance to our effort.

Having surveyed the entire trailer park, we collated the data and next began to work through the needs, doing all we could to meet them. For instance, one woman was in need of a refrigerator, so we found someone willing to donate the item and delivered it to her door. Such was our practice until every single request was met. Later, we discovered that nearly sixty windows throughout the trailer park were in desperate need of being replaced. For instance, many were broken or held together with duct tape, making it hard on the residents, both physically and financially. In response, we found a local window dealer to replace all of them for less than $100. We then enlisted a local dentist with a heart for God and for the Gospel. Working out of our trailer, Rudy Jolley served fifty-six patients in one day. At that time, he identified twenty-five of them to be in need of further, more complicated procedures. Over the next several months, rides were arranged and appointments made so that he could provide additional services; in the end, Dr. Jolley billed us $125—for everything!

As we began to develop relationships within the trailer park, we also learned that Latina women living there had significant needs. For instance, while their husbands were working long hours away from home, these women were left to care for the children, often without transportation and without understanding the area or having the means to do so. In addition, many had only recently arrived in the United States and could not speak English. Living in a foreign land apart from family and friends, they felt lonely, confused, and frustrated.

Led by Joy White, women from Mosaic stepped in to address these issues. They started El Club de Amistad (The Friendship Club) to provide relational encouragement, educational assistance, personal support, and spiritual growth. Through the club, Barbara Harris and others would take these ladies to appointments with doctors or to various assistance agencies and help them enroll. In addition, the women in Alexander were taught to drive, to cook American foods, and, eventually, to study the Bible by Elisabeth Ortega. For their children, the women of Mosaic also began to provide tutoring, and for four years now, Donna McFadden and others have been coming faithfully to the trailer on Monday afternoons. After snacks and drinks, the children complete their assignments, as tutors help each one of them according to their need. Because many of the parents have only the equivalent of a grade school education, they are grateful for our interest and desire to help lead their children to a brighter future. Even teachers at the local school have reported the difference these efforts have made.

From these humble beginnings, the people of this community have become one with us—our friends, fellow members of Mosaic, and, more important, followers of Christ. To date, we can say with certainty that twenty-six individuals living there have embraced the Lord by faith, together with another fourteen from a second trailer park in which Mosaic is also active. According to Cesar Ortega, all of them have come to Mosaic and received additional discipleship. Andres and Leonor Gaytan, for instance, have stood strong in the Lord, despite criticism from their family in Mexico. Teresa Rodarte accepted Christ and has begun to heal from the hurt of a father—a "Christian" minister who left his wife for another woman when Teresa was just a child. Another of the ladies turned to Christ after being physically and psychologically abused by her husband. She now has hope and prays for him.

Needless to say, this is what it is all about! Yes, the multi-ethnic church is uniquely suited for reviving faith, restoring hope, and revealing love to men and women from diverse ethnic, economic, and educational backgrounds to Christ.

Encourage the Greater Body

For planters and reformers, the pursuit of Christian unity should not be limited in scope to their own multi-ethnic church. I believe we also have a responsibility to pursue it with others throughout the city as well, that is, with other local churches and their pastors. Indeed, it is long past time for local church leaders to stop competing and start cooperating for the sake of the Gospel. And with this in mind, our vision for unity demands that we encourage the greater Body of Christ throughout the city and beyond.

I first experienced the encouragement of the greater body as a youth pastor in 1987, when I had the privilege of working with two collegiate students to establish Skatechurch[6] in Portland, Oregon. Having begun the work with about twelve students, a picture of one of them launching off a ramp on his skateboard was featured on the front page of the local section of *The Oregonian*[7] just seven weeks into the ministry. The following week, some 250 students were skating in the church parking lot! This "first of its kind" ministry has been led by one of those two collegiate students, Paul Anderson, for most of the past twenty years. At last count, more than 8,000 students have been exposed to the Gospel through Skatechurch in the Portland area alone, while over 17,000 have heard it proclaimed through their traveling skateboard demonstration team. Beyond this, the work has spawned perhaps as many as 200 other skate ministries throughout North America, Europe, and Australia and, through them, an untold number of decisions for Christ.

But in the context of our discussion, what I remember most is how encouraging the site of 250 skaters in a church parking lot became to other youth pastors I knew in the area. One told me that he made it a point to drive by Skatechurch on his way to his church just to be inspired. Another told me that the entire ministry gave him hope for the future of students and for the city of Portland. My point is that among our local network, Skatechurch was in no way perceived as a threat to other youth pastors—my friends and co-laborers in student ministry. And their genuine enthusiasm and encouragement in those days continues to serve as a model for me in relating to other churches, their leaders, and their successes.

Such is the spirit of unity that leaders of a healthy multi-ethnic church must not only champion but also embrace. Indeed, we must not only preach but practice oneness beyond our walls if we are truly to be men and women who encourage the greater Body of Christ.

Apparently, the psalmist David understood the value of such relationships:

> Behold, how good and how pleasant it is for brothers to dwell together in unity! It is like the precious oil upon the head, coming down upon the beard, even Aaron's beard, coming down upon the edge of his robes. It is like the dew of Hermon coming down upon the mountains of Zion; for there the LORD commanded the blessing—life forever. (Psalm 133)

When local church leaders embrace a spirit of cooperation and reject a spirit of competition, it leads them to become genuine partners in winning the city to Christ. For instance, we were honored to have pastors Marty Brown of Markham Street Baptist Church, Happy Caldwell of Agape Church, Arkansas Supreme Court Judge Wendell Griffin of Emmanuel Baptist Church, Tim Jackson of Celebration Church, LeRoy James of Faith United Church of Christ, Fr. John Medvick of St. Thomas Reformed Episcopal, Mark Schatzman from Grace Church, and Robert Smith from Word of Outreach, all of Little Rock, come to pray for Mosaic personally in the month of our official birth. At that time and in other ways, pastors T. J. Johnston of St. Andrews Church and Steven Arnold of St. Mark Baptist Church also blessed me personally and the church as well. Since then, I have become involved with other pastors in the area through Little Rock's Nehemiah Group, led by Ray Williams. And I especially value my relationship with Brother Paul Holderfield Jr., who leads Friendly Chapel Church of the Nazarene in North Little Rock, a forerunner in the Multi-Ethnic Church Movement that is still a healthy multi-ethnic church today, as it has been for the past forty years. In addition, I have just finished three sessions with leadership at St. Andrews Church, helping them to determine where they are currently and where they might one day be, as they, too, now desire to build a healthy multi-ethnic church.

Fulfill the Great Commission

Finally, the healthy multi-ethnic church must mobilize for impact with a firm commitment to fulfill the Great Commission (Matthew 28:19–20). As was true at Antioch (Acts 13:1ff.), missionary endeavor in a multi-ethnic church is not programmatic but flows from the congregation's very nature and being. In other words, believers from varying cultures and backgrounds will quite naturally desire for their own families and countrymen to come to Christ.

With this in mind, Wilcrest Baptist Church (WBC) in Houston, Texas, led by my good friend, Rodney Woo, provides a great model for multi-ethnic church missions and mobilization (see Chapter Thirteen). Given the age of Mosaic, WBC, like many other churches around the country, is much further along than we are in this regard. Nevertheless, with the help of fellow Mosaic, Hatley Hambrice, we have put together an excellent cross-cultural ministries team, as well as a solid developmental strategy to send missionaries to the community and abroad. Within the last year, we have launched three couples from Mosaic: one with five children to serve in North Africa, one from England to serve in Swaziland, and another from the United States to serve in Rwanda.

Therefore, the healthy multi-ethnic church will have a well-balanced strategy for global missions, based, in part, on Acts 1:8. However, growing cynicism, skepticism, and sectarianism in our world today increasingly threatens the credibility of those attempting to export globally what they do not embrace or experience personally in their own churches back home. Conversely, multi-ethnic churches must not become so heavily invested in the community that they see no reason to go abroad. At Mosaic, we believe it is possible to find a balance. In this regard, the vision of our cross-cultural ministries team is "to fulfill the Great Commission through the intentional support and mobilization of believers involved in cross-cultural evangelism and multi-ethnic church planting" across the street and around the world.

With church planting in mind, Jim Spoonts, the executive director of the Mosaix Global Network,[8] believes that "multi-ethnic churches need to multiply by sending their people into the city, region and world to share the Gospel, bring people together and plant new multi-ethnic churches." Like many, he believes that God is in these days relocating entire people groups throughout the world in unprecedented numbers. Therefore, Jim says, "The global Church has the opportunity not only to *go* cross-culturally but also to *welcome* people from other cultures who have now settled in their part of the world."

First Thessalonians 5:1–3 suggests that in the last days and just prior to "the Day of the Lord," the world will cry out for "peace and safety." And while some debate whether or not we are, in fact, living in the last days, what we can say with certainty is that the world today groans for peace. But I have some news worthy of reporting: the current United Nations Secretary General Ban Ki-moon cannot deliver in this regard. Neither can the current president of the United States, George W. Bush, nor England's prime minister, Gordon Brown, or Russia's current president, Vladimir Putin. In the United States, we might look in the future to Senator Hillary Clinton or Senator Barack Obama, but it would be a mistake, as much as it would be to think that former New York Mayor Rudy Giuliani or Senator John McCain could bring peace to the world if elected president of the United States in 2008. For only the *Prince of Peace* can bring peace to the world, and the Prince of Peace is none other than Jesus Christ, who once said, "If I am lifted up from the earth, [I] will draw *all* men unto Myself" (John 12:32, emphasis mine).

The fact is, Christ *has* been lifted up from the earth—no *ifs* about it! Therefore, *not all those who have been drawn unto him, now draw near to one another in his name?* Herein lies the real power and potential that we must recognize in order to fulfill the Great Commission in the twenty-first century. Yes, in the future we must speak with one voice, one heart, and one message in order to win the world for Jesus. And through multi-ethnic churches, we can do just that, as we diligently proclaim, and "preserve the unity of the Spirit in the bond of peace. [For] there is one body and one Spirit, just as also you were called in one hope of your calling; one Lord, one faith, one baptism, one God and Father of all who is over all and through all and in all" (Ephesians 4:3–6).

Amen, come, Lord Jesus!

Amazing Grace

At the time of this book's writing, the movie *Amazing Grace* (Bristol Bay Productions, 2007) was being shown in theaters. The film tells the story of "a young member of Britain's parliament, William Wilberforce, who was inspired to lead a long campaign for the abolition of slavery . . . in 1833."[9] Wilberforce's views were widely shaped and influenced by John Newton, a former slave trader and writer of the song known throughout the world as "Amazing Grace." Sometime before this, Newton had converted to Christianity in the aftermath of a violent storm at sea. Eventually, he was ordained a minister in the Church of England and began to write hymns for the benefit of his congregation.

In 1772, Newton wrote "Amazing Grace" under the title, "Faith's Review and Expectation." According to the film's Web site,

> It became perhaps the most popular song in history. It is a song that, with a few notes, lifts the heads of the hopeless and softens the hearts of the hardened. *Amazing Grace* was sung by both sides of the civil war and used as a requiem by the Cherokee Indians on the Trail of Tears. Civil rights protestors sang it defiantly during freedom marches and on that sweltering day when Dr. King shared his dream. *Amazing Grace* rang out when Nelson Mandela was freed from prison and when the Berlin Wall came crumbling down. [And] on 11 September 2001, *Amazing Grace* was sung to comfort a mourning world.[10]

"Grace has the power to transform, to right wrongs and to turn a man who once traded slaves into one who fought for their freedom."[11] Grace helps us to love beyond reason, hope without measure, and believe despite the odds. And within the context of a healthy multi-ethnic church, grace also humbles and inspires. In that environment, grace daily reminds us that no one is more important than another, "neither Jew nor Greek . . . slave nor free . . . neither male nor female; for [we] are all one in Christ Jesus."[12] Grace, then, expects us to live in such a way that the world may see our love for one another and come to know Christ as we do.

So with the healthy multi-ethnic church in mind, together let us sing these words from Newton's hymn: "I once was lost, but now am found, was blind but now I see."[13]

Indeed, the grace of God is amazing! The grace of God is glue.

---

o

Joy White

Although at a macro level, churches should commit themselves to mobilize for impact, it is in and through the mobilization of individuals—one life at a time—that the heart of a healthy multi-ethnic church is most clearly revealed. In this case, Joy White tells the story:

Our friendship with the women in Alexander, a small community just outside Little Rock, soon led to opportunities for us to serve their children. For instance, not long after we began El Club de Amistad, I met Sandra, the oldest daughter of a family with seven children. Her mother had shared her concern that Sandra was not doing well in school, and it did not take long for me to discover why. Often Sandra was kept home from school in order to baby-sit her siblings.

One day in the summer of 2003, I went to the trailer park to work with Sandra one-on-one and brought a few children's books to see how well she could read. Though technically Sandra was in the sixth grade, I soon realized that she could not read a complete sentence, even from a book as simple as *The Cat In the Hat*. Over the next couple of months, we began to meet regularly simply to read.

At the end of that summer, her mother wanted me to go to school with Sandra to get her schedule for the fall. When we got to the school, however, we could not find her schedule in the place where it should have been. Taking her to the office, I asked the counselor for some assistance. "Where can we find Sandra's schedule?" I asked. The counselor looked at Sandra sadly and replied, "Oh, honey, do you not know? You flunked sixth grade and will not be able to go on to seventh grade this year." Sandra wept, and so did I.

We began to work with the school in order to help Sandra move forward. I met with her teachers and promised to help get her to the point where she would be ready for seventh grade the following year. Others, too, including my daughter, Carrie, assisted in the effort. At one point, for example, we helped her write a talk for an English class and come up with a costume; we even went to the school (like proud parents) to see her presentation! Looking back, that was a most significant moment.

Because her own parents were not able to attend, she would have been the only child that day without someone to cheer her on. At the time of this writing, Sandra is in the ninth grade and just recently received her semester grades. All but one was an A! Of greater eternal significance, however, is the fact that Sandra received Jesus Christ as her Savior that first summer, while sitting in my car and learning to read. In the end, that's what it's all about!

PART THREE

ON PLANTING, REVITALIZING, AND TRANSFORMING

WITH A VIEW TO APPLICATION, the final three chapters of this book express the insights of leaders who understand the biblical mandate (Chapters One, Two, and Three) and have interacted with the core commitments (Chapters Four through Ten) within their local church contexts. Chapter Eleven provides my own additional thoughts, specifically directed toward church planters. In Chapter Twelve, Rodney Woo of Wilcrest Baptist Church in Houston, Texas, tells how he was able to revitalize a dying church around the multi-ethnic vision. And in Chapter Thirteen, Kim Greenwood and Pastor John Jordan from Village Baptist Church in Portland, Oregon, provide the transformational history of a healthy but otherwise homogeneous church and how it became multi-ethnic over time. At the end of this chapter, I also have provided a "A Continuum of Transformation" (pages 180–181) to further assist those considering how best to transform a church in incremental steps over time.

In addition, fifteen principles are embedded within the text of each chapter, as identified in bold type. These principles are drawn from the experience of the writers and are meant to provide the reader more specific understanding and guidance by way of application. At the end of each chapter, these principles are listed for quick and easy reference.

FOR THOSE PLANTING
A MULTI-ETHNIC CHURCH

*The miracle is not that we do this work, but that we are
happy to do it.*

—Mother Theresa

IN JANUARY 1984, I began working full-time as a pastor to junior and
senior high school students in Scottsdale, Arizona. With all the wisdom
and maturity of a twenty-two-year-old kid fresh out of college, I took the
job, reasoning, "I have nothing better to do." Six months earlier, my
dream of playing professional baseball had come to an end, for even
though my college career had some notable moments, it was said that
I ran like I had a piano on my back! Too slow, then, to continue playing
the sport I loved, I stumbled into my calling and spent the next eighteen
years ministering to young people. In all those years, I can honestly say
that I never once envisioned myself planting a church.

For one thing, junior and senior high school ministry was "the place to
be" for young, emerging leaders desiring to serve the Lord. Throughout
the seventies and eighties, it was (in most cases) the cutting edge of passion and innovation within the local church; beyond that, it was just
flat-out fun! Even into the early nineties, it was still where most of the
"mavericks" could be found. Yet by the mid-nineties, things began to
change. With revival sweeping the college campus, enabled in part by an
outpouring of God's Spirit on a new generation of worshippers, emerging
vocational leaders increasingly focused on college students. Soon many of

these innovators morphed their ministries into local churches, and a new era of church planting was on.

Abandoned to His Will

In those days, however, when the thought of planting a church did enter my mind, I would quickly dismiss it. "At nearly forty," I told myself, "I am too old and too tired to try! If I had wanted to plant a church, I should have started ten years ago." But the Holy Spirit would not let the issue die. For us, then, planting Mosaic was an all-or-nothing wager—an obedient choice that Linda and I made to place ourselves dangerously in the hands of God.[1]

In so doing, we stepped out in faith and away from the advice of some we respected greatly. In all honesty, we have had many rude awakenings since. Indeed, we have encountered all the opposition you might expect from those threatened by the prospect of a multi-ethnic church tearing down the walls erected by both human and demonic influence. Yet we press on, motivated by a deep conviction that God is with us, as evidenced by the stories of miracle and wonder you have read throughout this book.

With this in mind, **multi-ethnic church planters should recognize that their vision may not make sense to those closest to them. Well-meaning people will offer many good reasons why you should do something else; humanly speaking, they will be right.** In addition, planters should recognize that **multi-ethnic church planting is not for the faint of heart. It is something that should not be entered lightly and something to which you must be called.** For it is surely this calling that you will fall back upon, time and time again, as you join the movement that will, quite literally, change the face of the local church in the twenty-first century.

Beyond what I have already shared concerning the seven core commitments of a multi-ethnic church, let me speak further of them now in the context of church planting.

Embrace Dependence

Prior to making the decision to plant Mosaic and like most couples in vocational ministry, Linda and I patiently and prayerfully sought the will of God concerning the next season of our lives. For nearly eighteen months and while I continued my work with students, we consistently asked God to make our next "assignment" known. But when it came to actually considering what it would take to plant a multi-ethnic church and, more specifically, how we would survive financially, we made a very bold decision. In fact, it was through this decision that I first recognized the essential nature of the first core commitment, namely, embrace dependence.

Early on then, Linda and I not only discussed the possibilities but also the process by which we would determine God's will for us in the future. Most of the opportunities we considered involved established churches and, more important for a father of four, an established salary! Yet when it came to considering a church plant, there was no such certainty. Obviously, we would need money for ourselves and for our church. But from where would it come? In addition, we asked ourselves, "How can we rightly weigh this possibility against others in the absence of financial certainty?" I had been guaranteed three months severance (June through August, 2001) but after that, there was no way to know for sure whether or not we would have money to pay the mortgage, buy food, or otherwise support our family.

In light of this, we thought initially of approaching potential supporters (while still employed) and pitching the idea in order to secure financial commitments; then, based on their response, we would determine whether or not we should plant the church. However, we quickly realized this was not at all what God would have us to do. We knew that if we were to plant a multi-ethnic church, we would have to do so with the faith of Abram, certain only of our calling and being willing to obey. Once the church was established, it would be the only way to know for sure that God was with us, that we had, indeed, been called. Therefore, I believe that **multi-ethnic church planters must be willing to leave everyone and everything behind in pursuit of the dream. They must be willing to walk away from all that has made them feel significant and secure in order to follow God into the unknown.** If they are not willing to step out in faith, then they should not step out at all.

Fast-forward to May 17, 2001. After months of deliberation, all other doors of possibility had slammed shut. We knew then, beyond a shadow of a doubt, that God would have us plant a multi-ethnic church. So that afternoon I made a few calls, told a few friends, and invited their prayers; on June 1, we began the journey. Having chosen not to seek financial investors prior to making this decision, one of the first things I thought to do was prepare a support letter, for I would have only three months to discover the means to provide for my family. Amazingly though, I would never have to send it out.

Three weeks into June, a man invited me to come and share the vision with him. When I did (and to my complete surprise), he handed me a

$12,000 check to cover all of my projected start-up costs. Not only that, he did something more: he pledged a gift of $1,000 a month for the next four years in support of my salary! Before I could even process this encouragement, another man invited me to come the very next day to share the vision with a guest in his home. The guest never gave, but the man called me later that evening to pledge $1,000 a month for the next four years, as well! Three weeks later, a third man committed $500 a month, and near that time, another committed to do the same. At that point, Linda and I were completely blown away! For nearly six weeks, I had been meeting with others solely to share the vision, and I can honestly say that those meetings (other than the ones I've mentioned) had nothing to do with money. In other words, while I was out sharing the vision in obedience and faith, all the rest was being added to me from the One I served (Matthew 6:33). Recognizing God's favor, I went home and threw away the letters, having never sent one out.

By September 1, Linda and I were fully funded for four years, long enough to allow for the church to get established and eventually to absorb my salary. When all was said and done, the severance ran out, new funding kicked in, and we praised God for a support team consisting of—get this—only five individuals and two churches. We had fully embraced dependence, and God came through! That's why, again, we can confidently say with Paul, "Faithful is He who has called you, that He will do it" (1 Thessalonians 5:24).

Only by such clarity of calling, faith, obedience, and hope can we expect multi-ethnic churches to be successfully planted and sustained. Yes, it is God and God alone who must lead us in building *a house of prayer for all the nations*, and we must allow him to do so by embracing dependence. As I made clear in Chapter Four, **multi-ethnic churches are drastically different from all other forms of church and, as such, cannot be established through human ingenuity, self-directed effort, conventional wisdom, or church growth techniques. Apart from prayer, patience, and perseverance, you will not be able to get the job done.**

Take Intentional Steps

Prior to launching the church and as part of our decision-making process, I approached established pastors and spiritual leaders throughout Little Rock seeking their counsel and asking, *Is there a need? Is this the time? Am I the guy?* It was only after receiving their positive responses that I felt confident enough to move forward in planting a new and multi-ethnic church in our city. How wonderful it was to have many of these men come, as I mentioned in Chapter Ten, to endorse us in prayer at our formal, public birth. Tim Jackson of Celebration Church even brought us a gift of $1,000!

From the beginning, we made it clear that Mosaic desired to *cooperate* and not to *compete* with other churches in the capital "C" Body of Christ throughout Central Arkansas. I believe this set the foundation for a very favorable reputation in our city and beyond. With this in mind, **multi-ethnic church planters must value the intentional pursuit of unity with other pastors and local church leaders throughout a city, striving to build God's kingdom and not their own.**

I think, too, that established local church leaders throughout Little Rock, in particular, appreciated the fact that we chose not to advertise Mosaic according to common practices of many who set out to plant. For instance, I was told early on by someone who has helped to plant a number of churches throughout the United States that it would cost about $30,000 "to get your name out there and make it known." Yet we not only did not have any money for this, but initial members were all against this approach. Because we were striving to be a first-century church in twenty-first-century America, we asked ourselves, *How did the early church grow?* According to Acts 6:7, "The word of God kept on spreading [by word of mouth]; and the number of disciples continued to increase." Therefore, we determined that word of mouth would also be our strategy; we reasoned, "Unless the Lord builds the house, our money will be spent in vain." We decided then to wait on God to bring people to us—those moved by God's Spirit and not by glossy postcards featuring stock photos of people who, in fact, did not attend our church. This, too, was an intentional decision and I believe one that is potentially instructive for all those considering how to plant a multi-ethnic church by faith.

In addition, **multi-ethnic church planters should be commissioned (when possible) by leaders of an established multi-ethnic church that can serve as a model of the intended outcome.** In the early years, this will go a long way toward solidifying the credibility of your calling and your vision in the minds of others.

For example, I know of one planting team that set out guns blazing to build a healthy multi-ethnic church. They had diverse leadership, authentic relationships with one another, and an identified, strategic (diverse and underprivileged) area within their target city in which to plant the church. Indeed, they had a well-developed sense of vision, mission, and strategy. However, when the financial going got tough, they were unprepared. A decision was made to relocate the church in a more affluent area of the city. In part, this decision reflected the mind-set of the churches primarily responsible for their commissioning and training, which were, in this case, homogenous, White, suburban, and big. With this in mind, let me also say that **multi-ethnic church planters should be prepared; ethnic and economic diversity are two sides of the same coin.**

Along this same line, **multi-ethnic church planters must recognize that success is not to be defined by the number of people who attend but by the collective spirit of those who attend.** It is the unity and diversity of your congregation that will impress a world in need of Christ, not the size of your congregation. Indeed, do not compromise the vision for the sake of numbers, dollars, or buildings.

I've found it refreshing that multi-ethnic church pastors do not often speak of their congregations' size as much as they do of their congregations' diversity. For instance, my friend Sam Owusu pastors men and women from more than seventy nations at the church he planted in Vancouver, B.C.—Calvary Worship Centre. In case you're wondering, this represents more than one-third of the countries currently recognized by the United Nations (192) and by the U.S. State Department (a total of 193, including the Vatican). *Absolutely amazing!*

Empower Diverse Leadership

Of course, much was said concerning this commitment in Chapter Six. Yet, there are two other aspects I would like to touch on here.

First, **multi-ethnic churches are built on the sacrifice of leaders determined to yield themselves for the greater good. Such leaders recognize that the church is not about them; rather, it is all about others and all about the Lord.** The type of leaders you will want to find and empower are those like Treopia Bryant. Responding to our intention not to launch the church until at least three ethnically diverse individuals were on the payroll, Treopia became the first African American to serve on staff at Mosaic. She was hired to oversee the vitally important ministry of prayer. Yet two years later, we had the need but not the money to hire a student ministries pastor. Aware of this, Treopia approached me to surrender her own salary in order to make this possible. Best of all, she remained on our staff, as she does to this day, cheerfully serving without pay. Now that's a team player! For many more reasons, Treopia, together with her husband, Hubert, represents the very essence of Philippians 2:1–4ff.

In addition, I was fortunate to have a church-planting coach like Greg Kappas of Grace Global Network to guide me through the first eighteen to twenty-four months of our church plant. And one of the greatest lessons Greg taught me was not to empower leaders too soon. "People," he said, "will come to you initially for all kinds of reasons, and many of them will seem highly qualified to lead. Yet many, too, will be running *from a church* and not necessarily *to your church*." Therefore, Greg said, "be patient and time will tell. Allow the Spirit to be your guide." I can't tell you what great advice this was! For example, the very man who wants to be appointed quickly to some significant position of leadership will be the very man who was recently passed over for such a position in another church. It will be his sense of rejection or a desire to retaliate that leads him to your new work and not necessarily the vision.

I believe that as the Multi-Ethnic Church Movement gains momentum, people of all ethnicities will increasingly desire to be identified with it. However, not all of these will be heavenly minded. As I suggested earlier, many may be motivated more by agenda than by a biblical sense of calling. Others will come because it's "cool," because they are curious, or because they perceive it as somehow "politically correct," that is, "the place to be and be seen." Some might even come with a racially motivated agenda. My advice, then, is to avoid such men as these, no matter what the color of their skin. For they will not engage those different from themselves; they will not even desire to do so and, in the end, they will cause more harm than good. Therefore, **multi-ethnic church planters must not be too anxious to empower others simply to diversify their leadership teams.** Be intentional, yes, but be patient and somewhat cautious, too. Allow the Spirit of God to confirm in your heart those he would have to serve alongside you.

Develop Cross-Cultural Relationships

My relationship with Treopia has taught me a great deal about life, ministry, and culture from the perspective of an African American. Throughout the years, she has listened, advised, corrected, befriended, and been patient with me, for which I'm thankful. Best of all, she has demonstrated an unwavering commitment to the vision of establishing a church for all people. In fact, it is among my own staff that I have come to value and appreciate most the development of cross-cultural relationships. And it is often through them that I am led to others. For instance, by attending the funeral of one of her relatives, I first met Treopia's nephew, Amos Gray. Three years later, he became our youth pastor. Though an African American, Amos reminds me of—well, me! In a season where good youth pastors are hard to find, we are thrilled to have him at Mosaic.

My partner, Harry Li, is also my friend. Like myself and Linda, Harry and his wife, Melanie, embraced a journey of faith, courage, and sacrifice, leaving a wonderful home and tenured professorship at the University of Idaho, to share in all that is and is becoming Mosaic. Born in Tennessee, Harry is the son of Chinese immigrants; he met his wife and married in the United States. I cannot imagine a better partner to serve with from day to day. He is a man of great wisdom, spiritual depth, and personal integrity, through and through.

Inés Velasquez was a young student at Texas Christian University when a friend introduced her to the vision of Mosaic. She is bicultural; her father, Ali, is Nicaraguan, and her mother, now deceased, was from Spain. At the age of eleven, Inés began translating for her father in his work with short-term missionary teams coming to Nicaragua. Therefore, she is a very skilled Spanish-language interpreter. More than that, she passionately pursues cross-cultural competence. Inés is also passionate about developing cross-cultural relationships—so passionate that she married a White man on our staff, Rob McBryde, who is Mosaic's Pastor of—*get this*—Connection! Seriously, I have enjoyed my front-row seat, watching this couple mature in life and ministry before my eyes. They are completely devoted to the cause.

Likewise, Cesar Ortega and his wife, Elisabeth, joined us in 2003, selling all that they owned and leaving their native country of Honduras for Arkansas in obedience to Christ. Their love for Christ and desire to expand his kingdom was immediately evident, as was their gift of evangelism. Within the first six months of their arrival, nearly twenty-five individuals embraced Jesus Christ as their personal Savior in direct response to their witness. That's why we affectionately call Cesar, the Latin Billy Graham! For more than two years, I have also watched him serve the needs of the poor as Mosaic's Pastor of Benevolence. Beyond that, his work among first-generation Latinos is time consuming, emotionally draining, and spiritually challenging. Never once, though, have I heard him complain. He is a model to us all.

Larry Tarpley is a most valued volunteer. Twice a week, he sits at our front desk answering phones, folding bulletins, and representing the very heart of Mosaic to all those who enter our doors. Beyond this, he sings in the choir and serves those in need; he led worship in the summer of 2007 on a short-term missions trip in Siberia. Oh, and one more thing—Larry is blind.

Of course, I could go on naming the wonderful people I have come to know and love through Mosaic—a variety of people who have enriched my life and people, in kind, that I would not have met otherwise. It is such people who inspire my efforts and make me proud just to be a part of it all. Indeed, these wonderfully diverse people remind me daily of why I left the homogeneous church and why I do not regret it.

In short, **multi-ethnic church planters must surround themselves with individuals of diverse background, inviting them not simply to follow but also to guide them on the journey.** In other words, to reach diverse people you must walk daily with diverse people as a leader, learner, and friend. Program time, as well, for your people to play, have fellowship, and otherwise have fun together, for although relational connections are important to the life and health of any church, they are essential to the foundation and fabric of a multi-ethnic church. I'm not talking so much about small groups here, as I am about opportunities for your members simply to enjoy food, fun, and fellowship without the pressure of agenda. The principle is this: **multi-ethnic church planters must encourage their members to spend time with one another outside of Sunday mornings or small groups focused on a lesson.** You must recognize the essential nature of relationships in building a healthy multi-ethnic church and program time for your people to build them.

Pursue Cross-Cultural Competence

As discussed in Chapter Eight, the pursuit of cross-cultural competence is a never-ending task, yet one to which I cannot encourage you more. However, **multi-ethnic church planters should not feel as if they have to become experts in the language, culture, or customs of diverse people groups. The point is to humbly engage cultures in the church different from your own.** Yes, a sincere and humble heart in pursuit of competence is what others will appreciate most.

In fact, recently, I had to fill in as a worship leader at Mosaic. It was a last-minute deal and, literally, Linda brought my guitar just in time to plug it in and start the service. There was no time to rehearse, review the songs, or confirm the keys. Together with James Wafford, Mosaic's Minister of Music, I just forged ahead. However, one song on the play list that morning was supposed to be sung in Spanish. And it's a great song titled, "Magnifico Dios"—one our congregation has sung many times before. It's just that I had never led us in doing so because I don't speak the language. But when it came up on PowerPoint that morning, I just followed the words and sang the tune as best I could from memory. In the end, I really enjoyed singing the song in Spanish and in the future will probably do so again. What blessed me, though, was how wonderfully received my attempt was by Latinos in our church. For the next few days, they expressed great appreciation because their pastor was willing to attempt the song in Spanish. Again, it was sincerity and heart that had won the day and most certainly not my linguistic proficiency!

Promote a Spirit of Inclusion

As I have also mentioned, we must seek to accommodate diverse people who embrace the vision in order to become one in Christ. For instance, when we first printed bulletins, someone put the English version on one table and the Spanish version on another. In doing so, they must have reasoned, it might be easier for people to find the right one, depending on their language needs. Yet think about it: two separate tables, two separate groups; Inés and I quickly caught the well-intentioned mistake. Even at this level, **multi-ethnic church planters must re-examine everything they have previously learned, experienced, or assumed in order to avoid the unintentional creation of barriers. In the multi-ethnic church, they must remember that "my way" is only "a way" and not necessarily "the way" things should be done.**

Another way in which we have tried to promote a spirit of inclusion at Mosaic is by performing weddings on occasion during our Sunday worship service. For those new to the area without family in town or for those who might not otherwise expect much, this has been a real blessing. Typically, the brief ceremony begins with about fifteen minutes or so left in the service. The groom comes forward to stand at the altar as a song is played to set the mood. The entire congregation (more than would gather for most weddings) rises as the bride walks down the aisle. A brief word of explanation provides for what and why this is happening. The happy couple then recite their vows, exchange rings, and are pronounced husband and wife. After a kiss, they proceed up the aisle to the applause of the congregation, and everyone is dismissed to enjoy cake and punch—an instant reception!

Again, this has benefit for everyone involved. First, it helps to foster a greater sense of community within the church. In addition, it provides the couple a wedding, a reception, and great memories, all at no cost. Finally, it demonstrates our desire to accommodate the unique needs of people in our church by thinking outside the box. Such understanding contributes to the feeling people have when they enter our facility and, more important, when they interact with our members.

Mobilize for Impact

Make no mistake: the power of God is uniquely displayed when diverse people walk together as one in the local church. This is, as Francis Schaeffer said, the "final apologetic,"[2] and the sooner we recognize this, the sooner we will see faith revived, hope restored, love revealed, and the world transformed. Only in Heaven, you say? Maybe. But Jesus did teach us to pray, "*Thy will be done on earth as it is in heaven.*" Now either he was serious or he was not. If we take him at his word, I believe we should do more than just pray. Indeed, we should be willing to do all we can to establish unity and diversity (healthy multi-ethnic churches) on earth as well.

As at Antioch then, **multi-ethnic church planters must recognize the unique credibility of their message and their ministry. The vision, once established, will engender good will, even among nonbelievers. And this credibility will open doors for you—wonderful possibilities to extend the love of Christ within the broader community for social good.** Rather than run from such opportunities, you should run to them, cautious, yes, but in confidence, too. For through such efforts, the world will see the local church, "the way we always thought it should be," and come to know Christ as we do.

I am not so much talking about mobilizing for traditional missions, whether at home or abroad, as much as I am talking about advancing the good name and will of Christ to those outside the church locally. Each year on October 31, for instance, our church partners with the Little Rock Police Department to sponsor an annual Fall Festival for children and families. This year, some five hundred people are expected to attend the "trunk or treat"-style event. But, of course, there will be no overt attempt to present the Gospel or to promote our church in this otherwise secular environment. Neither will we seek compensation for the use of our facility. On that night, we will simply demonstrate our (Christ's) love for people in the community, apart from any overt attempt to share the Gospel. In so doing, we will further the notion that we are not only a church but, in fact, a *center of life* in this diverse and needy area of the city.

I believe that consistent community engagement resonates with the lost today, that is, with those more prone to see the church as interested only in itself and its own people or in advancing its own agenda. By faith, such involvement as I've described will position the multi-ethnic church for future spiritual impact, and you will be wise to advance this ball.

Tearing Down the Walls

Not long ago, the Berlin Wall divided what is now the city of Berlin into two halves, East and West. Having lived in Germany from 1989 until 1991, Linda and I had the opportunity to observe first-hand the stark contrast between what were, at that time, not only two separate cities but, in fact, two separate nations, namely, East and West Germany.

When we lived in what was then West Germany, the houses were well-constructed and clean, the fields neatly plowed and productive. West Germans drove cars made by Mercedes-Benz, BMW, Audi, and Volkswagen, and their outdoor plazas were well supplied and bustling with shoppers. In other words, West Germany was teeming with life.

On the other hand, East Germany in those years seemed dirty, industrial, and cold. Smoke poured forth from coal furnaces and, naturally, soot was everywhere. The atmosphere was dark and oppressive, and people seemed resigned to the fact that nothing might ever change. Indeed, it was this hopelessness, coupled with a knowledge that life was better on the other side, that caused many to try and breach the Berlin Wall, only to be shot at or killed by soldiers instructed to keep them trapped inside.

Is it possible that the local church has today become more consumed with providing life for those inside its walls than it is with helping others to get in? And are we not, in fact, perpetuating this separation through our incessant urge to erect big and insanely expensive buildings? How sad it is that so many are willing to invest more in bricks and mortar than they are of themselves in the lives of people outside the church and desperate to escape the condition of their existence, the dark oppression of their souls. For while those behind the latest "capital campaign" suggest that the money given "will help us reach people for Christ," far too often—and, again, let's be honest—these buildings, once built, merely keep those who have already been reached feeling happy, safe, separate, and worse yet, feeling (somehow) spiritually significant.

We must understand that the Devil himself is ultimately behind every wall of division we face today (Ephesians 6:12). Indeed, these walls have been carefully constructed through the centuries to keep as many as possible separated from the love of God. They separate the affluent in Christ (the saved) from the impoverished of this world (the lost). And just as tragically, these walls separate those who are Christ's followers from one another—Blacks from Whites, Asians from Latinos, professionals, white-collar workers, the working middle class from those without much, and the educationally advantaged from the disadvantaged, as well. So let me ask, *Where is the power or pleasure of God in that?*

Yes, I believe it's becoming outright hypocritical to go on proclaiming a message of God's love for all people from needlessly segregated pulpits and pews. *Do we really think the lost and cynical will respond?* And merely throwing Bibles, books, magazines and tracts, CDs, T-shirts, bumper stickers, Web sites, blogs, and podcasts over the walls from the comfort of our own sanctuary is not getting the job done. Like Reagan to Gorbachev in 1987, then, Jesus Christ stands opposed to such divisions (Ephesians 2:14–16) and expects local church leaders in the twenty-first century to *tear down these walls!*

○

Principles for Planting

1. Multi-ethnic church planters should recognize that their vision may not make sense to those closest to them. Well-meaning people will offer many good reasons why you should do something else; humanly speaking, they will be right.

2. Multi-ethnic church planting is not for the faint of heart. It is something that should not be entered lightly and something to which you must be called.

3. Multi-ethnic church planters must be willing to leave everyone and everything behind in pursuit of the dream. They must be willing to walk away from all that has made them feel significant and secure in order to follow God into the unknown.

4. Multi-ethnic churches are drastically different from all other forms of church and, as such, cannot be established through human ingenuity, self-directed effort, conventional wisdom, or church growth techniques. Apart from prayer, patience, and perseverance, you will not be able to get the job done

5. Multi-ethnic church planters must value the intentional pursuit of unity with other pastors and local church leaders throughout a city, striving to build God's kingdom and not their own.

6. Multi-ethnic church planters should be commissioned (when possible) by leaders of an established multi-ethnic church that can serve as a model of the intended outcome.

7. Multi-ethnic church planters should be prepared; ethnic and economic diversity are two sides of the same coin.

8. Multi-ethnic church planters must recognize that success is not to be defined by the number of people who attend but by the collective spirit of those who attend.

9. Multi-ethnic churches are built on the sacrifice of leaders determined to yield themselves for the greater good. Such leaders recognize that the church is not about them; rather, it is all about others and all about the Lord.

10. Multi-ethnic church planters must not be too anxious to empower others simply to diversify their leadership teams.

11. Multi-ethnic church planters must surround themselves with individuals of diverse background, inviting them not simply to follow but also to guide them on the journey.

12. Multi-ethnic church planters must encourage their members to spend time relationally with one another outside of Sunday mornings or small groups focused on a lesson.

13. Multi-ethnic church planters should not feel as if they have to become experts in the language, culture, or customs of diverse people groups. The point is to humbly engage cultures in the church different from your own.

14. Multi-ethnic church planters must re-examine everything they have previously learned, experienced, or assumed in order to avoid the unintentional creation of barriers. In the multi-ethnic church, they must remember that "my way" is only "a way" and not necessarily "the way" things should be done.

15. Multi-ethnic church planters must recognize the unique credibility of their message and their ministry. The vision, once established, will engender goodwill, even among non-believers. And this credibility will open doors for you to find wonderful possibilities to extend the love of Christ within the broader community for social good.

FOR THOSE REVITALIZING A DECLINING CHURCH

Rodney Woo
Pastor, 1992 to Present
Wilcrest Baptist Church, Houston, Texas

In the middle of difficulty lies opportunity.
—Albert Einstein

OF THE THREE POSSIBLE SCENARIOS BEING DISCUSSED IN PART THREE OF THIS BOOK, I believe it's the task of revitalization[1] that offers some of the more difficult challenges for building a healthy multi-ethnic church. However, I have not always believed this to be true. In fact, when asked several years ago which option—planting, revitalizing, or transforming—would be less difficult, I stated that revitalization was the path of least resistance. Yet after fifteen years on this journey, it seems to me now that multi-ethnic church planting is, in many ways, a much more viable option. Nevertheless, there will be an increasing number of homogeneous churches that will need to become multi-ethnic in the years to come, and I pray that Wilcrest's story will inspire those of you considering—or even now involved in—such work. Indeed, our story is proof of God's power and sustaining grace. Yes, the challenges of revitalization can be overcome, and God can use you to build a healthy multi-ethnic church!

History

Wilcrest Baptist Church was incorporated in 1972 and was established in the southwest part of Houston. During the "oil boom," this section of the city emerged as "a place to be" for young, White, middle- to upper-middle-class individuals. Through the years, church growth paralleled the growth of this community, and by the early 1980s, attendance had soared to nearly five hundred. However, in the middle of the decade, Houston experienced the "oil bust," and a decline in attendance at Wilcrest reflected the major transitions occurring in neighborhoods surrounding the church. By the early 1990s, attendance had plummeted to fewer than two hundred; "White-flight" influenced the decline, as people who had once moved in began to move out in seismic proportions. Soon, the all-White congregation at Wilcrest seemed somewhat out of place in an increasingly diverse neighborhood. In 1992, the church took a major step of faith by calling a twenty-nine-year-old man named "Woo" to lead them in light of changing times and demographics! It was then that, together, we began our journey of revitalization and toward seeing the nations gather "on earth as it is in heaven," to worship God together as one (Revelation 7:9).

When I arrived at Wilcrest, the twenty-year-old congregation was in a downward spiral that affected its attendance, finances, and morale. It was truly a critical juncture—one that would require a significant paradigm shift if the church was not only to survive but to once again thrive. Yet throughout this time, the people of Wilcrest maintained a firm sense of the church's original calling to minister in the southwest part of Houston. In light of this and the changing community as well, we soon realized our need to become multi-ethnic.

Personal Preparation

For me personally, many streams converged in those days and led me to embrace multi-ethnic ministry in Houston, Texas. First, God redirected my focus from mono-ethnic to multi-ethnic ministry by giving me new insight into his Word. Particularly, he ignited in me a passion to follow the pattern of the apostle Paul in preaching the unchanging Gospel to culturally diverse people. No longer was I content only to reach out to people of one specific ethnic group; I wanted to reach out to everyone through the local church.

In addition, my family heritage played a key role in shaping my understanding of future ministry in a multi-ethnic environment. My dad, who was half-Chinese, worked as a missionary in the inner city of Port Arthur, Texas. Through this ministry, he served Hispanic and Vietnamese people, as well as Americans, both Black and White. In fact, my mother-in-law (who is Hispanic) learned English from my father's inner-city ministry. This multi-ethnic mix within my own family encouraged me to see ministry increasingly through diverse cultural lenses.

Finally, God instilled in me at an early age a calling and desire to evangelize in light of the fact that all people everywhere desperately need the Gospel. In fact, some of my first experiences with evangelism occurred on Saturday mornings with my father. At the age of fifteen, for instance, I would often accompany him to the city jail to present the Gospel to inmates from varying ethnic and economic backgrounds. During this training period, God taught me to look beyond the color of a person's skin and to speak to the heart. Sharing the same experience in prison leveled the playing field among inmates, birthing within each prisoner one common vision: freedom! In the prison, I began to see that people of all backgrounds were spiritually imprisoned, stemming from their rebellion against God. Similarly, I began to see that people of all backgrounds shared the spiritual need to be set free (John 8:36; Galatians 5:1).

I also observed that prison guards kept the Black prisoners segregated from the White prisoners. Since in those days, all the schools, neighborhoods, and churches in our town were racially divided, I suppose those in charge thought it was the best way to keep from having any other difficulties with the inmates.

Even with a growing passion to preach, this situation was somewhat disturbing for me, as I was forced to share the same Gospel, from the same Bible twice—once for the Blacks and once for the Whites. I believe that it was in and through such experiences that God placed a vision for all people in my heart. One day, I hoped that I would be able to share the same Gospel from the same Bible to all people at the same time—to Blacks, Whites, Asians, Hispanics, indeed, to people of every nation, tongue, and tribe.

In spite of this calling I felt, I was serving an all-White congregation in central (rural) Texas before coming to Wilcrest. In this particular town, White people lived on one side of the railroad tracks and Black people lived on the other. In addition, an overwhelming majority of Hispanics living in this area were undocumented immigrants working as dairy farmers. During my eight years there, we saw God do amazing things, growing the church from an average of fifteen to over three hundred attending our worship service. Yet, it was only in the last two years that we earnestly attempted to enfold several non-Whites into the body of the church. But no matter how thoroughly I preached (encouraging the congregation to reach out to all of God's people), and in spite of my family's multi-ethnic mind-set, the attempt to transition was superficial and short-lived. I concluded that if a multi-ethnic congregation was to develop in that church, I was not the one called to get it done.

Soon, I learned of Wilcrest and, as I said, both of us would have to take enormous steps of faith. Wilcrest would have to trust God in calling a young pastor, and I would have to trust God to use me in revitalizing an established church in a transitional neighborhood.

Looking back, I can see how the seven core commitments affected the revitalization process at Wilcrest. Through the rest of this chapter, I'll interact with them and offer some additional insight for those seeking to revitalize an existing church around the multi-ethnic vision.

Embrace Dependence

To revitalize a homogeneous church around the multi-ethnic vision will require dependence upon the Holy Spirit at a level you may not yet have experienced in ministry. Of course, leading any church requires a good measure of faith; it's just that this calling requires a unique reliance upon the Lord in seeking to accomplish something that is otherwise unattainable apart from his involvement.

According to the Church Growth Movement, it is much easier to evangelize and disciple people who are ethnically, economically, and educationally similar to us. But in this situation, **those revitalizing a church will be challenged to share the love of God with people different from the vast majority of those already attending. At the same time, you will have to inspire the congregation to do so as well, and to adapt themselves to changing demographics. Finally, much of your new growth will likely come through conversions and not by way of those transferring their membership from another church, so be prepared.** There were several years at Wilcrest in which our baptism-to-transfer growth was 4:1! Although this is exciting, it is also challenging and can stretch a church beyond its understanding or resources.

Many of these new believers come with relational, emotional, and personal baggage. They may never have consistently attended a church or, at least, not since many years before. Adjusting to this, we stepped up our efforts in the area of member orientation and now include a class that I teach for new believers. In addition, we also try to connect new believers with mature ones individually, or to a small group consisting of others of their same age or stage of life.

An influx of new adult believers will also create a need for additional leaders, and to develop them will take much time and energy. Look for potential leaders in each and every person God sends to the church, and remember, it is never too early to develop leaders. In my case, I meet with several men in our church once every month or two in order to participate in their development as leaders. At any given time, I meet with twenty to twenty-five men in a three-month period. Perhaps five to ten will develop into effective leaders.

Such factors should keep reformers ever mindful of our great need for God as we seek not only to build but also to maintain a healthy multi-ethnic church.

Take Intentional Steps

Prior to calling me as pastor, there was only one thing Wilcrest had in mind: survival! **As a first step in the transitional process, the church began to ask critical questions, as should any church considering revitalization.** These questions included the following:

1. Will the church survive "White flight"?
2. If the church is forced to change, will it become radically different from the way it is presently?
3. What type of leadership is required to turn the church in a new direction?
4. Will there be so many changes that the church will lose its original identity?
5. If other races are incorporated into Wilcrest, can there ever be true fellowship among believers who are so different from one another?

Such questions led to **a period of self-evaluation, culminating in a weekend retreat for key members; I would recommend this as a second step for all churches in pursuit of revitalization.** As a result, **Wilcrest adopted a new vision statement to ensure that a multi-ethnic church would come to fruition:** "Wilcrest Baptist Church is God's multi-ethnic bridge that draws all people to Jesus Christ who transforms them from unbelievers to missionaries."

This vision statement laid the groundwork for our church to begin intentional, missionary outreach across ethnic lines by emphasizing a personal relationship with Jesus Christ. This emphasis represented a radical departure from the prevailing winds of church growth at the time. Rather than gauge our success in the future by how many people we could attract to the church, we determined to gauge our success by how many people we could send out as missionaries from the church, first into our own "Jerusalem" and then to "Judea, Samaria and to the remotest parts of the earth" (Acts 1:8).

Our staff has set a wonderful example. Our former minister to students, an African American, is now planting a multi-ethnic congregation that we are supporting with people and funds. Our next minister to students, an Anglo, is now working as a doctoral student and missionary in Europe; our current children's minister, a Korean, is about to leave for medical school in Mexico and desires to serve someday as a medical missionary in a third-world country.

Among the body, one of our lay members volunteered for five years in Swaziland and South Africa. In addition, we are sending out our members on short-term mission trips to their respective home countries. For instance, we are going to Honduras with our Honduran members, and in May 2007, we returned to the home village of one of our members from northern Nigeria, working in a predominantly Muslim area. We also work closely with a church in Cameroon, in the home village of another of our members, which, of course, excites the approximately twenty to twenty-five members of Wilcrest who are themselves from Cameroon.

Empower Diverse Leadership

It is important to realize that in the revitalization effort, these intentional steps cannot be taken all at once, rather they must be taken one after another over time. Nowhere is this truer than in following the core commitment of Empowering Diverse Leadership. Because God has called the church to be multi-ethnic, we believe it is essential that those seeking to revitalize a church call diverse representatives to join the new leadership team. This does take time, however. One of the early steps we took to this end was calling an African American to minister to our students. This step not only affirmed our vision statement but also provided visible evidence that we were, indeed, moving in the multi-ethnic direction. For until people see diverse leadership, statements like, "Wilcrest is a multi-ethnic bridge," are just empty claims.

To be clear, having one African American on our staff in no way made our church multi-ethnic, but it did move us one step forward and further away from being exclusively homogenous. Likewise, calling an African American as our minister to students did not immediately translate into African Americans flooding into our congregation. In fact, to most African Americans, we were in those days still too White! However, the relationship that the predominantly White church began to develop with our Black minister to students provided us all with much needed instruction on how to understand and to follow believers of varying ethnicity.

In addition, **those desiring to revitalize a church must be willing to ask new members for honest feedback concerning how they perceive the church to be reaching out to all people,** including in its staffing decisions. For instance, when we needed to call another staff member in 2000, I strongly felt that the person needed to be a non-White. There was an intense debate on whether we needed to limit our search to qualified people of color, or, more generally, seek the strongest candidate for the job, no matter his or her ethnicity, and thus open the possibility of adding another White staff member to our team. When I took the issue to some of our key non-White leaders, they responded that they did not care what color the person was as long as he or she had a vision and passion for what God had called Wilcrest to do. In my mind, I felt that hiring a non-White at this time was non-negotiable, but after hearing from our non-White leaders, I knew God would send the right person. Currently, then, we have a part-Chinese pastor, a Cajun minister of worship, a White minister to students, a Korean children's minister, a Black associate pastor, and a White preschool minister.

An important question to keep in mind, of course, is how the majority group is responding to these changes. It is more difficult to release leadership roles than to share leadership from the beginning. **In revitalization, it will be the majority group that will be called upon initially to sacrifice the most.** As the ones who have had in the past and who are now still in control, they are the ones who will have to determine to share or release it. This continues to be a primary area of struggle for some of our White members who have been with us throughout the entire transitional process. Sometimes they do not feel appreciated for the amount of sacrifice they have given to the multi-ethnic vision, or they assume they will be in leadership based solely on the longevity of their tenure as a leader. One of the steps we have taken to ensure they remain engaged is to involve them in mentoring emerging non-White leaders. In addition, we ask them to share leadership responsibilities, whether in a Sunday School class, as part of a church committee, or in another ministry assignment.

Develop Cross-Cultural Relationships

Most people in our congregation, particularly those who have been Christians for a long period of time or who have grown up in church, have in the past formed Christian friendships with others of their same ethnic background. In fact, prior to their experience at Wilcrest, most had never attended a church with people of other ethnicities. Michael Emerson, author of the book *Divided by Faith*, writes:

> People in homogenous congregations have little racial diversity in their circle of friends. Nearly nine out of ten people in homogenous congregations say that their two closest friends are the same race as they are, while just over half of those in multiracial congregations say that their two closest friends are the same race. Furthermore, 86% of those in homogenous churches say that either all or most of their friends are of their race, while only 25% of those in multiracial congregations say that most or all of their friends are of the same race.[2]

What is radically different about attending a multi-ethnic congregation is that members experience a steady exposure to believers of varying backgrounds, and each group brings so much to the Body of Christ. If we really believe that all people have been made in Christ's image, then we all carry the same divine resemblance (Genesis 1:26–27). To interact with someone who has been created in Christ's image demands that we see the face of God in his or her face, regardless of the color of skin. How sad it is that when we encounter people of different ethnic or cultural backgrounds, we are more prone and conditioned to focus on the differences than on the similarities.

In the revitalization model then, the development of cross-cultural relationships is more challenging because there are already social bonds in place. Either the established majority will initiate bridging the gap with newcomers, or ethnic-based subgroups will begin to develop. If this happens, it will likely lead to a pluralistic result, one in which there may, in fact, be several ethnic groups existing within the church that are spiritually and socially disconnected from one another. Thankfully, many of the people at Wilcrest have aggressively built bridges to those from different nations or ethnic background, and we have avoided this outcome. Yet there have been others who have left the church due to the influx of people who are ethnically or culturally diverse. Although they do not always share their reasons for leaving, I have observed that most who leave eventually return to a homogenous congregation. Some of those who have left claim that we have made too many accommodations for other ethnic groups and, consequently, that we no longer look like the Wilcrest they originally joined. Of course, it is always painful when people leave for such reasons. However, God has taught me that the task of revitalization is like a rigorous marathon and that I must remain thankful for those who have run a lap or two, only to pass the baton to others who come after them.

Pursue Cross-Cultural Competency

In reality, it is impossible for me to be completely competent in moving in and out of the more than forty different nations and cultures that currently make up the Wilcrest family. Because I come from a Chinese background, grew up in an African American neighborhood attending an all-White Baptist church, and have a wife who is Hispanic, I can easily relate to some. One of our recent converts, however, is from India, and my knowledge of his country is minimal. But when I took a mission trip with one of our sisters from northern Nigeria, my understanding of her culture was greatly enhanced. When an individual is operating within his or her own culture, of course, there are things that come naturally without any second thoughts. But **throughout the process of multi-ethnic revitalization, there is a constant need for cross-cultural interpretation and open, honest dialogue.** Nowhere is this more simply observed than in relation to various forms of greeting.

At Wilcrest, there is a man in his early seventies from Ethiopia. Every time I greet or attempt to embrace him, he shuns the otherwise open physical contact; he bows and addresses me as "Father" or "Abba." Because most of our new believers come either from no religious background or a Catholic tradition, this form of greeting has set off numerous alarms in my spiritual system! Yet this brother has been patient with me in explaining that because I am his spiritual leader, he is simply rendering respect for the position of the pastor. Therefore, on any given Sunday, while this man is bowing as a sign of respect, there are children knocking me over with their hugs! To hug the man would offend him; to require that the children bow in respect is not necessary, either. Although these are extreme examples, they indicate the need for us to pursue cross-cultural competency in dealing with the wide variety of people who will make their way to a multi-ethnic church.

The revitalization effort is fraught with risks but also filled with multiple opportunities for individuals to learn and grow, even through something as simple as a form of greeting. Unfortunately, **many established members will find the challenges of multi-ethnic revitalization insurmountable within the framework of "their" church. Consequently, they will actively avoid or oppose the multi-ethnic vision. Many more, however, will warmly embrace such cultural "collisions." These are the ones who give us encouragement and hope.**

Promote a Spirit of Inclusion

When Wilcrest embraced the multi-ethnic vision, the effects were not immediately apparent. In spite of what we said in print, those new to our service still observed us to be a predominantly White congregation. When our church finally crossed the first demographic barrier (when 20 percent of our people were not White), I thought we were well on our way. What I realize now but did not then is that we had morphed into an assimilation model—a model that welcomes diverse people but expects them to conform to the established majority in worship style, leadership, methodology, and vision. Yes, the doors are open for everyone but only to the degree that they understand and submit to the majority culture already in place. So, although we were increasingly diverse demographically, we had not yet integrated our leadership, our worship, or any number of other areas throughout the church.

I believe this is a real danger for those attempting to revitalize a church with a view to becoming multi-ethnic. When I initially began to see diverse people coming to Wilcrest, I immediately concluded that we were multi-ethnic in every way. In fact, by 2000, we were 60 percent White and had approximately twenty-five nations represented in our church. But in that same year, we received a written note from an African American visitor, and it was truly a wake-up call. Her observation primarily targeted our worship service and style. In part, she wrote:

> The choir was diverse. It looked to me to be about one-third non-White. But, the music was not only "White," but rather slow and traditional. I wondered why the non-White people are part of the choir. Who selects the music? Are there non-Whites who have input into the song and music selection? The worship style is not the least bit charismatic . . . I did notice a Black woman in the choir holding up her hands (to about waist level) and closing her eyes during one of the worship songs. It struck me that it probably took some courage to do even that, considering what, from my perspective, was a very rigid and conservative style . . . Personally I was disappointed, even sad about the disconnect that I saw between what the church claims to be and what, from my visit, it was. People who are non-White are welcome, I am sure, but they don't seem to be appreciated for what they can uniquely bring to the church or really included at every level. Given what I saw and experienced, I would not be able to invite other African Americans to Wilcrest.[3]

As a result of this painful assessment, we began to make adjustments. For instance, we became much more intentional in whom we appointed to committees, invited to teach Sunday School, asked to give testimonies or read Scripture, asked to lead congregational prayer, or chose to select songs and determine the style in which they would be sung. In revitalization, it will remain an ongoing challenge to bridge divides of expectation. But you must remain committed to doing whatever it takes to cultivate an atmosphere in which every person will be represented and celebrated.

It is often difficult to get an accurate read as to how well things are going if the non-majority's voice is not heard. It is vital, then, that reformers cultivate and maintain relationships with those in the minority in order to gather open and honest feedback concerning their perspectives.

Mobilize for Impact

One of our goals at Wilcrest is to send missionaries to each of the countries that are represented by members of our church body. We call this The Wilcrest Expression. This passion comes from Acts 1:8, where Christ commissions his disciples: "You shall be my witnesses both in Jerusalem, and in all Judea and Samaria, and even to the remotest part of the earth." Of course, the majority of our people's Jerusalem is Houston; their Judea is Texas; their Samaria is Canada or Mexico, and their "remotest part of the earth" is a country further south or across the Atlantic or Pacific Ocean. However, there are believers at Wilcrest for whom their own Jerusalem is actually across the ocean. As our church sends missionaries to the remotest parts of the earth, then, we must understand that we have arrived in another's Jerusalem. Likewise, we want our internationals to see themselves as missionaries here in America, in what is, for them, the "remotest part of the earth."

Many of our international members came to the United States in pursuit of the American dream, with all of its corresponding advantages, privileges, rewards, and freedoms. Yet as God has touched their hearts with the multi-ethnic vision, they now embrace "God's dream" of someday returning to their Jerusalem as a missionary.

When I first arrived at Wilcrest, I witnessed to a forty-two-year-old Vietnamese man. It was the fall of 1993. He told me he had to go back to Vietnam and ask permission from his parents to accept Christ and to leave the Buddhist religion. In the spring of 1994, he traveled to Vietnam for the first time in twenty-two years and told his parents of his intention to accept Christ. When he returned to the United States, he accepted Christ and I baptized him.

Upon his return from this monumental trip, he realized that he was a missionary to his own family, who were without Christ. It was fulfilling to watch, then, as an elderly lady in our church "adopted" this Vietnamese man. As a teenager, she had felt a call to missions but had never actually served on the international mission field. However, she fulfilled her calling by pouring her life and energy into people who came to America from different countries and providing a home for them. In the grand scheme of things, she did, in time, serve the foreign field; in this case, it was the people of Vietnam she served through this man into whom she poured the love of Christ. Consequently, his family in Vietnam did not hear the Gospel from a White Southern Baptist missionary but from one of their own family members!

By embracing revitalization, you can take a paradigm of missions already in place and exponentially expand the vision. For instance, it had been customary at Wilcrest for members to give to missions and to go on mission trips, but they had never been introduced to the biblical concept that we are to be missionaries right where we are. If we have been called to go, then we have been called to go wherever we find ourselves, whether in Houston or Honduras, Chicago or Cameroon, New York or Nigeria. Indeed, God has called us to be missionaries to the entire world and we, like Paul, are under obligation both to the Greek and to the barbarian, to both the wise and to the foolish.

I am thrilled to share that as of 2006, our church has sent missionaries to thirty different countries. Every time we send a missionary or a group of missionaries to a new country, we hang that nation's flag in the worship center as a visible reminder of who we are, of where we've been, and what is our continuing vision. We have sent missionaries to the following countries: Mexico, Canada, Honduras, Chile, Venezuela, Peru, Haiti, Portugal, Kenya, Swaziland, South Korea, China, Taiwan, Australia, Germany, India, Kazakhstan, Afghanistan, Scotland, South Africa, Nigeria, Cameroon, Caribbean Islands, and several places across the United States. Now when visitors come to our worship services, they will see people from all over the world in their native dress and see thirty different flags (sometimes their own) in a place of worship for all the nations. This missionary-sending atmosphere has both challenged and changed how many immigrants coming to reside among us now perceive the American dream. We have mobilized for impact, and we are, indeed, people of the dream!

Bringing the Mission to Our Doorstep

To watch God revitalize a church in a transitional community has been an overwhelming experience for me. Wilcrest has grown from a church in decline to a church trying to survive to what it is today—a dynamic, multi-ethnic congregation represented by forty-four different nations. Because God has designed every living thing to reproduce, now we must do the same. For a multi-ethnic congregation content to enjoy its diversity without attempting to reach out to the world's nations would contradict the very passion of God, who sent his Son to save the world. As Jesus told his disciples, "the Father has sent Me, so I also send you" (John 20:21).

Yes, Jesus has called the church to cross national, ethnic, religious, economic, social, educational, and all other cultural barriers for the sake of the Gospel. In the American context, I have observed that it is much easier and safer for us to address missions as a denomination or from the perspective of Christianity as a whole. All too many feel personally released from any further obligation if, for instance, they personally support a missionary, if their denomination is involved in work abroad, or if their own local church has sent members to the foreign field. Likewise, in giving money, many conclude that their responsibility to missions has been fulfilled and there is nothing more to be done at a personal level.

The apostle Paul, however, confronts this remote and impersonal mentality with his words: "I am under obligation, both to the Greeks and to the barbarians, both to the wise and to the foolish. Thus for my part, I am eager to preach the Gospel to you also who are in Rome" (Romans 1:14–15).

This same sense of obligation is also conveyed by John when he writes of Jesus, "he had to pass through Samaria" (John 4:4). In both instances, it is a divine mandate to proclaim the Gospel to all people. It is also interesting that this divine mandate required the Jews to reach out to people and nations that they had previously perceived to be unclean and unfit for the kingdom of God; in other words, they had to extend themselves beyond their own comfort zone. So if Jesus, himself, was led to the Samaritans and Paul was obligated to the Gentiles, what do you think that God requires of us? Since the same Spirit lives in the heart of each and every believer, we should recognize that he expects us, likewise, to be personally engaged in reaching out to other people and nations for the sake of Christ, whether at home or abroad.

o

Principles for Revitalizing

1. Those revitalizing a church will be challenged to share the love of God with people different from the vast majority of those already attending. At the same time, you will have to inspire the congregation to do so as well, and to adapt themselves to changing demographics.

2. Much of your new growth will likely come through conversions and not by way of those transferring memberships from churches, so be prepared.

3. As a first step in the transitional process, the church began to ask critical questions, as should any church considering revitalization.

4. A period of self-evaluation, culminating in a weekend retreat for key members, is recommended for all churches in pursuit of revitalization.

5. A new vision statement should be written and adopted to ensure that a multi-ethnic church will come to fruition.

6. It is essential that those seeking to revitalize a church call diverse representatives to join the new leadership team.

7. Those desiring to revitalize a church must be willing to ask new members for honest feedback concerning how they perceive the church to be reaching out to all people.

8. In revitalization, it will be the majority group that will be called upon initially to sacrifice the most.

9. In the revitalization model then, the development of cross-cultural relationships is more challenging because there are already social bonds in place. Either the established majority will initiate bridging the gap with newcomers, or ethnic-based subgroups will begin to develop.

10. Throughout the process of multi-ethnic revitalization, there is a constant need for cross-cultural interpretation and open, honest dialogue.

11. The revitalization effort is fraught with risks but also filled with multiple opportunities for individuals to learn and grow.

12. Unfortunately, many established members will find the challenges of multi-ethnic revitalization insurmountable within

the framework of "their church." Consequently, they will actively avoid or oppose the multi-ethnic vision. Many more, however, will warmly embrace such cultural "collisions." These are the ones who give us encouragement and hope.

13. In revitalization, it will remain an ongoing challenge to bridge divides of expectation. But you must remain committed to doing whatever it takes to cultivate an atmosphere in which every person will be represented and celebrated.

14. It is vital that reformers cultivate and maintain relationships with those in the minority in order to gather open and honest feedback concerning their perspectives.

15. By embracing revitalization, you can take a paradigm of missions already in place and exponentially expand the vision.

13

FOR THOSE TRANSFORMING
A HOMOGENEOUS CHURCH

Kim Greenwood
World Missions Assistant
with John Jordan
World Missions Pastor, 1993 to Present
Village Baptist Church, Beaverton, Oregon

Sometimes history takes things into its own hands.
—Thurgood Marshall

WHY MESS WITH A GOOD THING? This popular concept is meant to protect people from things that will potentially rock the boat of their lives; it is meant to save them money, time, and frustration. And yet, sometimes this concept is a powerful force of complacency, even within the church.

Village Baptist Church began as one man's bold vision to reach the needs of a growing new neighborhood called Marlene Village, in Beaverton, Oregon. It has grown into a multi-ethnic church with a significant global outreach and impact in the local community. Today, we continue to be a people of vision and faith, striving to live in a Christ-like way and reaching out to neighbors across the street and around the world in the name of Jesus.

The following is a brief look at our transformational process. It's a journey that continues to this day, as we strive to become a growing multi-ethnic church where believers and seekers from any culture feel welcomed and valued and have the opportunity to grow in their relationship with a loving God.

History

In 1949, before any members were gathered to worship, God provided for Village Baptist Church; the church received a $10,000 loan to buy land and build a building. By 1966, nearly 230 adults were involved, and growth was limited by existing facilities. In a letter to the congregation that year, Pastor Bob Luther cast the vision for a new sanctuary. In part, it read,

> We are privileged to live in the fastest growing residential area in Portland. We must plan for the future with vision and anticipation that God will use the instrument and testimony of this church to reach a multitude of our neighbors with the Gospel of Jesus Christ. It is so true, "Where there is no vision, the people perish." Let's attempt great things for God. Let's expect great things from God.

The heart and soul of this proclamation has been Village's legacy for over fifty years.

On March 5, 1967, our current sanctuary was dedicated. Through a responsive reading that day, the congregation dedicated the facility to God saying, "For the extension of Thy Kingdom through missionary endeavor and world-wide evangelism, for the up-building of the immediate community, and for the spreading of goodwill **to all men and all races.**"

By that time, a vision for global outreach had been established, and the congregation was supporting fourteen mission projects around the world. With room to grow, Villagers continued to connect with their neighbors and added seven new mission projects. The focus on outreach was inspiring life change and producing dedicated Christ-followers, both in Beaverton and around the world.

In 1969, Pastor Don Jensen was called to Village and began a remarkable career of service that would span twenty-eight years. In 1971, Pastor Jensen introduced a biblically based program for world missions called Faith Promise. Villagers learned of the great needs of our world and how they could play a part in meeting those needs through prayer and financial giving, as well as by supporting those who were called to "go."

In addition to this tradition of global outreach, Village has always desired to reach our immediate community for Christ. As the years passed, however, we began to notice that our congregation looked very little like the changing community around us. By the early 1990s, the community had experienced an influx of international students and workers brought here by opportunities for higher education, the high-tech boom, or seasonal agricultural needs. It soon became clear to us that the community inside our walls did not represent the community outside our walls. Something needed to change.

It did change—in 1990, when a man came to Village looking for a new church home, having left a church divided by conflict. He was frustrated, hurt, and angry; he was looking for a Bible-teaching church that was committed to unity in Christ. Impressed with Pastor Jensen's teaching, the man made an appointment to see him.

Over lunch, he asked profound questions about our church, expecting to stump Pastor Jensen with his questions, such as, "What is your mission?" and, "Why does your church exist?" Instead, he was surprised as Pastor Jensen clearly articulated Village's mission statement: "We exist to worship God, to teach the Scriptures, to care for one another and to proclaim the Gospel." In addressing our mission, Pastor Jensen simply told the man, "We exist to meet the needs of the community."

Of course, plenty of people have come to Village through the years. What makes this story worthy of note, however, is that the man in question is our dear brother Sooyoung Lee, a Korean. This meeting was a divine appointment and set in motion events that would literally change the face of our church and its future.

Initially, Sooyoung joined Pastor Jensen's small-group Bible study that met in his home. He appreciated the opportunity to get to know Pastor Jensen on a more personal level and was impressed with his approachability. Sooyoung and his wife, Hyunsook, also led small-group Bible studies for their friends, witnessing and seeing many of them trust Jesus as their Savior.

Soon the members of these groups began to ask the Lees why they attended Village instead of one of the growing number of Korean churches in the area. Sooyoung explained that it was the church's vision as well as the unity of the staff and congregation that drew him to Village. Many of these new believers decided to come and see this unity for themselves; today, they are leaders in our flourishing Korean Fellowship.

Likewise, the other ethnic fellowships at Village—those involving East Indian, Hispanic, and Chinese people—all began in the same basic way. Authentic relationships are foundational to transforming an otherwise healthy but homogeneous congregation into a healthy multi-ethnic church.

To cultivate these kinds of relationships, Village began to partner with International Students Incorporated (ISI), concentrating specifically on

Chinese and East Indian immigrants arriving in the Portland area. The program helped participants with issues such as housing, transportation, health services, and social networking. Meeting the real and felt needs of these students spoke volumes about Christ's love. As a result, many accepted Christ and were baptized at Village. In time, some returned to their homeland and became involved in ministry; others remained and found jobs in the community. Through this ministry, Village has established a reputation as a safe and welcoming place for people of diverse cultures.

Though the multi-ethnic church is clearly a New Testament reality, until now there has not been a book succinctly addressing the biblical mandate or identifying core commitments to help us get there in these modern times. Indeed, our metamorphosis has not been without bumps and bruises. Yet through it all, the Lord has been faithful, and we count ourselves blessed to be a part of his plan for the church in the twenty-first century.

In the following sections, we hope to share some of the valuable lessons we have learned through our own journey. Although the application of these commitments may take different forms in your church, they will need to be addressed functionally in order to help you successfully transform your current congregation into a healthy multi-ethnic church.

Embrace Dependence

As anyone who has led a church through a process of change knows, success often requires us to disregard the voices of those who criticize things that are new and different. This is especially true when attempting to transform an established, homogeneous congregation into a multi-ethnic church. Beyond our walls, even people and organizations in the community were critical of what we were trying to do and questioned our motives. Although many churches were renting their facilities to ethnic churches, we could find no other church in our area that shared our vision of becoming an integrated community of diverse fellowships, united in our vision for reaching the lost. But we pressed on.

Through it all, we learned to depend on God and to go forward by faith in spite of such objections. Therefore, in order to succeed, **transformational leaders pursuing the multi-ethnic local church must not yield to the voices that will surely challenge their vision.** Well-meaning people will question your motives or intentions, and you will cause them great confusion as you shake an otherwise comfortable spirituality. Some will feel threatened and try to defend the status quo or, worse yet, try to paint you as someone not in tune with God. Do not be surprised if even your closest friends do not understand why you want to rock the boat! In order to fulfill your mission, however, you will have to listen to the voice of the Holy Spirit and not to the voice of others, no matter who they are, what position they hold, or what they might mean to you personally.

As Village began to address the concept of becoming a multi-ethnic church, Pastor Jensen and the elders wanted to be sure that we were clear on God's Word regarding this focus. In 1997, they issued a positional statement clearly articulating the biblical mandate for evangelism and discipleship among the different ethnic groups living within our community. Through each new challenge and decision, we learned that **transformational leaders must articulate holy intentions and clear objectives in language that can be embraced by the body they seek to influence.**

Clear enunciation of the vision does not guarantee a smooth transition, but it most certainly helps. Regardless of the path an established church takes toward becoming a diverse congregation, **transformational leaders must allow the Holy Spirit to be the driving force and voice for change. Yes, it is Christ's vision for the nations that should guide and govern the decisions of those shaping the future of the local church.**

Take Intentional Steps

The process of transforming a historically White congregation into a multi-ethnic church requires transformational leaders to take certain intentional steps. A good first step is to gather information concerning the changing demographics of the community. Having done this, Pastor Jensen, together with World Missions Pastor, John Jordan, began to educate Village staff and elders about the various needs and opportunities resulting from the diversification of the area. As our leaders became more aware of such things, they began to specify in writing the core values and policies that would define our decision to make the change.

This led to the completion of a Multi-Cultural Ministries Plan Proposal in 1996 that was circulated among our leaders. In part, it read,

> The purpose of our ethnic ministries is to empower and equip Villagers to use their gifts, talents and resources to reach the various peoples within our community with the Gospel and to disciple them to accomplish God's global purpose.

This document also addressed issues pertaining to the core values of Village and defined how they might be applied in ministry among the varying ethnic groups of our community.

In 1997, a Multi-Cultural Positional Statement was completed and released to the congregation articulating a position on multi-ethnic ministries. Simultaneously, we began to address the issue from the pulpit. We updated the body concerning the process thus far and shared our vision for transformation into a multi-cultural church. During these days, we invited guest teachers to come and to further explore cross-cultural issues with our leadership team.

With this in mind, **transformational leaders should develop a written document that clearly articulates the purpose of embracing a vision for multi-ethnic ministry. Addressing the issue openly and honestly from the pulpit will go a long way toward winning the hearts and minds of the people.**

By 2002, we had changed the language of our core values to reflect the intentional shift to multi-ethnic ministry, and in 2004, our vision statement was refined to include the following declaration: "Village will be a church where cultures connect in unity as all people are included in our family."

In response to some of the challenges we faced in the early days of our transition, the God Help Us Committee was formed. Today, we call it The Multi-Cultural Committee. This group is charged with creating specific goals concerning worship, teaching, and ministry, in order to further explore how the various cultures at Village can work together to meet the needs of our growing and diverse church family. In addition, this committee is responsible for keeping the issues and goals of our multi-ethnic vision before church leadership. The group meets regularly to take the cultural "pulse" of the congregation and to define intentional steps for furthering the vision and reaching stated goals.

Enfolding people of diverse cultural background into an otherwise homogeneous congregation presents unique challenges and opportunities. By taking the time to define written policies and positions on the front end, transformational leaders will develop a common language and reference point from which to work in the future and to deal with unexpected challenges as they arise. Such guidelines ensure that diverse people are treated impartially, while the leadership exercises sensitivity and care in meeting the varying ministry needs of each culture.

Empower Diverse Leadership

In any model of transition, the important role of leadership cannot be emphasized enough. Yet before I continue, let me state clearly that **transformational leaders should move their congregations ahead in** incremental steps. Indeed, you will not want to split an existing church in the name of unity. Therefore, you should remain prayerful, purposeful, and patient throughout the entire journey of discovering and empowering diverse leadership.

Because the church will take its cues from its leaders, however, this area deserves prayerful consideration from the start. First and foremost, the entire leadership team (both vocational and volunteer leaders—staff, elders, deacons, for example) must be committed to the multi-ethnic vision if it is to succeed. Emerging ethnic leadership must also believe in the vision and make a firm commitment to the greater mission of the church. **Forging unity from diversity will require transformational leaders of diverse ethnic background to come together as one. All involved must passionately embrace the vision in order to lead the people with whom they have the greatest influence. There can be no hint of inconsistency, self-positioning, or diversion from the vision if it is, in fact, to take root and inspire change in the established church.**

With this in mind, empowering diverse leadership begins with finding "the right people." The following are qualities we would encourage transformational churches to keep in mind in their search for diverse ethnic leaders to join them on the journey.

First, **transformational leaders should look for diverse ethnic leaders who are firmly in line with the church doctrinally.** For instance, in assimilating diverse ethnic fellowships at Village, we have found that there are often cultural practices that arise in areas such as worship, communion, and baptism that are unique to the varying ethnic traditions. Sharing the same doctrinal positions among leadership has reduced these to questions of practice and not of theology. Thankfully, oneness of mind concerning these cultural issues is almost always achieved through further consideration, discussion, and prayer. However, you will not want to be working through cultural issues while wrestling over doctrinal ones as well. With this in mind, make sure that any ethnic leader you endorse (whether in a vocational or volunteer position of responsibility) understands and agrees with the vision, mission, and doctrine of the church.

Second, we have learned both from failure and success that it is best to find diverse ethnic partners who are bilingual. This is especially important when looking for someone to join the paid staff team. Because there is much room for misunderstanding, maintaining clear, open communication and accountability among the staff is vital for organizational progress. Without common language and understanding, the journey can be greatly impeded.

For example, in the early days of our Hispanic Fellowship, one of the key leaders spoke only Spanish. Consequently, we found it extremely difficult to communicate with him, and translation had to be arranged for any meeting of significance. In fact, one summer he left to visit his family in Mexico and never returned! This left us in a precarious position, without a leader and no real explanation for his decision not to return. Since then, we have avoided such problems by hiring only bilingual ethnic leaders who are able to communicate in English, the predominant language at Village.

It is also important that transformational leaders involve the ethnic ministry staff in other major ministries of the church. Their presence and involvement within the congregation as a whole affords them visibility, credibility, and increased opportunities for influence. It also makes the presence of different cultures an expected part of everyday church life.

Such involvement must be strategically designed in order to communicate that minority ethnic leaders have roles and responsibilities equal to that of the rest of the staff. Likewise, members of leadership who are in the ethnic majority need to be viewed as ministers among the other ethnic fellowships. This cross-cultural exposure empowers every member of the pastoral staff to minister effectively to the entire church body. It provides for everyone the opportunity to develop cross-cultural relationships and pursue cross-cultural competence.

Another challenge we faced early on was in understanding that there are different cultural standards and sensitivities that come into play regarding the issue of credentials. For instance, in the early days of the Korean Fellowship, Sooyoung Lee worked as a bi-vocational, lay leader of the fellowship. In time, he was given authority over the fellowship and held accountable by the church staff for certain leadership responsibilities. But he kept his day job and worked for Village in his free time during the week and on weekends.

Later, we named Sooyoung the "director" of the Korean Fellowship. Interestingly enough, there is not a word in the Korean language to accurately convey our use and meaning of the term *director*. At Village, we have multiple directors serving in different areas of ministry, for example, overseeing children, youth, women, and the arts. For us, it conveyed an individual's authority over a specific area of ministry and was applied to those who are not necessarily licensed or ordained as pastors. This, however, was a point of confusion and caused some concern for members of the Korean Fellowship, as the title of director in their culture is reserved for those working in the business world.

As the Korean ministry grew, Sooyoung became more pastoral in his functional duties. Soon his intent, as well as the intent of Village, was questioned by other Korean church leaders in our community because of his lack of credentials. Within the fellowship itself, too, there was a certain amount of anxiety over the fact that Sooyoung was not ordained. Over time, however, as the fellowship proved itself a credible ministry in the Korean community, Sooyoung's character and leadership skills were validated. The community recognized his commitment to the Lord and our commitment as a church to outreach and ministry to all people, without distinction.

Develop Cross-Cultural Relationships

Transformational leaders recognize that one of the most effective ways to inspire the development of cross-cultural relationships within the body is to model them as a staff. Because language often creates a barrier in communicating with first- and sometimes second-generation members of our ethnic fellowships, developing cross-cultural relationships of transparency and trust is often our greatest challenge. Yet the personal and professional interaction of a multi-ethnic staff speaks to the heart of who we are and what we value as a church.

Lay leaders, too, must be encouraged and equipped to extend themselves to diverse people within the body. Well-planned events that encourage the participation of all involved across ethnic lines will help to foster community. For instance, church picnics, concerts, and special events offer nonthreatening opportunities for interaction and should be planned with the entire, diverse congregation in mind.

Establishing a new cross-cultural relationship often takes bold initiative and a measure of self-sacrifice. Transformational leaders must light the way. At Village, Aleida Rivas, wife of Mauricio Rivas, pastor of Hispanic Ministries, is a wonderful model of someone dedicated to this commitment. She has actively sought relationships outside the Hispanic Fellowship by attending events for women provided for the greater body of Village. In addition, Aleida has helped to connect other Hispanic women beyond the fellowship by bringing them with her to these church-wide events. Although initial contacts may have us stumbling over words and working through insecurities, the chance to spend time with one another is appreciated by all involved. Together, we are moving closer to our goal of becoming a multi-ethnic church, filled with authentic friendships that transcend culture or preference.

Pursue Cross-Cultural Competency

From the beginning, Village has been global-minded and steadfastly committed to involvement in the Great Commission. This legacy afforded an important base from which to work toward the transformation of our church into a diverse congregation. Our consistent support of both short- and long-term ministry teams through the years has provided us with a natural platform to further educate the body about the diverse cultures living in our own community. However, studying different cultures is quite different from walking with them together as one. Most concerns can be addressed through relationships of transparency and trust, leading to adjustments in approach or programming. However, others run deep through culture and hold potential for conflict. These must be bathed in prayer.

With this in mind, **Ephesians 4:1–3 should serve as a guide to transformational leaders in their pursuit of cross-cultural competency.** In part, it reads, "Therefore . . . with all humility and gentleness, with patience, showing forbearance to one another in love, being diligent to pursue the unity of the Spirit in the bond of peace."

The willingness to invest one's heart, time, and energy in learning about cultural differences plays an important part in navigating the inevitable misunderstandings that surface when diverse people come together to pursue "the unity of the Spirit in the bond of peace." In our case, we encountered distinct cultural differences early on in dealing with divergent expectations related to the issue of child care.

Throughout our history, Village has employed qualified adult volunteers and, at times, even paid staff to provide child care for various events on the church calendar. Of course, this child care was available to the ethnic fellowships at all church-wide activities. But when the fellowships began to schedule their own events at the church from week to week, the assumption was made that they would not only provide for their own child care but also that they would utilize similar standards when enlisting others to help.

However, the care of children was loosely organized in the beginning by some of the fellowships and often left to older children in attendance. Although they did the best they could, these older children lacked training and oversight. Often, they were overwhelmed by the task. As a result, problems began to arise and the issue had to be addressed.

In another instance, a particular teacher-training event sponsored for teachers by our Children's Ministries cast some light on cultural differences related to classroom management. Stacey, a lay leader in the Korean fellowship, was attending the event designed to provide Sunday School teachers training in methods, classroom management, and church policies concerning behavioral issues. Soon the conversation turned to dealing with unruly children in the classroom. The children's ministry director instructed that if a child did not respond to a teacher's repeated requests for a change in disruptive behavior, the teacher was to call on the director, who would then go get the child's parents. In so doing, they would be asked to leave the worship service and to pick up their child from the class.

One of the teachers asked Stacey how Korean parents might respond to this corrective action. Not knowing for sure, Stacey sought the opinion of her small group later that week. After explaining the hypothetical scenario to Korean mothers, Stacey asked them what they would think if this were to happen to their own children. To a woman, they said that they would view it as a prejudicial reaction based on race. This was a quite honest and revealing answer! Since then, Village has made a concerted effort to develop well-reasoned policies and procedures for parents, children, and teachers and have taken pains to demonstrate that these policies apply to everyone and would never be used in a discriminatory manner. We are learning day by day to keep in mind cross-cultural understanding, experiences, and norms when developing policies.

Of course, it would have been easy for such conversations to slip into prejudicial judgments and accusations. Yet cross-cultural relationships between staff and lay leaders, coupled with our stated commitment to embrace all people, helped diffuse these potentially volatile issues. Ultimately, they were resolved in a spirit of humility and cooperation.

All of this happened in the early days of our journey toward transformation. At the time, many of the Korean families had previously attended homogeneous (Korean) churches and were still adjusting to working with Anglos in this area. Of course, most of the Anglos at Village were trying to get used to working with the Korean families as well and were struggling to become familiar with language and cultural issues. Thankfully, we have all made significant progress in this area, but we wanted to share this story as an example of how misunderstandings can happen if channels of communication are not well maintained and kept open.

Although we cannot anticipate every potential problem in dealing with these and other issues arising from our differences, **transformational leaders must pursue cross-cultural competency and maintain mutual respect for one another in seeking to understand and resolve cultural differences.** Demonstrating authentic consideration for one another and for our unique cultural distinctiveness speaks the language of love, not only to those within the body but also to those watching from the outside.

Promote a Spirit of Inclusion

The intent of our multi-ethnic vision has always been to see our members worship God together as one in a spirit of unity. The realization of this vision, however, has been challenged by the fact that many of our ethnically diverse members speak limited English, and our services are primarily conducted in English. Early on, the leadership of Village determined that this significant issue would not prevent us from pursuing our vision of becoming a multi-ethnic church. The challenge was to find the best solution to this problem.

To worship in one's first language is an important part of spiritual growth. After much prayer and consideration, we decided that the emerging ethnic fellowships should be allowed to conduct supplemental worship services in their own languages. Initially, there was some concern that members would only attend services offered in their first language and not any of the other, all-church worship services we conducted each week in English. In the end, through careful communication and the encouragement of all the ethnic pastors to make weekend services a priority, the members of these diverse fellowships did not substitute attendance at their weekly meetings for attendance on Saturday nights or Sunday mornings.

We also started simultaneously translating the weekly sermons into Korean, an idea Sooyoung resisted in the early days of the Korean Fellowship. Back then, the Korean Fellowship would meet immediately following the Sunday morning service, and Sooyoung would review the main points of the sermon and the main points during this meeting. For although many of the young Korean men had a working knowledge of English, many of the Korean women struggled to understand the weekly sermons in English. Consequently, they relied heavily on Sooyoung's sermon summaries to stay informed and connected.

One day, however, an older Korean gentleman approached Sooyoung in frustration and said, "You know, I really only understand about 10 percent of what the pastor is saying in the message." Sooyoung was surprised. Until then, he believed that the general proficiency of his people with the English language was approximately 40 percent. After asking other members of the fellowship about their experience, he concluded that simultaneous translation was a necessary step in keeping first-generation Koreans interested and attending weekend, corporate worship services.

Soon money for translation equipment was raised, and a volunteer translation staff was recruited to rotate through the services. The process was labor-intensive. By this time, we were holding Saturday night services to deal with general growth issues. Translators would attend the service Saturday night, taking copious notes and preparing an outline from which to work the following day. Receivers were provided on Sunday mornings in order to hear a live translation of the service. In time,

Sooyoung surveyed the women again and other first-generation members of his fellowship. He learned that the level of understanding and participation from the Korean Fellowship members had risen sharply as a result of simultaneous translation being offered.

The efforts and commitment of the church for translation equipment sent a clear message to the members of the fellowship: we care about you and your needs. This commitment to our brothers and sisters continues as we look to the future. In designing a new facility and sanctuary to be built in 2008, we plan to install equipment for simultaneous translation into multiple languages. The design includes features that will make it possible for everyone in the sanctuary to have a translation device so we can have speakers deliver their messages in languages other than English.

In addition to providing simultaneous translation, we translate all our key documents into the first languages of our ethnic fellowships. Being able to read the core documents of our church in one's own original language is essential for inspiring others to embrace the vision and mission of Village. For example, we translated nearly all the documents relating to our recent building campaign into Korean, Spanish, and Chinese. Banners designed for special events are translated into each of the languages of the fellowships, announcing to all who enter our doors that we desire to accommodate the diversity of our community. Ultimately, **transformational leaders should work hard to ensure that language is not a barrier that keeps people from coming to or remaining involved in the church.**

Furthermore, **committing to a spirit of inclusion requires transformational leaders to set the tone and to follow through with tangible signs for those in the minority. They must not feel as though they are an afterthought; rather, they must truly be an integral part of the entire church family.** These are often the steps that cost the most money, take the most time, or require the most creative thoughts. These are also the ones that will meet both the real and felt needs of people of diverse cultures seeking to dwell together in unity.

Mobilize for Impact

Being a multi-ethnic church in a very liberal-minded state like Oregon is something that often works in our favor. For instance, we have heard from individuals who attend our new-members class that the multi-ethnic element was a key factor in deciding on Village as a home church.

Many have said things such as, "I look around the room and see other people who look like me, and I like that." Or they will say, "I look around the room and see people who don't look anything like me, and I like that." The level of authenticity required of a multi-ethnic church appeals to many who want to experience unity in Christ, together with diverse friends and neighbors. It's encouraging to know that we can invite them to church, confident there will be others just like them there as well.

When members from our ethnic fellowships join their Anglo brothers and sisters for short-term missions, a clear message is communicated to our hosts in other countries. Our diversity, working together with a oneness of purpose, passion, and love, can speak profoundly, particularly in countries where centuries of racism and cultural divisions have existed. The humble witness of Villagers serving side by side, equally and sacrificially, gives them a picture of Christ's words in John 13:35: "By this all men will know that you are my disciples, if you love one another."

Often it is our ethnic fellowship members who are able to quickly build relationships and connect with individuals from the host country. Without many of our Western hang-ups or social concerns about stepping beyond our comfort zones, they are most likely the ones looking for language or cooking lessons or who feel comfortable just sitting down to visit with others (like Mary) rather than having to be active (like Martha) all the time. The more experience we gain in taking diverse teams on short-term mission trips, the more we will realize the value and the rewards.

A Place at Our Table

By no means has Village "arrived" as a multi-ethnic church. Indeed, we continue to struggle and at times to fail and to learn from our mistakes. But we do rejoice in how far God has brought us through the process of transformation. He has truly been faithful to accomplish that which he placed in our hearts to do (I Thessalonians 5:24).

Because Village had from the beginning a very clear and well-defined vision for sharing the Gospel with ethnically diverse people in other parts of the world, it was much easier to justify doing the same thing in our own community. We believe this foundational doctrine minimized excuses that might have otherwise challenged our desire to become a multi-ethnic church. If a church is so committed to reaching all people with the Gospel, why should the geography matter?

Of course, it does not matter whether we extend the love of God to people living in Senegal, India, or Beaverton, Oregon! For churches with a heart and foundation for global outreach and evangelism, a vision for transformation into a multi-ethnic local church should be a very natural and obedient step.

In our case, transformation began with a key relationship and progressed as God blessed that relationship. In time, he began to connect us with diverse individuals in similar ways. In coming to Village, people realize that ethnicity is not a factor that should keep us from connecting to God or to one another as brothers and sisters in Christ. Through it all, there has been a profound dependence on the Spirit for guidance and leadership. Although God did not keep us from the challenges and problems that naturally arose in our pursuit of unity, he did walk with us through them and grow us together in him. Today, there is room at our table for everyone!

---------- o · ----------

Principles for Transforming

1. Transformational leaders pursuing the multi-ethnic local church must not yield to the voices that will surely challenge their vision.

2. Transformational leaders must articulate holy intentions and clear objectives in language that can be embraced by the body they seek to influence.

3. Transformational leaders must allow the Holy Spirit to be the driving force and voice for change. Yes, it is Christ's vision for the nations that should guide and govern the decisions of those shaping the future of the local church.

4. The process of transforming a historically White congregation into a multi-ethnic church requires transformational leaders to take intentional steps. A good first step is to gather information concerning the changing demographics of the community.

5. Transformational leaders should develop a written document that clearly articulates the purpose of embracing a vision

for multi-ethnic ministry. Addressing the issue openly and honestly from the pulpit will go a long way toward winning the hearts and minds of the people.

6. Transformational leaders should move their congregations ahead in incremental steps. Indeed, you will not want to split an existing church in the name of unity.

7. Forging unity from diversity will require transformational leaders of diverse ethnic background to come together as one. All involved must passionately embrace the vision in order to lead the people with whom they have the greatest influence. There can be no hint of inconsistency, self-positioning, or diversion from the vision if it is, in fact, to take root and inspire change in the established church.

8. Transformational leaders should look for diverse ethnic leaders who are firmly in line with the church doctrinally.

9. It is also important that transformational leaders involve the ethnic ministry staff in other major ministries of the church.

10. Transformational leaders recognize that one of the most effective ways to inspire the development of cross-cultural relationships within the body is to model them as a staff.

11. Establishing a new, cross-cultural relationship often takes bold initiative and a measure of self-sacrifice. Transformational leaders must light the way.

12. Ephesians 4:1–3 should serve as a guide to transformational leaders in their pursuit of cross-cultural competency.

13. Transformational leaders must pursue cross-cultural competency and maintain mutual respect for one another in seeking to understand and resolve cultural differences.

14. Transformational leaders should work hard to ensure that language is not a barrier that keeps people from coming to or remaining involved in the church.

15. Committing to a spirit of inclusion requires transformational leaders to set the tone and to follow through with tangible signs for those in the minority. These must not feel as though they are an afterthought; rather, they must truly be an integral part of the entire church family.

A Continuum of Transformation

Like sanctification, the desire to build a healthy multi-ethnic church is one that requires patient and purposeful pursuit over time. For existing churches in need of revitalization or transformation, the last thing leaders want to do is split their churches in the name of unity! And this you will do if you move too quickly in the endeavor.

With this in mind, the following continuum provides a general overview of the process. By identifying your church with one of the levels or sublevels described next, you can see where your church is currently; you can also consider some of the logical next steps you might take in order to pursue the multi-ethnic vision. Examples are provided to describe the main thought of each level; plus (+) and minus (−) signs are used to convey the pros and cons of each step along the way.

The Homogeneous Church

0. Ground Zero: Self-Absorbed (cross-cultural blindness)

1. Level One: Obedience (cross-cultural awareness)
A. *Involved in Foreign Missions*
Church recognizes needs abroad.

> + Obeying Christ's command (Matthew 28:19, 20a)

> − Willing to cross the ocean but not to cross the street

B. *Involved in Local Missions*
Church recognizes needs at home.

> + The desire to "build a bridge to the community"

> − No desire, however, to "become" the community

2. Level Two: Friendship (cross-cultural sensitivity)
A. *Facilitation*
Church allows facilities to be used by an ethnic congregation.

> + A wise use of resources and a gesture of goodwill

> − A "welcome" into the building, but not into the body

B. Cooperation
Church participates with an ethnic or economically diverse congregation.

> + Showing potential for real relationship and understanding via project or pulpit sharing
>
> − Remaining in a "them" and "us" pattern

3. Level Three: Partnership (cross-cultural investment)
A. Church Planting
Church establishes an ethnic or economically diverse church in another part of the city or somewhere else.

> + Multi-ethnicity is truly a value, given the investment of time, talent, treasure.
>
> − Still the question, *Why not diversity here in our own church?*

B. Individual Assimilation
Church provides a small-group environment for those of a different culture within the overall structure of the church—a Sunday School class or specialized small group.

> + "Them" becoming "us"
>
> − "Them" still not "us"

The Multi-Ethnic Church

4. Level Four: Transformation (cross-cultural competency)
A. Accommodation
Church establishes new forms, for example, a multi-ethnic worship service option.

> + Will necessitate multi-ethnic leadership and cross-cultural competence
>
> − Will soon rival existing forms (*Are you ready for this?*)

B. Integration
Church strives to live out the seven commitments from the pulpit to the nursery and everywhere in between.

> + A healthy multi-ethnic church to the glory of God
>
> − There are still significant challenges ahead!

CONCLUSION

ALL THAT WE SHOULD BE

Now is the accepted time; not tomorrow, not some more
convenient season. It is today that our best work can be done.

—W.E.B. DuBois

ALTHOUGH GOVERNMENT AND EDUCATIONAL PROGRAMS, together with
the efforts of countless individuals, groups, and agencies, have long
sought to eliminate prejudice and the disparaging consequences of institutional racism still deeply embedded within society, it is time to recognize that such a dream cannot be realized apart from the establishment of
multi-ethnic churches that intentionally and joyfully reflect the passion
of Christ for *all* people of the world. For it is not the institutions of
government or of education that have been ordained by God to this task;
rather, it is the local church, the bride of Christ—we who are his people
(John 17:1–3, 20–23; Acts 11:19–26, 13:1, 16ff.; Galatians 3:26–28;
Ephesians 4:1–6; Revelation 5:9–10).

Concerning the movement of American Christianity toward racial
reconciliation in the 1990s, author Chris Rice wrote the following profound words:

> Yes, deep reconciliation will produce justice, and new relationships
> between the races. Yes this will lead Christians to become a bright
> light in the public square. But I have become convinced that God is
> not very interested in the church healing the race problem. I believe it
> is more true that God is using race to heal the church.[1]

Through the biblical transformation of our minds and wills, we will be
able to emotionally engage the concept of a multi-ethnic and economically
diverse local church. Indeed, we will not only come to understand the
passion of Christ for local church unity, as I have described throughout
this book, but we will desire to pursue it for the sake of the Gospel. Yes,

it is Christ's will that we become one with believers different from ourselves so that the world would know God's love and believe. As a by-product, society will be affected, "racial-reconciliation" will occur, and the church will be restored to a place of prominence in the minds and hearts of those outside its walls.

Indeed, this is the power of unity.

This is the Gospel of Christ.

NOTES

INTRODUCTION

1. Little Rock's Central High School was forcibly integrated in 1957, and as Mark Pryor writes in the Preface to this book, "Following *Brown* v. *Board of Education,* [the school's integration] endures as a major milestone of the civil rights movement." More information is available from www.nps.gov/chsc.

2. Technically, Fayetteville is the home of the Hogs (the nickname for the University of Arkansas Razorbacks). But you would never know it by the way people in Little Rock revere this team!

3. Former president Bill Clinton was born in Hope and raised in Hot Springs, Arkansas. He spent his early political years—as attorney general and later as Arkansas's governor—living in Little Rock.

4. DC Talk consisted of members Toby Mac and Kevin Smith, who are White, and Michael Tait, who is Black.

5. The song "Colored People" from DC Talk's album entitled *Jesus Freak* (Forefront Records, 1995) is a great example of this.

6. In addition, Dr. Bill Graham sent a personal greeting (by video) to the city of Little Rock, which was played for the crowd that day.

7. This is an excerpt of Promise 6 as found in the "Seven Promises of a Promise Keeper," available from http://www.promisekeepers.org/about/7promises, accessed 16 January, 2007.

8. NOW's entire paper entitled, "Myths and Facts About the Promise Keepers" is available from http://www.now.org/issues/right/promise/mythfact.html#racism, accessed 16 January, 2007.

9. The entire quote is available from http://www.ralphkeyes.com/pages/books/quote/excerpt.htm, accessed 8 August, 2007.

10. More information is available from http://en.wikipedia.org/wiki/Majority-minority_state, accessed 19 January, 2007.

11. More information is available from http://www.census.gov/ipc/www/usinterimproj/natprojtab01a.pdf, accessed 19 January, 2007.

PART ONE

1. Along this line, it is important to understand that prescriptive arguments are made throughout the New Testament in both direct and indirect ways. Indeed, while many are familiar with the differences between descriptive and direct prescriptive literature, far fewer are aware that *indirect prescription* is also a valid category of literary genre, one that concerns the concept of an ideal. In other words, often embedded within descriptive narrative literature and prescriptive literature with its commands, rules, and orders is a genre of thought (namely, indirect prescription) that clearly assumes the thing(s) being discussed as a commonsense ideal. Dr. Gregory A. Kappas defined this category of hermeneutics in a Th.M. thesis written in 1988 at Western Conservative Baptist Seminary entitled, *A Biblical Defense of Plural Proclamation in the Local Church*. In 1990, Dr. Kappas presented a summary of his thesis to the National Evangelical Theological Society at their annual gathering in San Diego, California, where it was subsequently received with receptivity and without any significant objection. The entire thesis is available online at http://www.tren.com/e%2Ddocs/search.cfm.

CHAPTER ONE

1. See Curtiss Paul Deyoung, Michael O. Emerson, George Yancey, and Karen Chai Kim, *United By Faith: The Multiracial Congregation as an Answer to the Problem of Race* (New York: Oxford University Press, 2003). The authors cite Mark Chavez, "National Congregations Study" (Tucson, AZ: University of Arizona Department of Sociology, 1999).

2. As to when and by whom this sentiment was first observed, religious scholar Martin Marty noted at the end of the nineteenth century, "White Protestants, however, did little to build bonds with [Black Protestant] churches, and racially there were at least two Americas or Christianities. Doctrinal and practical similarity counted for little. . . . Critics noted that the Sunday Protestant worship hour was the most segregated time of the week. Indeed, the once righteous churches of the North, after proclaiming triumph over the evils of slavery and the South, came during the next century to adopt southern styles of regard for Blacks and their churches, and there was little positive contact even within denominational families" (John McManners, ed. *The Oxford History of Christianity* [Oxford: Oxford University Press, 1990], 423).

3. Leon Morris, *Reflections on the Gospel of John*, Vol. 4 (Grand Rapids, MI: Baker Book House, 1988), 565–566.

4. Gerhard Kittel, ed. *Theological Dictionary of the New Testament* (TDNT) (Grand Rapids, MI: Eerdmans, 1985), as cited by Fritz Rienecker and Cleon L. Rogers, *Linguistic Key to the Greek New Testament* (Grand Rapids, MI: Zondervan, 1976, 1980), 255.

5. Fritz Rienecker and Cleon L. Rogers, *Linguistic Key to the Greek New Testament* (Grand Rapids, MI: Zondervan, 1976, 1980), 256.

6. H. E. Dana and J. R. Mantey, *A Manual Grammar of the Greek New Testament* (New York: MacMillan, 1927, 1955), 283.

7. See also Psalm 16:10; 49:15; 118:17; Isaiah 53:5; 61:1–2.

8. See also Genesis 12:3; 17:19; Jeremiah 23:5, 6; 31:31; Isaiah 9:1, 2; 42:1–6; 53:5; Joel 2:28.

CHAPTER TWO

1. Keith Green, "Jesus Commands Us to Go," from the album, *Jesus Commands Us to Go* (Sparrow Records: Produced by Bill Maxwell, 1984). Reprinted with permission of EMI CMG Publishing. All Rights Reserved.

2. I do not mean in any way to diminish the need for traditional foreign missions. The fact of the matter is we need to do both!

3. This was the case with Daniel, Hananiah, Mishael, and Azariah (see Daniel 1:1–7).

4. This can be inferred from Acts 10:1, where Cornelius is described as "a centurion of what was called the Italian cohort."

5. The term *Greeks*, as used here, does not refer merely to Greek-speaking Jews but to Gentiles as a whole. According to John McManners, "Hellenism meant not only speaking Greek as the main language of communication in the eastern half of the Mediterranean, but also [it refers to] games, gymnasia, theatre and the diffusion of polytheistic cult." (*The Oxford History of Christianity*, Oxford: Oxford University Press, 1990, 45–46.)

CHAPTER THREE

1. Some have tried to render "Greeks" here to mean "Greek-speaking Jews." Yet from the context of this passage and the book of Ephesians itself, this is most certainly not the case.

2. See Ephesians 3:21, where Paul specifically states that the glory of the Father is to be displayed "in the church and in Christ Jesus to all generations forever and ever."

3. These same values and attitudes can be seen in Paul's letter to the Colossians, where he explains that people of varying ethnic and economic background are united as one in Christ in the local church. "Here [in Christ and his church] there is no Greek or Jew, circumcised or uncircumcised, barbarian, Scythian, slave or free, but Christ is all, and is in all" (Colossians 3:11, NIV). Having prescribed the environment, Paul then draws his conclusion: "Therefore, as God's chosen people, holy and dearly loved, clothe yourselves with compassion, kindness, humility, gentleness and patience. Bear with each other and forgive whatever grievances you may have against one another. Forgive as the Lord forgave you. And over all these virtues put on love, which binds them all together in perfect unity" (Colossians 3:12–14).

Paul goes on to list other principles as well, urging the local church at Colossae to "let the peace of Christ rule in your hearts, since as members of one body you [have been] called to peace" (Colossians 3:15). This passage is not, therefore, a general description of the universal Church but very specific teaching concerning how diverse people are to walk as one in the local church.

4. The Greek word translated "left" (*aphiemi*) means "to depart, leave alone, forsake, [or] neglect." It can also be used of divorce, so the imagery here is very strong. In addition, the Greek phrase "your first love" precedes the phrase "you have left," making the first phrase very emphatic. More information is available from http://www.bible.org/page.php?page_id=3696#P34_11687, accessed 1 March 2007.

PART TWO

1. George Yancey, *One Body, One Spirit* (Downer's Grove, IL: InterVarsity Press, 2003).

2. More information is available from http://www.mosaix.info.

CHAPTER FOUR

1. An evangelist, too, George Müeller "was an ordinary man [with an] undeniable faith, implicit trust and love for God." More information is available from http://www.mullers.org/cm, accessed 7 December, 2006.

2. On November 27, 2001, Keith Green, who shaped an entire generation of worshippers, was inducted into the Gospel Music Association (GMA) Gospel Music Hall of Fame. More information is available from http://www.lastdaysministries.org, accessed 23 February, 2007.

3. This is referenced in a paper titled, "God's Quiet Conquests" at http://withchrist.org/1Cor1.28,29.htm, accessed December 7, 2006.

4. The term *Jewish Christians* is often applied to people who are ethnically Jewish but who have embraced Jesus Christ as Messiah and Lord.

5. Written in April 1984 by L. Robert Kohls, a paper titled, "The Values Americans Live By" is widely referenced on the Web. According to its introduction, Kohls was then the executive director of The Washington International Center in Washington, D.C. One source for the paper can be found at http://www.georgetown.edu/faculty/hac5/cs/values.htm, accessed 15 November, 2006.

6 The Arkansas River separates the city of Little Rock from the city of North Little Rock. So Harold is not too far away!

7. In our case, it was sending out one of our three teaching pastors.

8. This is wonderfully modeled for us in Acts 11:24, where Barnabus is described as just such a man, "full of the Holy Spirit and of faith." Indeed, is this not one of the reasons why God chose him to be a primary catalyst in the growth and development of the first multi-ethnic church at Antioch? (see also Acts 13:1).

9. "Without faith, it is impossible to please God" (Hebrews 11:6).

10. Henri Nouwen, *Clowning in Rome* (New York: Doubleday/Random House Inc., 1978, 13).

CHAPTER FIVE

1. See http://en.wikipedia.org/wiki/E_pluribus_unum, accessed 19 January, 2007.

2. A. Sims, ed., *An Hour With George Müeller: The Man of Faith to Whom God Gave Millions* (printed by Chapel Library, a ministry of Mt. Zion Bible Church, Pensacola, FL), as referenced by Randy Alcorn at http://www.epm.org/pdf/george_mueller.pdf, accessed 20 January, 2007.

3. *Encarta World English Dictionary* (©1999 Microsoft Corporation. All rights reserved. Developed for Microsoft by Bloomsbury Publishing, Plc).

4. George Yancey, *One Body, One Spirit* (Downer's Grove, IL: InterVarsity Press, 2003).

5. I am indebted to Gary L. McIntosh, whose understanding of the history and of current issues related to the Church Growth Movement made for an outstanding D. Min. course—even for "nay-sayers" such as me! For a good historical overview of the Church Growth Movement, see Gary L. McIntosh's introduction in *Evaluating the Church Growth Movement: 5 Views* (Grand Rapids, MI: Zondervan, 2004). In addition, Ralph H. Elliott, formerly the senior pastor of the North Shore Baptist Church in Chicago,

published an early but still somewhat relevant critique of the Church
Growth Movement titled, "Dangers of the Church Growth Movement,"
which appeared in the *Christian Century*, August 12–19, 1981, 799–801.
The article is available from http://www.religion-online.org/showarticle.
asp?title=1723, accessed 4 February 2007. Gailyn Van Rheenen offers a
more contemporary critique in "Contrasting Missional and Church Growth
Perspectives," available from http://missiology.org/mmr/mmr34.htm,
accessed 9 January, 2007.

6. My friends and fellow Mosaics, Hatley and Christy Hambrice, recently
   returned from a year in India. When asked about the situation today, they
   said, "The caste system is alive and well in India today. From the beggars
   on the street to students being accepted into colleges, caste and birth-
   right determine the options available to each and every Indian. In fact,
   India is the most segregated nation on the planet because the caste system
   has created an intentional separation of its people by language, wealth,
   customs, religious practices and education. And although the caste system
   is illegal in India today, job listings in the local newspapers still ask for
   applicants by caste. In addition, certain schools are open only to wealthy
   families and hospitals, too, are controlled by caste. In this regard, lower
   castes must get care at the free, over-crowded government hospitals while
   only those in a higher caste can receive quality healthcare from the clean,
   private hospitals."

7. Interested churches and their leaders will find help in this regard by referring to the "A Continuum of Transformation" on pages 180 and 181.

CHAPTER SIX

1. *Brown v. Board of Education of Topeka*, 347 U.S. 483 (1954).

2. *Encarta World English Dictionary* (©Microsoft Corporation, 1999).

3. To this point and in the future, we desire three different teaching pastors to
   share the pulpit.

4. Available from http://www.dartmouth.edu/~cwg/special/beaman.html,
   accessed 8 January, 2007.

5. The Philadelphia Eagles selected McPherson in the sixth round of the 1988
   NFL Draft. He was traded to the Houston Oilers in 1990, then went back
   to Philadelphia the following season. He also spent four seasons in the
   Canadian Football League with the Hamilton Tiger-Cats (1991–93) and
   Ottawa Rough Riders (1994).

CHAPTER SEVEN

1. Of course, this is true for all other faith-based houses of worship as well.

2. Is it any wonder that following the reference to peacemaking, the next three verses speak of persecution? (Matthew 5:10–12; see also John 15:18–20).

CHAPTER EIGHT

1. Basic, helpful information concerning the concept of institutional racism is available from http://en.wikipedia.org/wiki/Institutional_racism, accessed 4 February, 2007. Quoting from this site, "Two examples from U.S. history can help clarify the nature and effects of institutionalized racism. In 1935, the U.S. Congress passed the Social Security Act, guaranteeing an income for millions of workers after retirement. However, the Act specifically excluded domestic and agricultural workers, many of whom were Mexican-American, African-American, and Asian-American. These workers were therefore not guaranteed an income after retirement, and had less opportunity to save, accumulate, and pass wealth on to future genera-tions. [Second], the U.S. property appraisal system created in the 1930s tied property value and eligibility for government loans to race. Thus, all-White neighborhoods received the government's highest property value ratings, and White people were eligible for government loans. Between 1934 and 1962, less than 2% of government-subsidized housing went to non-White people. Both of these examples depend not on the individual, isolated, and idiosyncratic beliefs or biases of individuals, but rather on biases embedded in social structures and in institutions. Moreover, in the first example, no "race" was specifically named to be excluded from the Social Security Act, but the Act effectively allowed wealth benefits to accrue to certain racial groups and not to others. There need not be, therefore, any explicit intent associated with institutional racism in order for it to benefit certain races over others."

2. Perhaps this is a good time to state that the term *Hispanic* (as used in the United States) technically applies to people or things that come from Spain or Spanish-speaking countries in Central and South America, including Mexico, Puerto Rico, and Cuba. The term *Latino* or *Latina* (as used in America) is more inclusive and practically refers to men and women throughout Central and South America who speak either Spanish or Portuguese (as, for instance, is spoken in Brazil).

3. WordNet 2.0. (© 2003, Princeton University).

4. The National Council of La Raza (NCLR) is a private, nonprofit, and nonpartisan organization focused on reducing poverty and discrimination, and improving opportunities for Hispanic Americans. The continuum was presented and discussed at a seminar sponsored by Little Rock's Racial and Cultural Diversity Commission in 2004 and attributed to Christina López of NCLR. Attempts to locate López through NCLR in February 2007, however, were unsuccessful, as was the attempt to find anyone working there currently who could provide further assistance.

5. Available from http://www.med.umich.edu/multicultural/ccp/basic.htm, accessed 5 February, 2007.

6. Christina López, see note 4.

7. Available from http://www.med.umich.edu/multicultural/ccp/basic.htm, accessed 5 February, 2007.

8. Diane L. Adams, ed., *Health Issues for Women of Color: A Cultural Diversity Perspective* (Thousand Oaks, CA: Sage, 1995).

9. Available from http://www.med.umich.edu/multicultural/ccp/basic.htm, accessed 5 February, 2007.

10. Available from http://www.duke.edu/web/equity/cultural_competency.pdf, accessed 5 February, 2007.

CHAPTER NINE

1. Gregory Allen Howard, *Remember the Titans*, Boaz Yakin, dir. (Walt Disney Pictures, 2000).

2. More information is available from http://www.71originaltitans.com/hboone.html, accessed 17 January, 2007.

3. Actually, the original players, members of the T. C. Williams High School, 1971 State Champion Varsity Football Team, established the Titan Foundation in 2000, with the goal of providing scholarship funds to qualified T. C. Williams High School seniors for postsecondary education. More information is available from http://www.71originaltitans.com, accessed 17 January, 2007.

4. At Mosaic, each week a different individual or group leads music in our worship service. For example, one week our Gospel Choir takes responsibility for the music, followed the next week by a member of our church, Rachel Alford. On the following Sunday, Cesar Ortega sings songs in Spanish, followed the next week by James Wafford, III, Mosaic's current Director of Music, who leads the congregation in another way and style altogether. James, I might add, is a very gifted young man with a passion to

help singers and instrumentalists develop their gifts and skills to the glory of God. Not only do our worship leaders rotate from week to week, our teaching pastors do as well.

5. Josh McDowell and Bob Hostetler, *The New Tolerance: How a Cultural Movement Threatens to Destroy You, Your Faith, and Your Children* (Carol Stream, IL: Tyndale House Publishers, 1998).

6. WorldFest is an annual event sponsored by Little Rock's Racial and Cultural Diversity Commission (RCDC). It was created to help reduce prejudice in Little Rock and around Arkansas by bringing people together to experience and to learn more about the different cultures of our state. More information concerning the RCDC is available from http://www.littlerock.org/CityManager/Divisions/RacialAndCulturalDiversityCommission/AboutUs, accessed 1 March 2007. More information concerning WorldFest is available from http://www.rcdcworldfest.org, accessed 1 March, 2007.

7. "Lifestyle Evangelism" is a phrase coined in the 1980s by my wife, Linda's, uncle, Joe Aldrich, whose book *Lifestyle Evangelism* (Portland, OR; Multnomah Press, 1981) encouraged believers to build genuine, caring relationships with nonbelievers in order to develop common ground for the sake of the Gospel.

CHAPTER TEN

1. More information is available from http://www.hartsem.edu/events/churchgrowth.htm, accessed 3 March, 2007.

2. Ibid.

3. Luke 2:47; Matthew 7:28; Mark 1:22; Matthew 9:3; Matthew 12:23; Mark 2:12; Matthew 21:20; Luke 8:25; Mark 15:5.

4. In Little Rock, local government consists of a city board that includes the mayor, as well as city commissioners elected to represent various wards within the city.

5. Alexander is a small community just outside Little Rock.

6. For further information concerning the history of Skatechurch, see Mike Howerton, *The Relevant Church: A New Vision for Communities of Faith* (Orlando, FL: Relevant Media Group, 2004, chapter 4). Further information is available from http://www.skatechurch.org.

7. *The Oregonian* is the primary daily newspaper in Portland, Oregon, and the largest newspaper in the state by circulation.

8. George Yancey and I cofounded the Mosaix Global Network (MGN) in 2005. MGN exits to catalyze the growing movement toward multi-ethnic

churches by (1) casting vision, (2) connecting individuals and churches of like mind, (3) conferencing for the purpose of discovering and disseminating best practices, and (4) coaching pastors and ministry leaders with a passion to develop multi-ethnic local churches throughout the United States and beyond. More information is available from http://www.mosaix.info.

9. See http://www.cato-at-liberty.org/2007/01/31/amazing-grace-how-sweet-the-story, accessed 2 March, 2007.

10. More information is available at http://www.amazinggracemovie.com, accessed 2 March, 2007.

11. Ibid.

12. Galatians 3:28.

13. John Newton, "Amazing Grace," verse 2.

CHAPTER ELEVEN

1. From the song, "Living Dangerously" by Steve Camp, as recorded on the album, "Justice" released by Sparrow Records, 1989.

2. Francis Schaeffer, *The Mark of the Christian.* (InterVarsity Press: Madison, WI. 1970), 14. This entire work is available from http://www.ccel.us/schaeffer.html, accessed 22 February, 2007.

CHAPTER TWELVE

1. In this situation, a reformer determines to stimulate the rebirth of a dead or dying homogeneous church around the multi-ethnic vision.

2. Michael Emerson, with Rodney Woo, *People of the Dream* (Princeton: Princeton University Press, 2006), 96–97.

3. Ibid., 132.

CONCLUSION

1. Chris Rice, *More Than Equals* (InterVarsity Press, Downers Grove, IL, 261).

ABOUT THE AUTHOR

MARK DEYMAZ is the founding pastor of the Mosaic Church of Central Arkansas (www.mosaicchurch.net), where significant percentages of Black and White Americans, together with men and women from more than thirty nations, currently worship God together as one. A recognized leader in the emerging Multi-Ethnic Church Movement, he founded the Mosaix Global Network (www.mosaix.info) with George Yancey to help catalyze the movement and to connect leaders intent on the development of multi-ethnic churches throughout America and beyond.

Mark received his B.S. in psychology from Liberty University, an M.A. in theology from Western Seminary, and a D. Min. from Phoenix Seminary. Recently, he finished a two-year appointment as a commissioner on Little Rock's Racial and Cultural Diversity Commission. Visit markdeymaz.typepad.com to learn more.

Mark and his wife, Linda, live in Little Rock with their four children, Zack, Emily, Will, and Kate. Linda is the author of two books, including *Mommy, Please Don't Cry* (Random House, 1996), a 2004 Retailer's Choice Nominee providing hope and comfort for parents who grieve the loss of a child.

INDEX

A

Abdullah, J., 76

Accommodation: of Deaf and Hard of Hearing, 97–98; definition of, 59; intentionality attitude as part of, 60–61

Acts 1:8, 127, 159

Acts 2:42, 86

Acts 2 Fellowship (A2f), 86–87

Acts 6:7, 139

Acts 7, 15

Acts 8:5, 15–16

Acts 11:20, 20

Acts 11:24, 21

Acts 13:1, 23

Acts 16:14, 24

Acts 16:15, 24

Acts 21:15–22, 31

African Americans: learning from perspective of, 141; overcoming institutional racism against, 96–97; Wilcrest leadership among, 154–155

Agape Church, 126

Alcoholic Anonymous (AA), 66

Amazing Grace (film), 129

"Amazing Grace" (Newton), 129

American Sign Language (ASL), 97

American values, 47

Anderson, P., 126

Antioch Church, 21–23

Apostello (sent), 6, 10

Arkansas Asian Festival, 122

Arnold, S., 127

Assimilation, 59

Assyrians, 16

Athletes in Action (AIA), 44–45

Attitude adjustments, 60–61

B

B&B Trailer Park (Alexander), 123–124

Baha'i, 70

Baha'u'llah, 70

Barnabus, 20–21, 23, 24, 188n.8

Beatitudes, 90

Berlin Wall, 145–146

Boaz, 99

Body of Christ, 125–127, 156

Boone, H., 108

Brown, G., 128

Brown, M., 126

Brown, T., 78

Bryant, T., 76, 141

Bush, G. W., 128

C

Caldwell, H., 126

Calvary Worship Centre (Vancouver, BC), 140

Cane, S., 26

Caste system, 188n.6

Catholic churches, 4

Celebration Church, 126, 139

Central High School (Little Rock), 70

Chami, A. (Amer), 11–12, 92–93

Chami, A. (Ann), 92–93

Christians, as new term for Church members, 21–23